GODS & GOBLINS

A FIELD GUIDE TO **PLACE NAMES** OF **OLYMPIC NATIONAL PARK**

BY SMITTY PARRATT

Edited and expanded by:
GARY PETERSON and GLYNDA PETERSON SCHAAD

Published by POSEIDON PEAK PUBLISHING

Published by

POSEIDON PEAK PUBLISHING
4913 Upper Hoh Road, Forks, WA 98331
www.PoseidonPeak.com

Second Edition 2009

Printed by: Everbest Printing Co., Ltd., Nansha, China

Copyright ©2009 by Smitty Parratt
ISBN 978-1-57833-448-3
Library of Congress No. 83-73739

To order: 360-374-5254 or FAX 360-374-5266
Email: glynda@olypen.com

Book and cover design: Magdalena Bassett, www.BassettStudio.com
Photo scanning and restoration: DJ Bassett, www.HistoricPhotoPreservation.org

*To my best friend and partner, Shawn Kilpatric Parratt,
who has encouraged and supported me
for more than 32 years in our life journey.*

INTRODUCTION

The stories behind place names in the Olympic National Park collectively tell its human history. Most significant events in the recorded history of the Olympics (and a few obscure ones) resulted in the naming of a place or places.

Natives lived where they found food most plentiful and travel easiest. This was usually where rivers fed into the sea. The results of their occupying such land are visible on today's maps: 12 of the 13 major rivers draining the Olympic Mountains have Native names. Many coastal features, particularly in the northwest corner of the Olympic Peninsula, still carry Native names. Although there are claims by white explorers and settlers of being the first into the high country, there are 2,900 year-old basket fragments in locations such as Obstruction Point. These artifacts are considered definitive proof that Native Americans made use of and traveled into and through the Olympic Mountains.

The first non-native visitors came by ocean, sailing ships from distant ports around the world. Captain John Meares sighted and named Mt. Olympus while sailing for Great Britain on the Felice in 1788. Another Spanish seaman, Don Francisco Eliza, named Port Angeles (in 1791), calling it "Puerta de Nuestra Señora de Los Angeles."

Numerous ocean voyages by European nations resulted in the naming of most of the features along the Pacific shore, Strait of Juan de Fuca and Hood Canal waterways surrounding the Olympic Peninsula.

The Olympic Mountains region was one of the last in the contiguous 48 states to be colonized by Europeans. Settlers first arrived in the southern portion of the Olympic Peninsula in the early to mid-1800s; thereafter, they too imposed their names on the land.

THE PRESS EXPLORING EXPEDITION. Commonly referred to as the Seattle Press Expedition. Shown in this December 6, 1889 photo prior to their departure from Seattle are left to right: John William Sims, Dr. Harris B. Runnalls, Charles Adams Barnes, James Halbold Christie, John H. Crumback and Christopher O'Connell Hayes. These men traversed the uncharted interior of the Olympics in the horrific winter of 1889-1890. (University of Washington Libraries, Special Collection Neg# La Roche 10018)

Expeditions through the Olympics

Due to the roughness of the terrain, overland explorations of the Olympic Peninsula were delayed. The first major recorded explorations were by the six-man Press Expedition in the winter of 1889-90 and Lieutenant Joseph O'Neil's Army Expeditions in the summers of 1885 and 1890. Many places never before observed by the white man were named by these explorers. Lake LaCrosse, Mt. Bretherton and O'Neil Pass are the products of the expeditions of O'Neil. The Press Expedition and its sponsor, *The Seattle Press* newspaper, named the most features. Thanks to them, names such as the Bailey Range, Lake Margaret, Lillian River, Mt. Seattle, and Mt. Christie now dot the map. For further information about their journey, see *Across the Olympic Mountains: The Press Expedition, 1889-90*, by Robert L. Wood. The names of other explorers, such as surveyors Arthur Dodwell and Theodore Rixon, who hiked into the area in 1898-1900, are honored by a mountain pass deep in the Olympics.

Developers, loggers, politicians and adventurers - as well as friends of such people - have likewise been honored with place names in the Olympics. And finally, a glance at Olympic National Park place names reveals that many of them reflect the "melting pot" character indicative of the region's first visitors. Alckee Creek, Port Angeles, Bogachiel River, and Shi Shi Beach derive from the various languages spoken by early residents and visitors.

Name Origins

One such "language" was particularly instrumental in the ultimate christening of names throughout the Olympic Mountain region. Chinook Jargon, which evolved early in the nineteenth-century, flourished in this area virtually as a full-fledged spoken language for several decades. Developed basically from various Indian tongues, Chinook's "pidgin" dialect was used extensively as a means of communication between white visitors and local tribes. Thus, it was supplemented liberally with a somewhat haphazard selection of words from French-Canadian explorers, Hudson's Bay employees, and American trappers and traders. Among the many geographic features retaining a Chinook heritage are Alckee Creek, Hee Hee Creek, Kimta Camp, and Pelton Creek.

A number of Olympic names originated in myths, beginning with Mt. Olympus. The Valhallas, Mercury, Aphrodite, Aries, Kloochman Rock, and Enchanted Valley have mythical connotations which span the world and many centuries.

Man-made structures (Wellesley Peak, Altair Campground) and other remote parts of the world (Rialto Beach, Little Siberia), amusing occurrences (Three Prune Creek, Black and White Lakes), tragedies (Norwegian Memorial, Jeffers Glacier), and mistakes (Royal Creek, Diamond Meadows) - all are perpetuated in their Olympic names. Some remain unexplained.

Although people often like to be immortalized via place names, many have been content to christen an area because of some geographic feature or natural quality found there. For example, animals are honored at Eagle Lakes, Badger Valley, and Dragon Lake. Plants are recalled at Spruce Mountain and Devil Club Creek. Geological characteristics account for the names given Ruby Beach and Cannonball Island, while Baby Island and Aurora Ridge relate to innate qualities of the area.

Place names inevitably reveal the true history of the Olympics, at least as the white man's exploration of this region is concerned. Most of the names are logical; certainly they are diverse. When analyzed, they provide a genuine insight into the known history of the fabled Olympic Mountains. Place names tell a story, or more correctly, hundreds of stories of men and women who chose to live and work in this rugged part of the West and who tried in their own way to tame Mother Nature. In the process, these pioneers left behind something of themselves, or something of their culture and often something of their language.

Names found in the Park spring from many different tongues. The tales behind them often produce a smile, sometimes a chuckle. Just as often, they create a shiver of fear as the reader is able to empathize with the pioneer who faced such incredible danger and hardships. Whatever the reason, the names have one thing in common: Each is a vignette offering new insight into this magnificent, unspoiled segment of North America.

HOW TO USE THIS BOOK

This book is a large index. Place names of Olympic National Park are listed alphabetically throughout the text, with all appropriate data listed relative to each item. Following is an example of a typical entry, with a step-by-step description of how to find pertinent information about it.

GOBLINS CANYON, GATE; MT. OLYMPUS (6F). One of the Park's most extraordinary landmarks, "Goblin Gates" was named by the 1889-90 Seattle Press Expedition. Mapmakers later altered the spelling to "Goblins Gate." Here the Elwha River swerves at a severe right angle and tumbles into a narrow cliffside opening. Resembling two large gates such as might have been found on a medieval castle, the rock portals appear to reach out and suck the waters of the Elwha into their grasp, only to send them plummeting down a precipitous canyon in a headlong rush to sea level.

It is the eeriness of Goblins Gate, however, that is noteworthy. Perpendicular canyon walls, usually immersed in shadows, somehow combine to fire one's imagination. Many visitors to Goblins Gate are able to squint their eyes and easily visualize demons, goblins, and various other monsters lurking within the rock-strewn canyon.

Press Expedition member Charles Barnes described it thus: "...like the throat of a monster, silently sucking away the water" and as a "multitude of faces... with tortured expressions." Numerous visitors have described a wide variety of animals they have been able to "see" along the walls of Goblins Gate, ranging from rats and buffalo to elephants and apes.

There have been two bridges which crossed the 20-foot chasm at this point. One was washed away in high water around the turn of the century. Another became a weather-beaten hazard, and was removed by Chris Morgenroth in 1935. 12, 195, 207, 207.5

1. <u>GOBLINS CANYON</u> is the first feature in this section upon which the discussion is based. The name is underlined, indicating that it does not appear on U.S. Geological Survey maps - or any other maps - even though it is or has been in general use. NOTE: Entry referring to mountain peaks are followed by the mountain's elevation in parentheses.

2. GOBLINS GATE, having the same place-name origin, is also found under this heading. It is NOT underlined, because it can be found on conventional maps.

3. If you examine the MT. OLYMPUS map (See **INDEX TO SECTIONAL MAPS**), you will find one or both of these features there.

4. (6F) is the coordinate, or key, to where you will find **GOBLINS CANYON** and/or **GOBLINS GATE** on the MT. OLYMPUS map. NOTE: Some entries contain more than one map reference. In those cases, the geographic features being described overlap, and can be located on such maps. Coordinates are shown for all such entries. All features listed in the book can be found on maps found in the **INDEX TO SECTIONAL MAPS**.

5. The body of the entry describes whatever information could be found relative to the christening of the geographic feature.

6. Numbers shown at the end of the entry refer to specific sources in the Bibliography found at the end of the book.

Bibliography/Maps

The bibliography section at the end of the book lists alphabetically all sources used in gathering information for this book. Each place-name entry is followed with a key to sources in the bibliography. In the bibliography, sources from personal communications are followed, whenever possible, with their "qualifications" as a source in parentheses to provide as much credibility to that information as possible.

This section begins with an "INDEX TO SECTIONAL MAPS." The index map shows what is defined as Olympic National Park for the purposes of this book. It is an index to 18 detailed maps (from the United States Geologic Survey Olympic National Park map) which follow alphabetically. All maps include a scale in miles and an indication of true versus magnetic north. All place names in the book can be located on a map at the end of the book; all places labeled on maps in this book are discussed in the book. Place names for which no information was discovered are listed in the text and shown on the maps.

Place Names along Pacific Coastal Stretch

Place names along the Pacific coastal stretch, but not actually in Olympic National Park boundaries, are included in this text.

"Shelters" vs. "Camps"

It is important here to make a distinction between the terms "shelter" and "camp" as used in this book.

Geographic features designated on maps as "shelters" may or may not be the site of actual shelters at this time. Such sites did contain actual structures when these base maps were created, but at the time this book went to press many had deteriorated and/or had been removed; this is even more the case in the 2009 printing. Nevertheless, any place so designated is a good campsite; the term "camp," therefore, is fast becoming preferred terminology among backcountry travelers.

Because of the very nature of the subject, and because some of the facts were culled from dim memories, errors may have crept into the text. Also, there are times when more than one version of a story was told, each purporting to be the tale behind a particular place name. When this occurred, and no definite proof could be found, all versions were listed. If you discover an error or have additional information, please contact the author or publisher; we will include it in the next edition.

This book includes more than 600 separate listings of place names. Thus, the information provided here is thought to be more detailed and inclusive than in any other source available to date.

ACKNOWLEDGEMENTS

The preparation of this reprint required the efforts of many. All shared a common desire to prevent the loss of historical knowledge. Specifically, I would like to thank Director Kathy Monds of the Clallam County Historical Society and Jacilee Wray, Gay Hunter and Paul Gleason at the Olympic National Park Cultural Resource Center for their invaluable support of this project. For wonderful vintage photographs used in this second edition, I would like to thank the Clallam County Historical Society, Marilyn Lewis, the Olympic National Park, the Peterson Family, Adeline Smith and the University of Washington Library Special Collections. For scanning and restoration of these photographs thanks goes to D.J. Bassett at historicphotopreservation.com. For the book's layout, design and cover I would like to thank Magdalena Basset, at bassettstudio.com.

Copious amounts of well-deserved credit for this updated reprint go to life long-friends, Lou Salsbury and Chiggers Stokes who worked with and inspired the author. Without their assistance this project would not have happened.

Also important to this edition were Keith Spencer, expert on Olympic Mountain ascents and Stan Fouts west side historian, both of whom poured over the manuscript to suggest updates and corrections.

Historians Gary Peterson and Glynda Peterson Schaad provided information and editorial help in addition to orchestrating layout changes, publishing and printing.

The bibliography of this book is a veritable "who's who" of those who participated in and wrote the history of the Olympic National Park. To all, I am greatly indebted

The greatest thanks, however, goes to my best friend and mate, Shawn. She inspired me to continue through the four years of research leading to this book's first printing. She was my companion as we became the first couple (she the first woman) to hike all 675 miles of Olympic Trails, the Olympic coastal strip and all major cross-country traverses in the Park. This allowed us to view firsthand many places in the Olympic National Park and to verify the natural attributes used in their naming.

—Smitty Parratt

Smitty Parratt Biography

At six-months Smitty Parratt was packed by his ranger father to a log cabin in Glacier National Park. Thus began a lifetime of learning the natural and cultural history of national parks. Smitty graduated Magna cum Laude with a degree in biology from the University of Redlands in California and completed graduate work at the University of Wyoming in 1976 earning a Masters Degree in Zoology and Physiology. Early assignments with the National Park Service took him to Great Smoky Mountains National Park, Lassen Volcanic National Park and Death Valley among others. However, it was the nine years between 1979 and 1988 that Smitty remembers as pure magic for him and his wife, Shawn. It was during this period the couple hiked all the trails of the Park and researched and wrote the book, *Gods & Goblins*. Many of the pioneers who shared their adventures are no longer with us but largely due to Smitty's vision and diligence these stories have been captured to be shared by all.

GODS & GOBLINS

A FIELD GUIDE
TO PLACE NAMES OF
OLYMPIC NATIONAL PARK

ABBEY ISLAND; DESTRUCTION ISLAND (3G). Abbey Island, visible from the popular Ruby Beach area, was named by Coast Surveyor James Lawson in August or September of 1866. Lawson so designated the outcropping of land "from its appearance," akin to a monastery or church. 64,120

ADELAIDE PEAK (7,300'); TYLER PEAK (2C). Kent Heathershaw of Southworth and Robert McKee of Seattle named the peak in 1958 for Adelaide Degenhardt, who made the first ascent of this mountain in 1944. They wished to show the importance of the Degenhardts in opening up the Needles as a rock climbing area. 140, 169, 184.5

AHLSTROM PRAIRIE; LAKE OZETTE (2E). The prairie was created by fires set by Ozette Indians who burned the land to produce forage for deer. Lars Kristopher Ahlstrom (1872-1960) homesteaded on the prairie in 1902, after having spent his childhood in Sweden. Ahlstrom was a true pioneer and the westernmost white resident in the contiguous United States for 56 years. The Swedish homesteader returned home one day in 1916 to find his two-story home destroyed by a runaway brush fire. Undeterred, he replaced it with a three-room cabin.

Lars often played his accordion at lively gatherings of the Lake Ozette settlers. The popular bachelor hiked to Ozette twice weekly for mail, supplies and companionship. Most of his income was from fall and winter jobs in mills or logging camps. Ahlstrom laid most of the original puncheon planks along the Indian Trail to Cape Alava, and later spent much of his spare time maintaining that popular path. Hikers going to Cape Alava before 1958 were often welcomed by his cheerful greeting. He left the area only after a foot infection in 1958 forced him to return to Port Angeles, where he died in 1960, at the age of 88. 105, 120, 156

ALCKEE CREEK; MT. TOM (3G). The word "Alckee," meaning "by and by," derives from the Chinook tongue, which was a trade, or pidgin language. It was a combination of several Indian languages, French and English, and was effectively used in carrying out business between the Indians and white traders. 120

ALEXANDER ISLAND; LA PUSH (8B). It is thought that Alexander Island may have been christened by early sea explorers, but there is no way to verify this fact. Some residents believe the island was named for the Vaudeville magician and oracle, Claude Alexander Conlin who built what became known as Alexander's Castle on the bluffs above Rialto Beach. Parties he hosted there during prohibition were legendary for their excesses. Alexander began his career in Gold Rush Skagway, Alaska as mob boss Soapy Smith's lieutenant in charge of prostitution enterprises. Later after leaving the North, he worked the theater chain begun by his Dawson City friends, Alexander Pantages and Klondike Kate. Using the stage name "The Great Alexander—The Man Who Knows," Claude wowed audiences and identified "marks" to be later fleeced with a little help from fellow stampeder J.E.L. James, owner of the Mora Hotel (see Mora Campground). Advertised activities for this secluded location ran the gamut from fishing to séances at which the bereaved could contact their dearly departed. 26.5, 63, 76.5,109, 154

A

ALLENS BAY, SLOUGH; LAKE OZETTE (3C). A Peterson family first homesteaded here in 1893, building a two-room 14' by 18' cabin from one huge cedar log during the summer of that year. One of the rooms was a grocery store, the only store at the lake for three years. The Swan Post Office was established at Allens Bay in 1894. Mrs. Peterson was the postmistress until 1899, during which time the mail was delivered once a week. It is said that the resourceful Mrs. Peterson often had to dress like a man in order to milk the family cow. The beast was accustomed to being milked by men only - and was quite aggressive toward the fair sex.

The actual naming of Allens Bay and a neighboring trail took place after the area's second homesteader (and postmaster) A.C. Allen drowned while crossing the lake. He was carrying a heavy load of mail to nearby settlers when his boat was capsized in a sudden storm. 4, 21, 120

ALPHABET RIDGE; MT. Tyler (5G). This east-west ridge with numerous summits and spires is located between Warrior Peak on the south and Charlia Lakes on the north. Summits included, from east to west explain the name of the ridge: A Spire, Cloudy Peak, Zee Spire, Why Spire, Ex-Spire, Curiosity Peak, Etcetera Spire, Infinity Tower, and Finite Tower. 146.5, 184.5

ALTA CREEK; KLOOCHMAN ROCK (8F). Alta is Chinook (see ALCKEE CREEK) for "now" or "at the present time." It is claimed that the creek was named for the wife of George Shaube, a homesteader at Smith Place. He wrote that it was, "named for my wife, a daughter of Ray Northrups (sic), who, at the age of 16 years led a party consisting of his mother, three younger brothers, and two sisters, with all their worldly goods, including livestock...via steamer to Clallam Bay, and then over the old Burnt Mountain Road to Sappho, then by trail to the Queets, and settling at Clearwater in 1897." 120, 156, 178, 192, 207.5

ALTAIR CAMPGROUND; JOYCE (5A). Named for the *U.S.S. Altair*, which was named for the star Altair that appears in the constellation Aquila. The U.S.S. Altair was a repair ship for a destroyer squadron of the Pacific Fleet. The crew liked to camp at Altair. 12, 14, 82, 83.5, 120

ANDERSON CANYON, RANCH (See RICA CANYON).

ANDERSON CREEK, GLACIER, MOUNT (7,321'), **PASS**: MT. STEEL (6F). The Mt. Anderson massif, which drains into Hood Canal, the Pacific Ocean, and the Strait of Juan de Fuca, was christened in approximately 1890 by Lt. Joseph O'Neil, who named it in honor of his Commanding Officer, Colonel Thomas M. Anderson (1836-1917).

The mountain was also referred to on some maps as "The Brothers" and "Pyramid Peak." Mt. Anderson was first climbed in August of 1920 by Fairman B. Lee and his party. The shelter near Anderson Pass has been referred to as "Camp Siberia," or "Little Siberia," because of cold winds which descend from nearby snowfields and glaciers. 12, 15, 71, 169, 195, 207.5, 208, 209

ANDERSON FIELD; SALMON RIVER (2B). In 1906 George Anderson filed for this claim consisting of 160 acres in the southwest corner of section 26. It is still referred to today as Anderson Field, although there is some nearly-obliterated evidence of pre-1906 occupation in the area. 203

ANDREWS FIELD; KLOOCHMAN ROCK (1D). The area was first occupied (from the early 1900s until 1922) by six members of the Bill Hunter family. Hunter was a mail carrier with a wife and four children. He would get together with another local resident, Charley Streator (see STREATOR FIELD) and often play the violin at dances. Later (1924-44) the area was occupied by the John Andrews family, for whom it was named. Mrs. Andrews, the former Alice Anderson, had previously settled (1902) with her parents in the Queets Valley and remained on the Anderson homestead until her marriage to John Andrews in 1924. Andrews Field is shown as Andersons Field on some maps, due to the Andrews-Anderson marriage.

The land at Andrews Field supported hay and pasture, as well as a 1/2 -acre vegetable garden, orchard (apple, apricot, pear, plum, and prune trees), and Himalaya blackberries. Animals kept there included 150 chickens, 50 turkeys,

ANDERSON BRIDGE AT GOBLINS GATE. At this point the El-wha River swerves right and tumbles into an extremely narrow cliffside opening. The fact there was no bridge at this point after 1935 places this photograph by Grant Humes prior to that date. (Olympic National Park Collection)

Below: LARS AHLSTROM. Lars' claim on Ozette Lake was at one time the western-most homestead in the continental United States. (Olympic National Park Collection)

50 cattle, 6 peacocks, 4 horses, 2-3 pigs, ducks, and guineas.

Buildings on the land included two houses, woodshed, turkey coop, chicken coop, guest house, and a barn. The barn still stood when this book first went to press in 1984, but was down by Sept. 1999. The clearing was originally virgin spruce timber and now offers an excellent view of Kloochman Rock. 64.5, 152, 184, 203

A

ANTELOPE CREEK: MT. OLYMPUS (7F). Grant Humes and other area residents referred to this stream as "Canyon Creek" in the early 1900s. Suddenly the name "Antelope Creek" mysteriously appeared on various maps and a sign was installed to that effect where the creek crosses the Elwha trail. There never have been antelope here-but then, neither are there badgers in Badger Valley. 51, 106, 141, 152, 207.5

ANTRIM RANGE; KLOOCHMAN ROCK (4A), QUINAULT LAKE (4G). This name, no longer in use, honors Frederick S. Antrim of Aberdeen, the first man to meet the six-member Press Expedition as they emerged from the wilderness into the Quinault Valley in 1890. (see INTRODUCTION.) 167, 207

APHRODITE (6,254'); MT. OLYMPUS (4B). Kent Heathershaw and an Olympic College party named this peak in 1965, following the original theme established by the naming of Mt. Olympus, "Home of the Gods." In Greek mythology Aphrodite is the goddess of love and beauty, the daughter of Zeus, and the counterpart of the Roman goddess Venus. The first ascent was in 1964 by members of the Olympic College climbing class. 69, 140, 146.5

APOLLO (7,168') (see MT. MATHIAS)

ARIES (6,400'); MT. OLYMPUS (4B). This peak was named by glaciologists Richard Hubley and lean, bearded Edward LaChapelle (chief glaciologist of the University of Washington Department Of Atmospheric Sciences) in preparation for the International Geophysical Year in 1955. The name was in keeping with the theme of Mt. Olympus as "Home of the Gods."
Aries, the Ram, is a constellation and the first sign of the Zodiac. Aries was sacrificed to Zeus, who in turn transformed him into a constellation and placed him in the heavens. 69, 140, 169, 202

THE ARROWHEAD (7,000'); TYLER PEAK (2C). This difficult-to-climb 120' spire in the Needles was named for its shape by Keith Spencer and Kent Heathershaw in 1958. 140, 184.5

ATHENA (7,350'); **ATHENA II** (7,250'); MT. OLYMPUS (3B). This peak may have been originally called Mt. Reid by the Seattle Press Expedition in honor of Whitelaw Reid of the *New York Tribune*.
The peak may have been named after the 1938 first ascent by D. Dooley, G. Martin, B. Peterson, and B. Scott, following the "Home of the Gods" theme. The first ascent of Athena II may have been on September 22, 1890, by Bernard Bretherton, Nelson Linsley, and Private John Danton as part of the Lieutenant Joseph O'Neill expeditions. Athena, in Greek mythology, is the goddess of wisdom and invention. Athena II, just southeast of Athena, was named by Robert L. Wood during area field trips in the early 1970s. 69, 120, 140, 146.5, 169, 207.5

ATHENA'S OWL (7,000'); MT. OLYMPUS (3B). Athena's Owl peak resembles an owl with its two "ears" protruding upward. Richard Hubley and Edward LaChapelle named it in preparation for the 1957-58 International Geophysical Year in keeping with the theme of "Home of the Gods" established by the original naming of Mt. Olympus. In Greek mythology, Athena and her owl stayed as close together as are these peaks. 169, 207.5

AURORA CREEK, PEAK (4,700'), **RIDGE**; LAKE CRESCENT (5B). August 1908, while atop the ridge they were later to name, Chris Morgenroth (District Ranger), Theodore Rixon (surveyor) and Glyde Chapman (packer for the Sol Duc Hot Spring Resort development project) thought they were witnessing searchlights from a flotilla of battleships due to enter the Strait of Juan de Fuca. Rixon was first to realize the spectacular show enjoyed by the trio for over an hour was the Aurora Borealis. So impressed were they that over breakfast the next morning local landmarks were christened with the name Aurora.

On occasion one can see the Northern Lights from Forks and other locations in the vicinity. Aurora Ridge is indeed a spectacular viewing platform for this phenomenon of nature.

A Makah legend says that the Northern Lights came from a tribe of dwarfs who lived many moons' journey north of the Olympic Peninsula. The dwarfs, as the story goes, were evil spirits who were only half as tall as a canoe paddle. They made their home on the ice, living on seals and whales. These frightening little people often dove into the freezing water and caught whales barehanded. Whale blubber was then boiled over huge fires built on the ice, thus creating the Northern Lights. 39, 62, 62.5, 138, 154, 175

BABY ISLAND; LAKE OZETTE (4B). Containing less than one acre, this is the smallest island on Lake Ozette. By way of comparison, nearby Tivoli Island has 22 1/2 acres and Garden Island has 7 1/2 acres. 152

BADGER VALLEY; MT ANGELES (5E). Two versions exist of how this area received its name. Some old-timers think that early visitors hiking through the valley saw Olympic marmots, mistook them for badgers, and promptly christened the site Badger Prairie (later, Badger Valley). There is no evidence that badgers have ever lived on the Olympic Peninsula.

Another story claims that the valley was named by Forest Ranger Frank Vincent (1870-1947) for a horse named "Badger" sometime between 1910 and 1920. His stepdaughter, Marian Taylor, was the first woman to ride a horse (Badger) up Sentinel Peak in the Dosewallips. It is worth noting, however, that the horse never made it all the way up to Badger Valley!
51, 120, 190

BAILEY RANGE; MT. OLYMPUS (5D). On April 27, 1890, the range was named for William Bailey, owner and publisher of the *Seattle Press* newspaper. Bailey's paper sponsored the 1889-90 Press Expedition, the first fully recorded journey through the heart of the Olympic Mountains. (See INTRODUCTION.)

The Bailey Range was first traversed by Billy Everett, who in 1885 at the age of 16 reached Cream Lake Basin. Some claim he was the first to ascend Mt. Carrie and Mt. Fitzhenry, located along the range. 12, 120, 169, 207

BALDUR (5,750'); MT. OLYMPUS (1A). This peak was climbed in 1971 by a party of Bremerton climbers, R. Beckett, D. Haley, G. Kelsey, M. Lennox, D. Michael, H. Pinsch, D. Stevens, and R. Yekel. The christening of the peak as "Baldur" by Pinsch and Kelsey was a direct reference to Norse mythology, wherein Odin's second son of that name is the god of sunlight, spring and joy. According to legend, Baldur was fair and wise, as well as physically beautiful, and loved all things. He lived in a mansion called "Broad Gleaming," which only the pure could enter. Baldur was inadvertently slain by mistletoe hurled at him by the blind god Hodr, who was in turn deceived by the evil Loki. The naming is in keeping with the "Home of the Gods" theme earlier established. 69, 78, 140, 169, 184.5

THE BANDERSNATCH (5,300'); MT. STEEL (8D). Donald N. Anderson of Bremerton christened this 150' spire on "Jabberwocky Ridge" during his ascent with Jim Richardson and Eldin Rogers in 1958. The name referred to the fierce, imaginary animal in Lewis Carroll's *Through the Looking Glass*. Stanza 2 of "The Jabberwocky" in *Through the Looking Glass* says of the Bandersnatch:

> Beware the Jabberwock, my son!
> The jaws that bite, the claws that catch!
> Beware the Jubjub bird, and shun
> The frumious Bandersnatch!
> The king, when asked to "stop a minute," says that is impossible. He might as well try to stop a Bandersnatch.

Fit 7, verse 3, 4, 5 and 6 in *The Hunting of the Snark*, also by Lewis Carroll:

> But while he was seeking with thimbles and care,
> A Bandersnatch swiftly drew nigh
> And grabbed at the Banker, who shrieked in despair,
> For he knew it was useless to fly.
>
> He offered large discount- he offered a cheque
> (Drawn "to bearer") for seven-pounds-ten;

But the Bandersnatch merely extended its neck
And grabbed at the Banker again.

Without rest or pause-while those frumious jaws
Went savagely snapping around-
He skipped and he hopped, and he floundered and flopped,
Till fainting he fell to the ground.

The Bandersnatch fled as the other appeared;
Led on by that fear-stricken yell;
And the Bellman remarked "It is just as I feared!"
And solemnly tolled on his bell.

The peak named for this mythical beast is a difficult Olympic ascent in isolated terrain. 36, 37, 140, 169, 184.5

BARNES CREEK, POINT; LAKE CRESCENT (7B). This point is a delta of sediment from a glacier which overlaid this point during the Pleistocene Epoch, one million years ago. There are two stories told regarding the naming of Barnes Point and Barnes Creek. The first says that Paul Barnes, brother of the Press Expedition explorer, Charles A. Barnes and Sarah Porter Barnes (their mother) settled on the point in 1890. By another account Pierre Barnes, a Seattle patent attorney, and his brothers pioneered in the area naming Marymere Falls and applying their name to both the stream and point. 126, 207, 207.5

BARRINGTON FIELD; SALMON RIVER (7D). The site was occupied in the 1890s by Thomas Killea, from 1908 to 1913 by a man named Barrington (from whom the name derives), and from 1915 for an unspecified time by a Mr. Cooper. The seven-acre field included a small orchard; it has returned to its natural state. 203

BEAR PASS; MT OLYMPUS (5B). Grant Humes and a friend camped in the Dodwell-Rixon Pass area in August of 1907. They attempted to climb Mt. Olympus, but were forced to descend because of stormy weather. When returning to camp, it is said they happened on some bear tracks and followed them back to their camp via "Bear Pass," which saved several hours. In Humes' own words: "In returning to our camp of the previous night, we discovered a shortcut, by following the tracks of a bear in the snow through a narrow pass, which saved about two miles of difficult going." 20, 99, 185

BEARGUT VALLEY; MT. ANGELES (6F). It is said that a 1912 hunting party traveling through this area carried as part of its weaponry, "a large cannon" (gun). With this weapon, the "hunters" shot a bear, hereafter the unfortunate animal rolled about 1,000 feet down a mountainside spilling internal organs everywhere; hence, the name Beargut Valley. 114

BEE CREEK; SPRUCE MTN. (6D). Wild honeybees are rare here. Perhaps early trail builders stumbled on a yellow jacket or hornet nest and in their excitement called them "bees." 152, 154

BELVEDERE (7,528') (See MT. CLARK.)

BELVIEW CAMP; MT. STEEL (3B). The term "Belview" derives from the word "belvedere," meaning a structure "commanding a view." As used to describe this site, it refers to the splendid view south of Six Stream Valley and Five Ridge. It is not known who affixed the name to the area. 53, 69

BEN LAKE; MT. STEEL (5D)

BENSONS POINT; LAKE OZETTE (5D). The Andrew Benson family were early homesteaders at this site. The name stems from their early occupancy. 3, 107, 193

BICENTENNIAL PEAK (6,722'); MT. STEEL (4F). Mike Doherty of Port Angeles is thought to be the first climber to ascend this mountain, in 1970. It was named in honor of the 1976 United States Bicentennial. 140

Above: BILLY EVERETT, HERB CRISLER AND MT. OLYMPUS. Here two venerable mountain men pause to enjoy the landscape.
(Olympic National Park Collection)

Below: BLUE GLACIER. So named for the bluish tint of its crevasses by the Seattle Mountaineers in 1912. Photograph circa 1925. (Marilyn Lewis Collection)

Above: BLUE GLACIER. These two women are on a Klahhane Club outing circa 1920. Note Glacier Pass in the upper left corner of the photograph. (Clallam County Historical Society Collection)

Below: AMOS B. CAMERON FAMILY. The family is pictured here at their Blue Mountain homestead. Amos, a mountain man of considerable reputation blazed the first trails into the Cameron Valley and with his wife contributed 14 students to the local school district. (Clallam County Historical Society Collection)

BIG CREEK; MT. CHRISTIE (2C). A 30-foot-wide river, 5-6 feet deep, sinks underground at one point, leaving nothing but a dry creek bed downstream (it rarely contains water and only during times of extreme high runs). After its underground journey, the river resurfaces farther downstream. When it emerges, it is noticeably wider and deeper than before it dipped beneath the surface, accounting for the term "underground passage" which appears on some current maps. 58, 120

BIG FLAT; MT. TOM (3B). Here one will find a huge, flat area made up of a series of small meadows and wooded areas. 152

BIG LOG CAMP; MT. STEEL (4C). This camp, along the North Fork of the Skokomish River, was named for the large foot log that spanned the river at this site. 27, 53

BIG RIVER; LAKE OZETTE (5E). The river was first settled in July, 1890, by a party of Scandinavian immigrants, including Nils P. Andrews, Ole Boe, and 16-year-old Ole Klaboe.

The area around Ozette is deluged with winter rain. Consequently, when travelers came through, they frequently were unable to cross the swollen, turbulent river; thus the name Big River was applied. Paradoxically, the summer flow on Big River is so light that it becomes a narrow stream one can actually jump across. 120, 149

BIG ROCK (See SHELTER ROCK).

BILLY EVERETT LAKE; MT. OLYMPUS (6D). The lake was named in 1945 during a trip by Billy Everett, Herb and Lois Crisler, "Chappy" Chapman, and Carol Preston. By naming the lake for him, Billy's friends honored him for his achievements. Everett was the first man to traverse the Bailey Range and was one of the very earliest explorers and hunters in this region. See EVERETT PEAK.) 95, 141, 173

BIRKESTOL POINT; LAKE OZETTE (4B). A Norwegian family, the Birkestols, settled in the area. Tom Birkestol settled at the south end of Lake Ozette and his mother, Mrs. Anna Birkestol, settled at what is now Birkestol Point. 107, 120, 193

BLACK AND WHITE LAKES; MT. STEEL (5C). According to geologist Ralph Arnold, the name derives from nearby Camp Black and White, which in turn was named by early elk hunters for a brand of whiskey of that name. Apparently one in the party was sober enough during their sojourn here to mark the name prominently on a tree. There was also a Black and White Mine on Mt. Gladys which is said to have produced gold, manganese, and copper from 1907 through the 1940s (see GLADYS DIVIDE). 120, 159, 204

BLACK GLACIER; MT. OLYMPUS (2C). Commonly called Mud Glacier in the 1940s and located between the Blue and White Glaciers, its name refers to the dark color cast upon it from rocks and dirt falling onto its surface from the cliffs above. 152, 185

BLACKWOOD CREEK, LAKE; MT. TOM (4F). Al J. Blackwood, an early county government contract surveyor (some claim he was a prospector and trapper as well), arrived in Port Crescent in 1891. Blackwood Creek and Lake Blackwood were named for him shortly thereafter. All that is known for certain concerning the dates is that the names had already been applied prior to the Dodwell-Rixon surveys that began in 1898. 91, 120, 156

BLIZZARD PASS; MT. OLYMPUS (4B). In 1907, the Mountaineers were caught in a blizzard here during their first ascent of Mt. Olympus. Founded that year, their first annual outing was to the previously unclimbed Mt. Olympus. They planned to go up the Elwha into the Queets Basin and then up the mountain. Two weeks before the outing, however, Belmore Brown, Hershel Parker, and William Clark of the Explorers Club (an exclusive New York City club affiliated with the American Geographical Society), used William Humes' 35-mile trail, paid for by and built for the Mountaineers, to try to beat them up the mountain. The Explorers named "Explorers' Pass" and climbed the Middle Peak, which is not actually the highest peak of the Mt. Olympus massif.

In mid-July of 1907, the Mountaineers, with 65 climbers, used the trail William Humes built for them and traveled to

Queets Basin. On August 10, they climbed over Explorers' Pass but were forced to turn back because of the previously mentioned blizzard. Demoralized by their encounter with the gale, Asahel Curtis wrote:

Once out from the protection of the snow ridge, exposed to the full fury of the gale and everyone's hope sank. Through the pass at its head a thirty-mile gale was blowing, whirling the snow along as it fell...The Party appeared suspended in the heavens on the edge of some great cloud, with a white desolate world forming out of the chaos.

The retreat bugle was sounded and Companies A through D reversed their course back down the Humes Glacier toward Queets Basin. In memory of their adventure, the Mountaineers re-named the pass "Blizzard Pass."

A party of 11 climbers consisting of Miss Anna Hubert, (see HUBERT GLACIER), L.A. Nelson, W. Montelius Price, Professor Henry Landes, Professor Charles Landes, Professor T.C. Frye, Professor F.M. Plumb, Professor Weaver, J.B. Flett, E.E. Richards, and A.W. Archer returned to climb East Peak and West Peak on August 13, 1907. They were the first to officially climb the highest point in the Olympics. 10, 48, 169, 185, 207.5

BLOOMS BAY; LAKE OZETTE (3E). Blooms Bay was named for an early homesteader in this area. It is not known who affixed the name or when it was done. The house he built was moved in 1901. 107

BLUE GLACIER; MT. OLYMPUS (3C). The bluish tint of the crevasses, accentuated in the ice fall area, is the source of this name. It was christened and first explored in 1912 by Edward W. Allen in company with Charles Farrer, Earl Rice, and a Mr. Stuart (first name unknown), all of the Seattle Mountaineers Club. 91, 120, 152, 207.5

BLUE LAKE; MT. OLYMPUS (1F). The name of this lake derives from the deep blue color of the water. 152

BLUE MOUNTAIN (6,077'); MT. ANGELES (8F). During summer months, a soft, blue haze seems to hang over this peak, providing the source of its name.

A devastating fire in 1891 destroyed much of the Dungeness/Blue Mountain area. The blaze was so widespread and intense that 30,000 acres were laid bare. Winds created by the flames actually blew off the roof and door of a local settler's cabin. 120, 166

BOB CREEK; KLOOCHMAN ROCK (5F). The name is believed to honor Bob McKee, a bachelor who had a cabin across from the Smith Place (see SMITH PLACE), located about five miles downstream. 104

BODELTA ISLANDS (198'); LAKE OZETTE (1F). The Makah name for these two islands is "baditta," pronounced "ba-di 't-ta," a word for which there is no known English translation. The islands had the largest breeding colony of seagulls (about 2,500) on the Olympic coast in 1959. 120, 121

BOGACHIEL LAKE, NORTH FORK RIVER, PEAK (5,474'), **RANGER STATION**; SPRUCE MTN. (3E), MT. TOM (6E). The word is a corruption of the Quileute words bo' qwa tcheel el, meaning "gets riley after a rain," "muddy waters," or (less likely) "big river." In the summer of 1892 Chris Morgenroth, with a neighbor, left his homestead on the banks of the upper Bogachiel River to explore its headwaters (this home later became a U.S.F.S. Bogachiel Ranger Station). On the fifth day of the expedition the two reached the summit and named Bogachiel Peak. In his autobiography, *Footprints in the Olympics*, Chris credits the grandeur and beauty that overwhelmed him that day with beginning his life-long affair with the Olympics that made him such a force behind the Park movement.

Four decades later, on September 16, 1934, at the direction of Preston Macy, Assistant Chief Ranger at Mt. Rainier, Chris Morgenroth and Charley Anderson began construction of a fire lookout on Bogachiel Peak. Outfitters Minnie Peterson and Micky Merchant (see Mink Lake) packed camp and building materials for the project from Sol Duc Hot Springs. 12, 50, 62.5, 154, 155, 156, 171, 180

BOOT BAY; LAKE OZETTE (5C). The bay closely resembles the outline of a boot when viewed on a map or from the air. 120

BOSTON CHARLIE'S CAMP; MT. OLYMPUS (3D). Boston Charlie was born in the 1860s and homesteaded the lower Elwha River where Harold Sisson later owned property. Called Boston for his adoption of some white ways, Boston Charlie was a mountain man and the last medicine man of the Klallam people. Boston Charlie frequented Olympic Hot Springs for spiritual cleansing long before they were discovered by white people. Located at the east end of the Catwalk was one of his favorite campsites, one that became known as Boston Charlie's Camp. Boston Charlie continued to roam the Olympics into his later years and his encounter with a mountain being similar to a Sasquatch is part of Klallam oral history.

Boston Charlie became foster father to relative Billy Everett after Klallam native, Mrs. John Everett, died giving birth to Billy. Under Boston Charlie's tutelage Billy Everett became a mountain man and explorer of considerable reputation. 51, 140, 179, 210.5

BOSTON SWAMP (Meadow); MT. STEEL (1G). This beautiful, spacious, but swampy, area is located about one-half mile beyond the Elwha River crossing and just below Chicago Camp. It was the first meadow one encountered after leaving the Elwha and provided spectacular trailside views of the ridge tops on either side of the valley. Because it is too wet to tramp through until August or September of each year, and because of potential damage to its terrain, the Elwha Trail has been routed away from it.

There are many theories as to the origin of this name, but none could be documented. Some think early mountaineers may have named the spot for the East Coast city of the same name. Others believe the name was applied by Native Americans, for the word "Boston" was a Native term for "white man." Thus it may have been done as a compliment (because of the picturesque view), or as a joke (because it is, after all, only a swamp). Still others theorize that Boston Swamp may honor old Boston Charlie, who is said to have camped here many times. Noted wildlife photographer Herb Crisler stayed here for long periods of time during the 1940s, and maintained a lean-to on the spot. 46, 51, 106, 150, 182

BOULDER CREEK, CREEK CAMPGROUND, LAKE, NORTH FORK CREEK, PEAK (5,600'); **SOUTH FORK CREEK;** MT. OLYMPUS (2G), MT. TOM (8G). Boulder Creek was named for the many boulders along its course. Other features were named because of their proximity to the creek. Boulder Peak was probably dubbed Mount Agnus by the Seattle Press Expedition members during their 1889-90 trek through the Olympics, so named to honor Felix Agnus, a Baltimore, Maryland publisher. This name fell into disuse, and was replaced by the term so common in local usage, Boulder Peak. Boulder Hot Springs, named in 1907, is now called Olympic Hot Springs. 120, 179, 207.5

BOULEVARD CREEK; SPRUCE MTN. (4D). This stream has a boulevard-like look, flowing, as it does, through a flat, open area where the trail crosses it. 29, 154

BOVEE(S) MEADOW; LAKE CRESCENT (7B). Mr. and Mrs. Bovee lived in this area during the 1950s. The Bovees owned Lake Crescent Lodge, which they later sold to the National Park Service. This property includes the dead hulk of what was once the world's largest grand fir. The last building was removed in the late 1960s. 49, 122, 157, 191

BOWMAN CREEK; MT. ANGELES (1E). During the 1890s and on into the first decade of the twentieth-century, a hunter named Bowman maintained a small cabin near the old Elwha trail. Located along a small stream, the cabin had an outside fireplace and was Bowman's base of operations for extensive hunting forays into the nearby hills. His residence there for at least five years assured the name of the stream.

Nevertheless, the 1889-90 Seattle Press Expedition members apparently named it Kate Creek, an application which did not take hold with local residents, and which did not appear on any permanent maps of that era. (It is not known to whom the Expedition members referred when they called the stream "Kate.") A letter from M.D. Humes to his brother Will on February 8, 1898 (mailed, interestingly enough, from the old McDonald stump post office) verifies that he had hunted with Bowman in that section of the woods just a few days earlier. Bowman was still living and hunting there in 1903, when Will Humes wrote to M.D. Humes that "...our friend Bowman was in there a few days previous and saw them and got a fine bull. The place was almost to the head of Lost River..." This letter was written at a time when Bowman evidently was working for the U.S. Forest Service, enforcing rules dealing with grazing permits. He had begun work for that agency in approximately 1899.

The well-known hunter later settled on 40 acres at Madison Creek, on land previously occupied by a settler of that name. Bowman "proved up" the land- something settler Madison and another man named Schmitt had not done. (See MADISON CREEK.) 26, 100, 179, 207

BRAGI (5,450'); MT. OLYMPUS (1A). This 170-foot high pinnacle first climbed in 1978 honors a character from Norse mythology. Bragi is the god of poetry and husband of the fertility goddess, Idunn. 69, 78, 120, 140, 146.5, 169

BRIDAL VEIL FALLS; see MADISON CREEK.

BRIDGE CREEK; MT. OLYMPUS (2E).

BROKENFINGER CREEK; THE BROTHERS (4G).

THE BROTHERS (6,866'); THE BROTHERS (4E). The mountain with twin spires was discovered in May of 1792 by English naval explorer George Vancouver, who viewed it from Hood Canal. Captain George Davidson of the U.S. Coast and Geodetic Survey named it in 1856 for members of the Fauntleroy family. He was in love with Ellinor Fauntleroy and thought he could impress her father and her by naming the peaks in honor of her brothers, Arthur and Edward Fauntleroy. Arthur Fauntleroy later became a civil engineer and died in 1884 at the age of 40. Edward did not live as long. He was employed as an aide to Captain Davidson on the Pacific Coast, and was not yet 20 when he died in 1861. George named Mt. Ellinor, north of Lake Cushman outside Olympic National Park, for his fiancée a year before their 1858 marriage.

The first ascent of the lower north peak via the Duckabush approach was in 1908 by William R. Hill and his brother, Clinie E. Hill, football players at the University of Washington and members of Phi Gamma fraternity. The first ascent of the higher south peak was in 1912 by six University of Washington students and instructors, Ira L. Collier, Orville P. Cockerill, William M. Dehn, Walter H. Fish, Edward D. Goldsmith, and Harlan L. Trumbull. They also used the Duckabush approach. The Board of Geographic Names rejected a Seattle resident's proposal to change the name to The Brothers Kennedy for John and Robert, in 1967. 70, 120, 130, 155, 169

BROWN CREEK, POINT; DESTRUCTION ISLAND (4E). Named for James Brown, early settler. Brown settled near here at the mouth of Kalaloch Creek in 1892. Two relatives, Bessie and Robert W. Brown, moved to a nearby site a few years later. 120, 207.5

BRUSH CREEK; SPRUCE MTN. (7D).

BUCK LAKE; MT. STEEL (6E). This body of water was originally named Indigo Lake by an O'Neil Expedition scouting party (Bretherton and Yates) on August 19, 1890. That name appears appropriate, for the water is a deep blue color, enhanced considerably by the steep cliffs rimming the lake. Early trappers or hunters began referring to it as Buck Lake, and it remains so today. 120, 152, 208

BUCKINGHORSE CREEK; MT. STEEL (2G).

BUNCH CREEK, LAKE, FIELD; MT. CHRISTIE (3A). Honored here is the Bunch Family, Jack, Jasper, and John. Jack and Jasper were two very early homesteaders in the Quinault area above the lake and below the forks of the Quinault River. John Bunch, a cousin, lived nearby. 59, 94, 167

BURDICK CREEK; MT. ANGELES (8B).

BURKE RANGE; MT. ANGELES (3A), MT. STEEL (4F). Judge Thomas Burke of Seattle, an important figure in Western Washington during the late 1800s, was honored here by the Seattle Press Expedition during the first fully recorded trans-Olympic trip in 1889-90. 169, 207

BURNT MOUNTAIN (4,910'); PORT ANGELES (4A). A terrible fire swept over this region in the late 1890s, scorching the earth all the way from the Elwha River to Deer Park. Now somewhat overgrown again, the mountain is clearly visible from Dungeness and several other vantage points nearby. 114

BUTLER CREEK; MOUNT ANGELES (6C).

CACHE CREEK; MT. ANGELES (8B).

CAKE ROCK; LA PUSH (3F). The name derives from its cake shape, which is quite obvious to the observer. 120, 152

CAKESOSTA (ROCK); LA PUSH (5D).

CALAWAH RIVER, (SOUTH FORK); SPRUCE MTN. (3E). "Calawah" is derived from a Quileute word, "Kayloway" ("ca la wa") and pronounced "Ka' la wa." The word means "middle fork" or "middle river." As shown on the 1896 Gilman National Geographic map, it was spelled Killiwah. 12, 73, 120, 161, 180

CAMERON BASIN, **CREEK, GLACIERS, MOUNT** (7,192'), **PASS**; MT. ANGELES (5C), TYLER PEAK (1E). It is thought that Cameron Basin was originally named "No Place," or "Camp No Place," by Lt. Joseph O'Neil during his 1885 expedition into the interior of the Olympics. The camp was the deepest penetration by O'Neil's pack animals on that journey. It is a tribute to outfitter Minnie Peterson's skill and tenacity as an outfitter that in August 1965 at age 67 while packing for the Sierra Club, Minnie brought two riding horses and eleven fully loaded pack horses across Cameron Glacier and Pass without incident.

   The name "Cameron" was applied to these geographic features by a map sketcher employed by the U.S. Forest Service. Amos B. Cameron, for whom they were named, was one of the earliest settlers in this area, having arrived on the North Olympic Peninsula around 1899. For 41 years he homesteaded in the Deer Park region, all the while hunting, packing and ranching. A noted hunter, Cameron was reputed to have killed seven cougar and 23 bobcats in one year.

   He forged the first trail into Cameron Basin and named the Lower Cameron (camp area) "Boone Valley," for Emerson Boone, one of his fourteen children. Today, there are still descendants of Amos Cameron living in Clallam County. 12, 32, 33, 34, 94, 101, 135, 153.25, 169

CAMP BALTIMORE (Baltimore Bottom); MT. ANGELES (1E). It is not certain how Camp Baltimore received its name. Two stories are told, either of which might be true.

   Some believe that C.D. Sisson and one of the Humes brothers, either M.D. or Will, guided and packed into this area a party of wealthy persons from Baltimore, Maryland. Thereafter the spot was called Baltimore Bottom or Camp Baltimore.

   Another version, however, claims that the first climbing party with a recorded climb of Mt. Olympus, the Seattle Mountaineers, named several areas after large U.S. cities. Some of the Mountaineers on that particular climb were cosmopolitan with a few from Baltimore, thus the name. 94, 114, 179

CAMP BEAUTY, LAKE, PASS; MT. CHRISTIE (4F). Merle D. Schmid was one of 16 boy scouts who in August, 1930 hiked across the Olympics. The 16- to 19-year olds and their 40-year-old guide started at North Fork Quinault and ended up at Brinnon 15 days later, having climbed seven peaks - including Olympus and Anderson - along the way.

   Enroute, the scouts located a then-unnamed body of water, and decided among themselves that it was such a beautiful spot it should be called Lake Beauty. After three years of intense discussion with U.S. Forest Service and State of Washington officials- during which time they had to convince all parties that the lake really was a lake and not a snow pocket - the officials gave their approval to the name. Later, in 1932, the young men received permission from the U.S. Forest Service to plant eyed (fertile) trout eggs in the lake. They did so, carefully securing the eggs in wet moss and packing them over the Olympics' difficult terrain to Lake Beauty.

   Camp Beauty was a Herb Crisler encampment, the "headquarters" from which he filmed elk and other natural scenes for several Disney Studio motion pictures. At one time it was common for food to be stored at the camp. Crisler camps were removed in the summer 1985. It should be noted that Camp Beauty is difficult to find.

   Robert L. Wood named Beauty Pass in August 1964. 64.5, 95, 152, 172, 207.5

CAMP CREEK; MT. TOM (2F). The U.S. Forest Service is thought to have established a camp or base here while constructing the well-known Bogachiel Trail. 154

CAMP DAVID JUNIOR; LAKE CRESCENT (4C). Dr. Louis Dechman established a beautiful health spa/resort at this site in 1912. Originally dubbed Eugenika in honor of the "goddess of the better race," Dechman later changed the name of his sanatorium to Qui Si Sana, Latin for "Here Find Health."

Louis Dechman was a splendid promoter with a deep belief that good health - even perfect health - could be attained with a balanced regimen of outdoor exercise, good diet, and relaxation. The doctor's treatments involved deep breathing, positive thinking, and quiet meditation. The resort became quite popular with Clallam County residents - especially housewives who left their dishpans to follow the charismatic Dechman's formula to good health.

Qui Si Sana was fabulously beautiful during Dechman's time there. Elaborately landscaped with exotic, imported shrubs, it featured terraces, pools, fruit orchards, rock gardens, and statuary artistically placed throughout the grounds. The lodge itself was ornately furnished and presented a restful atmosphere to the suave Dechman's many guests. Furniture was of the finest hickory, and there were magnificent antler chandeliers made of elk horn imported from Germany.

Dechman's sanatorium flourished for several years, but in 1917 he became involved in a court fight over water rights to an adjoining stream and Dr. David Thompson acquired the land. The resort closed forever. Many years later Dr. Thompson donated the land to Clallam County with the provision that it be used for the recreation of youth and that it be named after his son David, Jr.

Some of the statuary erected by Dechman is still visible on the grounds of Camp David, Jr. The original buildings, however, have since been torn down and replaced by a new lodge now operated by the Clallam County Parks Department, which retains jurisdiction over it. Groups wishing to rent Camp David, Jr. may do so by applying to the Parks Department at the Clallam County Courthouse. 25, 108, 195

CAMP MARION; MT. ANGELES (8B). Camp Marion was named in honor of Marian "Vincent" Taylor (Marion is a misspelling that has been perpetuated for decades), who was the step-daughter of well-know settler and forest ranger, Frank Vincent. Back-country packers, Frank and Marian hunted and packed up the Dosewallips from 1910 to 1920. Marian began helping her stepfather when she was but a young lady, about age fifteen, and later became the first woman to ride a horse to the top of Sentinel Peak (see also BADGER VALLEY). Her well-known, large, white horse, Badger, did the honors. Marian traced her ancestry as a descendant of S'Klallam Chief Ste-tee-thlum through E'owitsa (little sister) in the great Chief's "House of the Seven Brothers." 12, 190, 113.75

CAMP PAN; MT. OLYMPUS (3B).The camp, about 300 feet above the Hoh Glacier and on a rocky table, likely takes its name from Greek and Roman mythology. Pan was a lustful, woodland god, with the ears, horns, tail, and hind legs of a goat. Pan was the son of Hermes and Dryope, and was the god of flocks and shepherds. Pan invented the seven-reed pipe, naming it after the nymph Syrinx, who turned into a reed to escape him. Pan competed with the god Apollo (see APOLLO and MOUNT MATHIAS) in a music contest and lost. Pan was known to cause terror amongst mortals, thus the word "panic," as in Panic Peak (6,860') on the Snow Dome (see SNOW DOME). 69, 78, 140, 169

CAMP PLEASANT; MT. STEEL (5C). This breeze-swept, bottomland campsite by the North Fork Skokomish River is comfortable and most pleasant; thus the name. Being three miles up the old trail, it was formerly called "Threemile." 53, 74, 209

CAMP SIBERIA; (see ANDERSON PASS)

CAMP WILDER, MOUNT (5,198'); MT. ANGELES (2A). The mountain was called Mt. Barnes by the Seattle Press Expedition. Early passersby put signs on trees in this area to name it. The signs were made by positioning fire-heated wire in the form of letters onto boards, thus burning the words into the wood permanently.

The first sign read "Bean Camp." By 1940 the area, initially a hunting camp, was signed "Crackerville". This name lasted for years and honored an incident in which a horse in a pack train became uncontrollable and bucked off its load of crackers.

The present camp name was derived from a group of families from Tacoma (Clark, Hardy, Oliver). The Tacomans camped at the mountain base annually in the 1920s and 1930s. It is not known to whom the name Wilder refers. 51, 64.5, 94, 137, 141, 207.5

CANNINGS CREEK; MT. CHRISTIE (4A).

Above: CANNONBALL ISLAND. Some names are deceptive, as are appearances. There are no true cannon balls on Cannonball Island. (Olympic National Park Collection)

Below: CAMP WILDER. Camp Wilder, located along the Elwha, was known as "Crackerville" when this photograph was taken in 1910. (Olympic National Park Collection)

Left: BOSTON CHARLIE. Boston Charlie, the last medicine man of the Klallam people, roamed the Olympics throughout his entire life. A camp on the Catwalk in the Olympic National Park is named in his honor. Photograph circa 1920. (Adeline Smith Collection)

Below: CIVILIAN CONSERVATION CORPS TENTS IN CAT CREEK BASIN. Cat Creek Basin served as CCC headquarters for the Corps trail building effort to reach the Cream Lake region of the Hoh Valley. Photograph circa 1939. (Peterson Collection)

CANNONBALL ISLAND; LAKE OZETTE (1F). The original Makah Indian name for this island was "wa-ye-?iq," pronounced "wa'h-yeah-iq." Warriors would often go to the island to play a game designed to improve accuracy with the bow and arrow. Known as a "hoop game," it consisted of having one man throw hoops (made of twisted limbs) into the air while others tried to shoot arrows through them while they were airborne.

Cannonball Island has been called other names throughout the years. Some early maps labeled it "tskawahyah," while others knew the place simply as Indian Island.

The present name describes cannonball-like sandstone concretions (masses of mineral matter, usually found in rock, of a composition different from that around it), perhaps formed by wave action interacting with the aqueous solution in the rock. Some archaeological excavations were made on Cannonball during 1967. Also, one can find an old, abandoned Coast Guard cabin on the island's summit. 120, 121

CANOE CREEK; KLOOCHMAN ROCK (6A). Before there was a road on the north shore of Lake Quinault, a canoe landing just a little below the mouth of this stream served those north shore residents using this means of transportation. It was known as Higley's Landing (see HIGLEY CREEK) and was the main settlement in the area. 59

CANYON CAMP; MT. ANGELES (2E). There is a natural canyon here with high, pronounced cliffs on the west side of the Elwha River. It is not known who assigned the name to this camp. 75

CANYON CREEK; MT. TOM (6F). The creek descends through a canyon. Canyon Creek Shelter, often called Sol Duc Falls Shelter, was constructed in 1939 and remains an excellent example of Civilian Conservation Corps workmanship. Just past Appleton Pass Trail junction, on a Douglas fir tree is a CCC inscription-"9-14-33 CCC F O Wagner." 64.5

CAPE ALAVA; LAKE OZETTE (1E). The westernmost geographical landmark in the contiguous United States. Named by Manuel Quimper in August 1790 for Jose Manuel de Alava, Commissioner for Spain at the 1790 Nootka Convention. Originally, Quimper intended the cape to be called "Hijosa" and the cove just south of it to be called "Boca de Alava." The term "Alava" was transferred from the bay to the cape in 1792 during the voyage of Dionisio Alcala-Galiano and Cayetano Valdez. The name Alava is both a family and province name in Spain. As a Spanish name, it is accented on the first syllable, unlike the accepted pronunciation today, accenting the second syllable. 12, 55, 120, 131, 155

CAPE JOHNSON, CREEK; LA PUSH (3F). A Makah Indian name for this point is "xi-xap" pronounced "xee-xap," meaning "a point." Another name for the point is "xacoc'u?a," pronounced "xa-chi-t'su-wah," meaning "a deep hole" in the Makah language. The Quileute Indians called the area "ta-qwa-at," meaning "big curve in the bay." The name first appeared as a feature on Captain George Vancouver's map on April 29, 1792.

It is thought that the cape was named for a Swedish or Norwegian fisherman who was lost when his boat wrecked in a storm on the rocky point.

On October 4, 1893, the Chilean bark *Leonore* found herself in a gale just south of Cape Johnson and piled onto the rocks. Many crew members jumped overboard but were smashed against the side of the boat by huge waves. Within a half hour, the vessel broke into pieces, and a few survivors drifted to shore on the debris. 118, 120, 121, 180

CARROLL ISLAND; LAKE OZETTE (2A).

CASTLE IN THE CAT; MT. OLYMPUS (3E). This unusual name refers to a cabin—still standing at the time this book first went to press in 1984, and in remarkably good condition—located in Cat Basin, near Cat Peak. Heavy snows crushed the cabin in the winter of 1998-1999. It was so christened by Herb Crisler in 1944, while he was there with his wife and a California youth visiting the family. Cat Peak itself is clearly visible from the "castle," which incidentally, has the words "Castle in Cat" inscribed upon it.

While camping in this area in 1981, the author listened to the shrill bugling of elk, experiencing the same thrill Crisler must have felt when such a challenging roar echoed over the valley floor. 64.5, 95, 152

CASTLE SPIRES (5,800'); MT. STEEL (6B). This peak on Sawtooth Ridge was christened by Neil Jacques of Bremerton at the time he made the first ascent in 1952 along with Louis Nothweng and Roy Smith. It certainly is an appropriate name. Turret-like towers reach skyward from this massive rock formation. 140, 169, 184.5

C

CAT CREEK, PEAK (5,940'); MT. OLYMPUS (3E). This stream was dubbed "Wildcat Creek" by members of the Press Expedition (see INTRODUCTION) on the morning of February 28, 1890. The group stayed on the banks of the stream for over two weeks during their journey, and on that particular day one of the men killed a bobcat at the juncture of the creek and the Elwha River. On the same morning, a wolf was killed in that vicinity, an incident which quite possibly accounts for the naming of nearby Wolf Creek. Both Cat Creek and Wolf Creek now drain into man-made Lake Mills; the sites of these two incidents are now under water. Cat creek drains both Cat Peak and Cat Basin. Near its headwaters lies Herb Crisler's cabin, "Castle in the Cat" (see CASTLE IN THE CAT), and Catwalk, a narrow ridge guarding the north Bailey Range entrance. In the late 1930s headquarters for the Parks' trail building effort into the Bailey Range was located in Cat Basin. The CCC crew was led by foreman Julian McCabe. The trail crew worked both east toward the Baileys and west toward the High Divide from this central location. The camp was made up of four crew tents and a cook tent that housed the 300 lb. stove outfitter Minnie Peterson packed to the Basin from Sol Duc Hot Springs. On her weekly supply trips Minnie dropped food at Cat Basin for the cook, and then continued to the trail's end with dynamite and other supplies.

In the early days of the project the cook was pleased to find a very simple solution to the camp's refrigeration problem; that is, until the local population of black bears zeroed in on the smell of smoked bacon and ham emanating from a snowfield near the camp.

By the time war came and Minnie pulled the Cat Basin camp, McCabe's crew had pushed the trail to within two miles of the Cream Lake traversing the steep slopes of Cat Peak and the southern flank of Mt. Carrie. 12, 18, 128.5, 153.25, 169, 207

CATS EARS; TYLER PEAK (5A). Its two peaks look like a cat's ears. 140

C.B. FLAT; MT. TOM (7E). Hoh ranger C. Bud Hanify favored the campsite on these flats. He was honored here in 1974-1978 in conjunction with his retirement. Hoh Lake lacked suitable flat camp spots and was overused from trampling and fires, so Bud put an outhouse on the flats to encourage use there. 43, 51, 79, 211

CEDAR CREEK; DESTRUCTION ISLAND (5G). This brackish, tea-colored stream flows through several cedar swamps, a fact which accounts for the unusual shade of the water - and the name. Although part of the stream was originally called Minnie Creek (for early homesteader Minnie Skofstad, circa 1890), the Gilman National Geographic map named it Piper Creek in 1896. Over the years, however, the natural physical properties of the creek, coupled with its location in the numerous swamps, caused local residents and other to unofficially name it Cedar Creek. The name caught on and remains today. 63, 73

CEDAR CREEK; LAKE OZETTE (4B). There are many western red cedar trees growing near this creek, thus the name. Ole Birkestol homesteaded upstream on this creek in 1891. His brother, Ivan, settled on the coast near the mouth of the stream. 120, 196

CEDAR POINT; LAKE CRESCENT (5C). Heavy western red cedar growth in the immediate vicinity prompted the naming of this point of land jutting into the water along the north shore of Lake Crescent. 152, 175

CHATEAU CAMP; MT. ANGELES (2C).

CHICAGO CAMP; MT. CHRISTIE (7G). It is uncertain how Chicago Camp was christened. It is likely that a group of hunters from Chicago, Illinois, stayed at this spot for several weeks in 1906. C.D. Sisson and Grant Humes guided such a group at that time, and a photo of the hunting camp from Humes' collection depicts several men loaded with camera gear and rifles standing before a canvas wall tent and a sign that says "Chicago Camp." 51, 64.5, 94, 106, 120, 179, 207.5

CHICAGO CAMP. Hunters at Chicago Camp 1906. (Olympic National Park Collection)

CHICKEN-EATER HILL; MT. ANGELES (1G). Although many a chicken (novice) skier "eats it" (falls) on this slope, the origin of the name is 1,000 miles distant, in Yosemite National Park, California. There, it was common for non-skiers to drive to Yosemite's Badger Pass Ski Lodge to lounge on the veranda and eat chicken on Sunday afternoons. These people were locally referred to as "chicken-eaters." When Park Ranger Dave Houston was transferred to Olympic National Park from Yosemite in 1967, he brought the expression with him. Referring to the arrival of non-skiers at Hurricane Ridge during the skiing season there, he often said "there's a lot of chicken-eaters coming up." The term was catchy, and by the time Houston left this area in 1973, it was commonly used to describe a particular brand of non-skier, 'tuber and sledder. The steep, quarter-mile descent just west of Hurricane Ridge Lodge warrants careful maneuvering no matter what mode of travel one chooses.

The following excerpts (stanzas 1, 4, 6, and 16 from a poem (1975) by rangers Jack Hughes and Janet Kailin bring this local lore to life:

> I got out of the Army
> For I tired of wars that kill
>
> Now I find the action worse
> On Chicken-Eater Hill...
>
> With laughter and excitement
> The air will quickly fill
> Hysteria and madness
> On Chicken-Eater Hill...
>
> The innertube went off the track
> Its passengers did spill
> And flew into the forest
> On Chicken-Eater Hill...
>
> To finish the report
> Rangers pick up ink and quill
> And add to the thick files
> On Chicken-Eater Hill...

There was a time when Park Rangers carried Kentucky Fried Chicken from nearby Port Angeles up to the lodge and conducted lighthearted parties around the fireplace.

Along the winter ski route from Chicken-Eater Hill to Hurricane Hill, many of the areas have been given names appropriate to conditions found there. "Windy Corner" (exposed to severe winds, but commanding a breathtaking view), "Watch Out" (a narrow slot where two-way traffic merges perilously), "Wipe Out" (where many a cross-country skier does just that), and "Exclamation Point" (where skiers may suddenly find themselves airborne!) follow in rapid succession. Then, slightly northeast of the picnic area in the Ridge compound, "Picnic Pass" (a hill adjacent to Picnic Area A) prepares the cross-country buff for "The Toilet Bowl," originally dubbed "Idaho Bowl" by Ranger Eric Burr (though, in truth, it is nowhere near Camp Idaho). Ski instructor Neal Brodien liked to refer to the Toilet Bowl as "Valley of 10,000 Falls" because it was thought that student Vern Bessey fell that many times while learning the snowplow turn. The unusual bathroom appellation "Toilet Bowl" was suggested by seasonal employee Pam Rouvalis because of its proximity to the restrooms of the above-mentioned Picnic Area A.

On Hurricane Hill itself, skiers confront "Steep and Icy," a steep and often icy side-slope 1/3 mile from the road end and "The Bowl" nearly a mile from the road end, a place popular with more advanced skiers working on their telemark. See map below concerning these places. 20, 94, 152

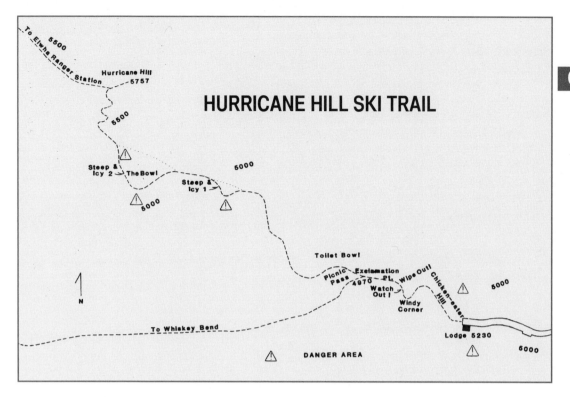

HURRICANE HILL SKI TRAIL

CHILEAN MEMORIAL; LA PUSH (4F). A small rock monument here marks the spot where 20 people died on November 26, 1920. A Chilean ship, the *W.J. Pirrie,* was being towed as a lumber barge by the *Santa Rita*. As the vessels neared Cape Flattery, they were assailed by 90-mile-per-hour winds and were driven shoreward. In order to escape certain disaster for his own ship and crew, the *Santa Rita's* captain was forced to cut the towline about 800 yards from shore - and the *W.J. Pirrie* was crushed on the offshore rocks. Two survivors lived to tell the tale after clutching frantically to pieces of the broken ship. Five men and one woman had previously died in a shipwreck nearby on October 4, 1893. Their Chilean vessel, the *Leonore* was enroute from Irique to Puget Sound and encountered gale-force winds just offshore. Forced onto rocks, it was quickly smashed to pieces.

Because of the two disasters, this section of shoreline is often referred to as the "Beach of the Dead." 120, 127, 144

CHIMNEY PEAK (6,911'); MT. STEEL (4F). The name refers to the presence of a square chimney-like tower on the west side of the peak. It was first climbed in 1941 by Toivo J. Nelson of the U.S. Geological Survey. Fifty-one years earlier, Charles Barnes and James Christie of the 1889-90 Press Expedition named this peak "Old Snowback" for its appearance on April 19, 1890 as viewed from the north. This name fell into disuse as the descriptive, presently accepted name Chimney Peak was circulated. 120, 169, 207, 207.5

CIRCE (6,874'); MT. OLYMPUS (3B). Circe is at the junction of three rock ridges which separate the Hoh, Humes, and Jeffers Glaciers. Named by glaciologists Hubley and LaChapelle in keeping with the mythical god theme already set with Mt. Olympus and in preparation for the International Geophysical Year, Circe refers to an enchantress in Homer's *Odyssey*. Circe was the daughter of Helios and Perse and was considered a witch-goddess. She tried to change Odysseus and his companions into swine by means of a magic drink, but succeeded only with the companions. Odysseus was protected by a magic herb given him by Hermes (see HERMES), and thus immunized, was able to convince Circe to reverse her spell over his friends. 69, 78, 140, 169

THE CITADEL (7,378'); (see MT. WALKINSHAW).

CLALLAM COUNTY. The county encompasses the northern portion of the Olympic Peninsula and is illustrated in eleven quadrangles at the end of this book.

    The Clallam tribe called themselves, "Nu-Sklaim," later corrupted to Klallam for the Elwha Natives and S'Klallam for Jamestown and Port Gamble Natives. Its meaning is brave people, strong people and/or a big, brave nation. It is also said to be derived from the Makah name for the Klallam tribe, "Klolub," meaning a clam, and "aht," meaning a man. The Territorial Act of April 1854, officially created Clallam County. 11, 12, 101, 120, 121, 152, 155, 201.

CLAYWOOD LAKE, MOUNT (6,836'); MT. ANGELES (5B). Lt. Joseph O'Neil named the mountain for his superior officer, Major Henry Clay Wood. Wood was at the time Assistant Adjutant General, Department of the Columbia, and was the man who signed the orders authorizing O'Neil's 1885 expedition into the Olympic wilds. Henry Clay Wood fought in the Civil War and received a Congressional Medal of Honor. Mt. Claywood, originally two words, marks the 1885 Expedition's deepest penetration from the north. 12, 120, 169, 208

CLEAR LAKE; MT. TOM (7E). Due to its subalpine setting, the lake is typically clear, thus the name. It is not known who applied this name, or when. 152

THE CLEAVER (5,500'); MT. STEEL (6B). Located on Sawtooth Ridge, the name is descriptive of its narrow, sharp-edged profile, which resembles an upside-down meat cleaver. 140, 152, 184.5

CLIDE CREEK; MT. TOM (7D). It is thought that the name applied to this stream was so assigned to honor Clyde Shore, West End Clallam County pioneer. For many years Shore was a store owner in Forks, Washington, until moving to Black Diamond, where he raised quarter horses on the Diamond Divide Ranch. During his lifetime, Clyde Shore held positions on the Forks School Board, Clallam County Board of Commissioners, and the County Clerk's office. 154, 178.5

COAL CREEK; LAKE OZETTE (4F), KLOOCHMAN ROCK (2E). According to legend, Coal Creek used to flow directly into Lake Ozette before early settlers diverted it to flow into the Ozette River (part of the "Panama Canal" fever of the time). When Coal Creek is running high, the Ozette River is sometimes flooded near its source, actually flowing backwards into Lake Ozette. The name "Coal" is thought to refer to the color of the water, which is extremely dark from oil and natural gas seepage throughout the area. There is another Coal Creek upriver from Andrews Field along the Queets Valley. 64.5, 147, 152

CONSTANCE CREEK, LAKE, MOUNT (7,743'), **PASS**; THE BROTHERS (4G), TYLER PEAK (4A). This is the third highest peak in the Olympic Mountains and was "discovered"- first sighted from Hood Canal - by English explorer Captain George Vancouver in May 1792. The peak was first climbed on June 26, 1922, by Robert Shellin and A. Earl Smith.

The mountain massif was the site of a plane crash on September 9, 1941, when a military aircraft plowed into its northeast side, killing all six aboard.

    "Point Smith" (7,100'), a spire just south of the Constance north chute and 1/8 mile west of the main ridge, was named in honor of A. Earl Smith (See above).

    "Point Shellin" (6,850'), is a wall approximately 100 yards north of the South Constance chute on the main ridge. It honors R. Shellin, who accompanied Smith to the top of the peak in 1922.

    "Point Harrah" (7,000'), 1/8 mile south of the South Constance chute and 2/3 mile northeast of Lake Constance honors D. Harrah, who was the leader of the 1939 Inner Constance first ascent.

    Mt. Constance was named in 1856 by Captain George Davidson (see THE BROTHERS), who was in charge of the U.S. Coast and Geodetic Survey here for nearly 50 years. The name was selected to honor Constance Fauntleroy, the sister of his soon-to-be bride, Ellinor Fauntleroy. The christening of this peak was significant, since it was only the second major Olympic mountain given a name (Mt. Olympus was the first).

    Within the next few years, Captain Davidson was to name other geographic landmarks in the area. Among the most important were Mt. Ellinor (outside the Park north of Lake Cushman) and The Brothers - once again referring to the Fauntleroy family, (his wife Ellinor and her two brothers).

There is a fair amount of information available about Constance Fauntleroy. We know that she was born in Indianapolis, Indiana, on January 15, 1836, and, except for the five years spent abroad studying in German schools, lived her entire life in the Midwest. Married to George Runcie, Constance was the founder of the Minerva Club, thought to be the first permanent women's club in America. A prolific author, Constance wrote numerous poems as well as several books of prose. Later, she penned operas and cantatas as well. In light of her brilliant career, it seems appropriate that this high peak in the Olympics (as well as the lake and creek on its flank) should bear her name. (See DOSEWALLIPS for a Native legend relating to Mt. Constance.) 10, 39, 58.5, 70, 120, 130, 155, 169, 184.5

CONVULSION CANYON; (see GRAND CANYON).

COUGAR CREEK; MT. OLYMPUS (3G). An early resident in the area (possibly Billy Everett or Tom Ferrill) killed a cougar on this creek. 179

COUGAR CREEK; MT. TOM (5D). According to veteran Olympic horse-packer Minnie Peterson, this stream received its name (the source is unknown) because a cougar was killed along its banks. The event probably occurred in the earliest days of the white man's exploration of the area. 154

COWAN CREEK; JOYCE (8B).During the 1890s, a man named George Cowan was a superintendent at the Filion Mill (now the site of Angeles Millworks) in Port Angeles. George and some of his friends owned a mine on the western slope of Hurricane Hill. The men erected a cabin near the junction of the Elwha Ranger Station trail and Hurricane Hill meadows. It is thought that Cowan may have also owned the mine alongside the creek flowing down the northeast side of Hurricane Hill that now bears his name. 179

COX VALLEY; MT. ANGELES (3G). Originally called Coxe's Valley with a long "e" pronunciation, the name refers to E.C. (some sources claim his initials were A.E.) Coxe, an early settler who built a cabin and settled here in the 1890s. Legend has it that he once slid thousands of feet down into the valley on a frying pan! It is not known why he did this or how but reliable sources attest that he never repeated the remarkable descent. Coxe had dreams of building a ranch in the valley but settled for a modest home. 12, 114, 120

CRAG CREEK; TYLER PEAK (1A)

CRAZY CREEK; THE BROTHERS (1E). Some unknown Olympic National Park employee named the creek for its many short and erratic tributaries, especially near its source. 91

CREAM LAKE, BASIN, LAKE CREEK; MT. OLYMPUS (5D). Billy Everett discovered and named this lake sometime between 1885 and 1890 while exploring the Bailey Range. He also discovered the Olympic Hot Springs and ran the business established there. The "cream" in the name refers to the permanent, milky color of this lake - a phenomenon of nature caused here by "scouring" of permanent snowfields. This creates movement of fine particles into streambeds, which ultimately wash into the lake. As the author can attest from personal observation (September, 1982), the water in Cream Lake is distinctly cream-colored and extremely cold. There is also the point of view that the name fits very well because this area could well be "The Cream of the Park." 94, 115, 120, 152, 169, 173, 195

CRISLER CAMP; MT. OLYMPUS (5D).This was the fourth of six permanent camps that well-known nature photographer Herb Crisler established in the Olympics during the 1940s. The camps were removed in the summer of 1985 and Crisler passed away in December of the same year. All the camps were strung south along the Bailey Range and Skyline Ridge areas and were Crisler's bases of operation for his extensive film-making. Much of his work was ultimately purchased by Walt Disney and made into popular films of that day, including the splendid "Olympic Elk." 64.5, 95

CRISLER'S HOTCAKE CAMP (WINDY HOLLOW); MT. OLYMPUS (2E). Herb Crisler called this campsite "Windy Hollow" in the fall of 1921, after he had been caught in a blizzard there and had to run around the fire all night "to keep from freezing."

Undaunted, he built another shelter, and then did something mere mortals wouldn't try: He packed a massive,

Above: HERB CRISLER AT CAMP. In the Olympics circa 1935. (Olympic National Park Collection)

Below: HERB CRISLER AT HOME IN THE OLYMPICS. Headquartered at the Grant Humes homestead in the Elwha Valley, Crisler and his wife Lois made their summer home the high Olympics and their mission photographing its life and landscapes. Crisler's *Olympic Elk* was released by Disney in 1952. (Olympic National Park Collection)

Above: HERB CRISLER in the field circa 1940. (Olympic National Park Collection)

Below: CASTLE IN THE CAT. Billy Everett is pictured here with Herb Crisler at Crisler's Castle in the Cat Creek Basin, one of his many cabins and supply caches in the Olympic interior. Everett, known as Mowich Man (great hunter in Chinook Jargon) was an early explorer of the Bailey Range and Cream Lake country. (Olympic National Park Collection)

125-pound stove top all the way from Olympic Hot Springs over Appleton Pass to Windy Hollow. He considered the giant griddle ideal for making hotcakes, thus the new name, Hotcake Camp. In later years, he would build a detached guest shelter and pack in extra sleeping bags to the site - which became his photographic headquarters for eight years. As with his other camps, they were removed in 1985, the same year he died. 64.5, 95, 141

CRISLER LAKE; MT. OLYMPUS (5D). Herb Crisler camped at this large lake. Here and in other locations along the Bailey Range, he filmed footage for the movie "Olympic Elk," released in 1952 by Disney Studios. 95, 141

CROOKED CREEK; LAKE OZETTE (5D). Winding and twisting its way through rugged terrain, Crooked Creek is beautifully shaded by overhanging foliage and is aptly named. It is not known when the stream was christened, or who did the honors, but local residents note early in this century that it followed a more tortuous route than neighboring creeks, so it would appear the name evolved quite easily into common usage. 152, 196

CROSS CREEK; LAKE CRESCENT (4B). Very likely the name is associated with Charles Cross, postmaster at Fairholme in 1898. The Fairholme post office was closed on May 15, 1902. 166

CRYSTAL PEAK (6,896'); MT. STEEL (4G). Originally called Mt. McCullough by the Seattle Press Expedition (for J.B. McCullough of the *St. Louis Globe-Democrat*) in 1890, this peak is now known more appropriately for material found there. Quartz and other silicates are imbedded in rocks along the ridges of Crystal Peak; no precious stones have yet been found. It is not known when the name change occurred. 94, 169

CRYSTAL RIDGE, CREEK; MT. OLYMPUS (3G). Numerous rocks with coarse crystalline structure were noted on the ridge by hikers such as Harold Sisson and Keith Thompson, leading to the eventual naming. The author personally observed this in November of 1981. 179, 195

CUB CREEK; MT. ANGELES (8C).

CULTUS CREEK; SPRUCE MTN. (3D). The word "cultus" is Chinook for "worthless" or "good for nothing." (See ALCKEE CREEK and HADES CREEK.) 90, 93, 101

DARKY MINE; MT. STEEL (5C). Named for a black man, Joseph W. Moss, who, along with partners Smith Keller and George Thomas (both white men), owned what was thought to be a gold mine here from the late 1890s until approximately 1925.

Nobody was ever completely certain whether the Moss-Keller-Thomas operation was a viable mining venture or merely a shallow shaft the men drove into a hillside for the sake of appearances. Some observers at the time believed the "mine" was actually a non-producing, pie-in-the-sky scheme used by Moss to tap the wallets of various Seattle investors. In fact, it was said by some that the agreeable, well-liked black man, who rode a horse virtually everywhere because he was too fat to walk, led the "good life" by means of his imaginative winter-summer schedule. He "mined" the pockets of Seattle's wealthy during the winter months and "mined" only beer and fish during the summer!

The name "darky" was affixed to the landmark by other Caucasian pioneers. 27, 53, 74

DEAD MAN'S GAP; TYLER PEAK (4A).

DEAD MAN'S GULCH; MT. OLYMPUS (4G).

DECEPTION CREEK, MOUNT (7,788'); TYLER PEAK (2C). Forest Ranger G.A. Whitehead of Quilcene, along with Roy Strom, named the mountain because of confusion climbers experience finding routes on the mountain in cloudy weather. The creek name comes from proximity to the large mountain. Mt. Deception, the second highest in the Olympics, originally was named Mt. Holmes by the Seattle Press Expedition (see INTRODUCTION) for John H. Holmes of the *Boston Herald*. 60, 120, 210

DECEPTION DIVIDE; MT. OLYMPUS (7A). The 1889-90 Seattle Press Expedition named this Deception Divide because at this spot they were deceived by unusual, previously uncharted terrain. Members believed they were still on the direct route over the Olympics when they veered westward onto the Goldie River. This passage, which led up to the divide, revealed the mistake they had made. They had ascended the wrong river valley and pass and were forced to descend, then climb the correct divide. 207

DEE LAKE; MT. STEEL (8F). Dick Pargeter, Dosewallips seasonal ranger, hiked here with his wife Dee during the summer of 1955. Since the lake was still unnamed at the time and because Pargeter was enchanted with the secluded location, he promptly named it in honor of his wife.

At the time this book was written, the U.S. Geological Survey Board had not yet officially approved the name; thus it does not appear on topographic maps. 151

DEEP CREEK; MT.OLYMPUS (4G).

DEER BAY, POINT; LAKE OZETTE (4E). Deer often were found here by pioneers; thus the name. 196

DEER CREEK; MT. OLYMPUS (3G).

DEER LAKE; MT. TOM 96F).

DEER PARK, CAMPGROUND, RANGER STATION, ROAD; MT. ANGELES (8F). The area was named by a trapper and his partner who frequented Deer Park prior to 1900. The name reflected the fact that hunters could always find abundant deer in the park-like meadows. In the 1930s a road was built and the area was used as a winter ski facility for many years. 12, 31, 115, 120, 205

DEER RANGE; MT. OLYMPUS (6G). The Seattle Press Expedition (see INTRODUCTION) named this area while camped here from March 17 to 20, 1890. Deer were bountiful throughout the region, a fact which obviously impressed the explorers. 207

DELABARRE CREEK, MOUNT (6,024); MT. CHRISTIE (8G), MT. STEEL (1F). W.F. Delabarre was a Port Angeles banker in the early 1900s. Seeking to help the Seattle Mountaineers, he pledged that he and the Port Angeles Commercial Club would financially assist the Mountaineers' 1907 expedition into the interior of the Olympics. Later, accompanied by Asahel Curtis and W. Montelius Price, he scouted a new trail to Mt. Olympus on behalf of the Seattle-based group. On that journey, the men crossed the stream that now bears Delabarre's name.

The peak at 5,024; was originally called Mount Taylor by the 1889-90 Seattle Press Expedition, in honor of Colonel Charles Taylor of the *Boston Globe*. Later, the designation "Peak 6024" replaced "Mt. Taylor" on maps. Most references now refer to peak 6,024 as Mt. Delabarre. 120, 184.5, 207.58, 94, 96, 120, 195

DEL MONTE RIDGE; TYLER PEAK (2B). Billy Del Monte was a popular black cook perhaps from the West Indies, at the Seattle Boy Scout Council's Camp Parsons during the 1920s. Some of the scouts, who were first to ascend the nearby ridge, christened it in 1926 in honor of Del Monte. 58.5, 120, 169, 207.5

DELL RAY CAMP; SPRUCE MTN. (5D). In the early 1950s outfitter Dell Ray packed members of the Port Angeles Archery Club to this hunting camp situated, at the time, in a large in-holding of Forest Service and private land within the bounds of the Olympic National Park on the south side of the Bogachiel River. In 1953 most of this nearly 6,000 acre parcel, the ocean strip, and Queets corridor, were added to the Park. In the early 1960s Dell went to work for Lloyd Beebe at the Olympic Game Farm. While at the farm Dell played bit parts in Disney movies, *Lobo* and *Charlie the Lonesome Cougar*. 160.5, 182

DENNIE CREEK; MT. STEEL (6G). During the summer of 1955, Dosewallips seasonal ranger Dick Pargeter, accompanied by his younger brother Dennis ("Dennie") Pargeter, undertook a long loop hike up the Main Fork Dosewallips River to Hayden Pass, cross-country to Sentinel Peak and Silt Creek, then up this stream toward Mt. Anderson. They enjoyed the area, and decided to affix Dennie's name to the stream. The name has not been officially approved by the U.S. Geological Survey and does not appear on topographic maps. 151

Above: DEER LAKE. Micky Merchant, Minnie Peterson's assistant is packed up and headed for the Bogachiel Peak fire lookout construction project, September 1934. (Peterson Collection)

Below: EEL GLACIER. This glacier dominates the North side of Mt Anderson. (Olympic National Park Collection)

DESPERATION PEAK (7,150'); TYLER PEAK (5B). The first ascent of this peak was made in 1940 by Ingals, Henderson, Carlow, and Dooley. According to their report, the climb was fraught with waist-deep snow, avalanches, and "other spring horrors," which made the men "desperate to get up something or anything." The name was applied by Neil Jacque. 140, 169, 184.5

DESTRUCTION ISLAND; DESTRUCTION ISLAND (1F). A number of deaths have occurred on the mainland near this island. In July of 1787, six English sailors from the *Imperial Eagle*, captained by Charles Barclay, landed at the mouth of what is now known as the Hoh River and were killed by Natives there. Barclay named it "Destruction River" for this massacre, and, shortly after, explorers transferred the name to the island. The river was later renamed the Hoh River.

A similar event had occurred on July 14, 1775, when Spanish Captain Juan Francisco de la Bodega y Quadra sent seven sailors aboard the *Sonora* to shore just south of the Quinault River. The sailors were to bring back water, firewood and a new topmast for the ship. They were armed with muskets, cutlasses, and some even with pistols, cartridge boxes, and several hatchets for chopping firewood and larger wood for the mast. While attempting to beach their boat, the sailors were attacked by 300 Natives. After two hours of fighting, the sailors succumbed one by one to the victorious Natives who carried off portions of the sailors' bodies and salvaged the iron from the boat.

Natives called this island "Hob to la bish," pronounced "hob to la bish," of Salish origin, either Quinault or Lower Chehalis. The Quinault tribe also called this island "ta tchist qu," pronounced "ta' tchish qh," the meaning of which is unknown.

According to Makah legend, long ago when the world was new, Destruction and Tatoosh Islands were husband and wife. They lived together near the mouth of the Hoh River. They had many children, which were big and little rocks along the coast. The parents often quarreled and finally, after a very bitter dispute, Tatoosh left her husband. She put all of the children into her boat and paddled north along the coast. The farther she got, the angrier she became toward her husband. When she got to the place now called Point of the Arches, she said to her children, "You will probably grow up to be just like your father," and threw them all overboard!

Then, paddling alone, she rounded Cape Flattery, stopped, and made her new home on what is now Tatoosh Island. Her children, islands unto themselves, lie in the water just a few miles south, a place we now know as the Point of the Arches. 39, 73, 120, 120.5, 134, 155, 156, 180

DEVIL CLUB CREEK; SPRUCE MTN. (2D). "Devil's Club" is a rugged, spiny plant that grows in great abundance along this lowland stream. It is not known who applied the name to the creek or when it was done (see HADES CREEK). 29, 60

DEVIL'S BACKBONE; MT. OLYMPUS (5G). Devil's Backbone is a steep, craggy ridge overlooking the roaring Elwha River. Downriver settlers named it sometime before 1890, when Seattle Press Expedition members (see INTRODUCTION) traversed it during their journey through the area. 207

DEVILS POINT; LAKE CRESCENT (7C). Originally, the awesome amphitheater-like bay, with perpendicular cliffs around it was called "Devil's Bathtub" or "Devil's Wash Basin." Later, the common local usage changed it to "Devil's Punch Bowl." The nearby tip of land jutting into Lake Crescent derives its name, Devils Point, from these locally-applied appellations. 138, 141

DIAMOND MEADOW, MOUNTAIN (6,800'); MT. STEEL (7G). There are two explanations for the naming of this mountain and the meadow nearby. The first one says that because the easternmost high point along the ridge between the West and Main forks of the Dosewallips is "diamond" shaped, the peak was originally called Diamond Mountain. This spot is now known as Piro's Spire, for Robert F. Piro (see PIRO'S SPIRE), and when that name was applied, the term "Diamond Mountain" was shifted westward two miles. Obviously, the Meadow is named for its proximity to the mountain directly above it. Another account, though, says that the name honors Edward Diamond (see HONEYMOON MEADOWS), who traveled extensively in this area during the late 1800s and the early part of this century. Diamond was a game warden at South Union. 57.5, 94

DICKEY RIVER; LA PUSH (5F).The name comes from the corruption of a Quileute word for this stream, "diswo dat stada," "dichoh dock-teacer," or "de tho date t doh," pronounced "da to dotch't doh." The name was also applied to a branch of the tribe living on the river, and meant "people who live on the first branch of the Quillayute River" or "people who live on the dark water." 93, 120, 180

DIFFICULTY HILL; MT. OLYMPUS (7F). Seattle Press Expedition (see INTRODUCTION) members first encountered this hill just south of the Lillian River (see LILLIAN RIVER) on April 3, 1890. Steep and hazardous, they found it extremely difficult to climb, especially since they were leading their pack mule "Dollie." Even today, with a cleared trail one can follow, the average hiker will agree that the name is most appropriate. 207

DISCOVERY PEAK (4827'); MT. CHRISTIE (6A)

DISMAL DRAW; JOYCE (1B). This narrow, dreary spot is the first of several camping areas one encounters above Barnes Creek after the trail leaves the creek bottom. The draw is approximately 3/4-mile and 600 feet above the stream and is among the bleakest, most depressing places imaginable. Trees and moss dominate the foliage, obscuring vision on all sides. Also contributing to the gloom, several huge, fire-blackened firs and numerous small, dead trees dot the landscape. There is virtually no undergrowth.

Trail-crew member Al Cunningham named the spot in 1962, nailing a sign to a tree to make it "official." 46, 209

DODGER POINT (5,753'); MT. OLYMPUS (8D). Sanford Floe, a district ranger in the U.S. Forest Service named this mountain for fellow employee "Dodger" Bender (his first name is not known). Bender had given the Forest Service many years of faithful service - many of them at the lookout named for him. During that time, he fought fires on Long Ridge and in the Elwha Valley. It is rumored that Dodger Bender accidentally discovered a backwoods still during Prohibition days and was knifed for his trouble. As a result of this incident, he lost a lung and died a few years later of complications. 26, 94, 108, 120, 153.5, 169, 173

DODWELL-RIXON PASS (4,750'); MT. OLYMPUS (6B). Professor Herschel C. Parker, Belmore H. Browne, and Walker G. Clark, while attempting a first ascent of Mt. Olympus in July 1907, named this pass for Arthur Dodwell and Theodore Frederick Rixon. The three men believed that the Dodwell-Rixon Survey team, famous for mapping 3,483 square miles of the Olympic Forest Reserve during a three-year time span, were the first white men to pass that way, in approximately 1900. A short while later, however, a Seattle Mountaineers' team found in the pass area a Royal Baking Powder tin containing a record on a torn magazine page, proving that a party of climbers from the Port Townsend area had been there in 1894. Nevertheless, the name of the pass remained Dodwell-Rixon.

Theodore Rixon, who lived from October 10, 1861, to April 19, 1955, was born in Staines, Middlesex County, England. He was present in the Olympic area from 1897 to 1900, 1907 to 1935, and 1940 to 1949.

During their 1898-90 survey of the Olympics, Dodwell and Rixon had four assistants, including one DeWitt Sisson. Difficult terrain ruled out horses, so the men carried 100-pound packs, but no bedding. Therefore, they slept out in the open or under trees. At times they constructed crude wickiups (brush huts), building fires in front of them to provide warmth. Once, they were immobilized in a blizzard on Mt. Olympus for 11 days.

On another particularly memorable occasion, in bitter-cold weather, the men were forced to straddle a log over the Dosewallips River for an entire night with the 100-pound packs still on their backs!

Rixon maintained a detailed diary throughout all of his explorations. He was quite a fisherman, as well. In fact, his name is still in record books as the man who caught the largest Beardslee Trout ever taken from Lake Crescent - 23 pounds. 12, 58.5, 94, 120, 179, 188

DONAHUE CREEK; MT. STEEL (5C). An early miner named Donahue built a cabin near Eight Stream (see EIGHT STREAM) and worked throughout this area from the turn of the century until 1938. It is not known who affixed the name to this stream. 53, 159

DOROTHY CREEK; MT. ANGELES (1E). According to Sandy Floe, son of U.S. Forest Service Ranger Sanford Floe, his mother and father named Dorothy Creek for one of their two daughters, who were Dorothy and Maxine. Everett Frisbee, who worked on the U.S. Forest Service trail crew in the 1920s and 1930s, claims he named this creek for his daughter, Dorothy. (See WILDROSE CREEK.) 51, 64.5,

DOSE MEADOWS; MT. ANGELES (5B). Rudo Fromme, U.S. Forest Service Supervisor, named this picturesque site for the small shelter which District Ranger G.A. Whitehead built at the head of the Main Fork Dosewallips River. Dose, pronounced "Dosie," is a nickname for the longer, more colorful name of the river. (See HUNGRY GUT HILL concerning the four-mile approach to Dose Meadows.) 68, 152, 190

DOSEWALLIPS CAMPGROUND, RANGER STATION, RIVER, WEST FORK; MT. ANGELES (8B), THE BROTHERS (3G), MT. STEEL (8G). Dosewallips Campground was first called Camp Muscott (see MUSCOTT CREEK, CAMP). August Case first noted the Dosewallips River in June of 1841.

The name Dosewallips comes from Twana Indian mythology, in which Dos-wail-opsh is a legendary man who turned into a mountain that is at the river's source.

There is also a S'Klallam legend about Dosewallips. It tells of the "Great Changer," whose name was Doquebatl. Doquebatl was a powerful spirit who transformed a mythical S'Klallam Chief into a mountain which now forms the headwaters of the Dosewallips River.

Two other legends from the S'Klallam tribe, each differing on various points, carry the story further. One tells of a Native who had two wives who fought often. Once, when the husband intervened in a wife-to-wife struggle, one of the wives, Takkobad, scratched her husband's face, creating the cracks near Jackson's Cove on Hood Canal. For punishment, the Great Changer turned one wife into Mt. Rainier and her son into Little Tahoma. He turned Takkobad's husband into a peak in the Olympic Mountains.

Another story relates that long ago when mountains, stars, and rocks were living things, Dosewallips, a mountain on the west side of the Hood Canal, had two wives. They were jealous and fought often. Finally one of the wives, Takkobad, filled her basket with food and crossed over to the other side of Puget Sound. While passing over the Skokomish River, she dropped a piece of salmon, which fell in the water. Ever since, salmon have run up the Skokomish River. When Takkobad reached the area known today as Olympia, she dropped bulbs of blue camas (wildflowers), which spread throughout the region, and a great camas prairie was formed. Finally Takkobad gathered some fire and threw it across the sound at the head of the other wife. The fire burned all the trees off the second wife's head and she is now called Mt. Rainier. Takkobad herself is known today as Mt. Constance (see CONSTANCE CREEK). 27, 39, 50, 155, 180

DOUBLE PARKING; MT. ANGELES (3G). About 11 miles up Hurricane Ridge Road toward the lodge, the driver will encounter two parking areas which double as lookout points. They are quite near to one another and are known simply as Double Parking. At this point the road is sometimes closed during winter months, because of heavy snow and the danger of avalanches which could bury both car and driver.

There are, in fact, seven distinct avalanche paths which cross Hurricane Ridge Road in the 3 1/4-mile stretch just beyond Double Parking. All have been assigned unofficial names by Olympic Park personnel and should be easy for the visitor to sight. They are" "Waterfall" (0.3 miles), where a waterfall cascades from the cliff above; "Through the Trees" (0.4 miles), where the avalanche path is difficult to see through the trees; "Old Faithful" (0.6 miles), which faithfully avalanches every year, sometimes more than once in succession (because it is fed by several faces); "Siamese Twins" (1.5 miles), with two similar swaths side by side; "Goat Creek" (2.0 miles), a large swath where mountain goats are frequently observed; and "Big Brushy" and "Little Brushy" (at 2 1/4-miles), one large and one small chute choked with brush (slide alder). See map of avalanche swaths. 20, 94, 152

DRAGON LAKE; MT. TOM (5B). There is no certainty as to how this body of water received its name, though it may have been because visitors observed large numbers of dragonflies here. However, another possibility exists. The lake is shallow and is a veritable breeding ground for salamanders, such as newts, which present a dragon-like appearance. Some observers think that a government survey party passed through the area and named it for the insect population. 63, 154

DRUM'S CABIN; MT. ANGELES (2D). Though the structure for which it was named no longer exists, this area was the site of a cabin completed in 1929 by Truman Drum and his son Bill. The men lived in the Tacoma area, where Truman sold farm gear, animal feed, and seed. Since the actual location of the cabin was so far into the National Park area (it is 26 miles from Highway 112, or a two-day hike), the Drums had to secure a special-use permit and build the structure over the course of two summers. Recalling the time he and father spent there, Bill Drum says they often stayed overnight at the Humes Ranch on their way in and out of the interior. 43, 54, 58.5

DUC POINT BAY; CAPE FLATTERY (3F).

HURRICANE RIDGE ROAD Avalanche Swaths

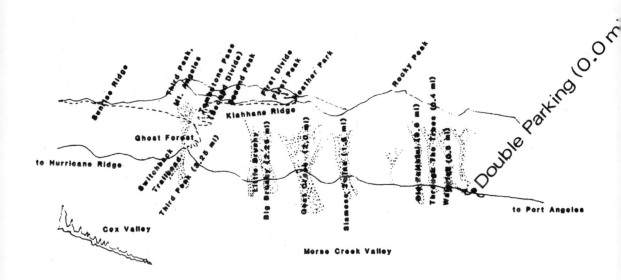

EAGLE CREEK, LAKES, POINT; LAKE CRESCENT (4B). This stream drains into Lake Crescent at what is known as Eagle Point. It is not known whether eagles actually nest in the vicinity or just visit at certain times of the year, but they are frequently observed here. These three landmarks, therefore, bear the name "Eagle." Eagle Lakes on Aurora Ridge was named by Ranger Chris Morgenroth, Theodore Rixon and Glyde Chapman while scouting a proposed trail from Lake Crescent to Olympic Hot Springs in August of 1908. 62.5, 75, 94, 138, 205

EAGLE POINT; MT. ANGELES (3F).

EAGLE RANGER STATION; MT. TOM (5G). (See SOLDUC RANGER STATION)

EAGLE POINT; LAKE OZETTE (4D). Eagles commonly have been seen here and may nest in the area, thus the name. 83

EAST BEACH (PICNIC AREA), ROAD; JOYCE (1C). This is a beach on the east end of Lake Crescent; thus the name. Beginning in 1909 ferries departing from the resort hotel dock located here carried passengers to Fairholme, Lyre River and other resorts on the lake. 8, 152, 179

EAST PEAK (MT. ANDERSON) (6,200'); MT. STEEL (6G). This summit is east of, but closely associated with, the Mt. Anderson massif. (See MOUNT ANDERSON and EEL GLACIER.) 152

EAST PEAK (MT. OLYMPUS) (7,780'); MT. OLYMPUS (3B). This is the easternmost of three high spires of Mt. Olympus, capping the massif. In 1907 the Seattle Mountaineers called it "The Sphinx Head" for its unusual appearance. 23, 152

EAST TWIN CREEK; MT. TOM (1C). This stream flows into the Hoh River less than 150 meters east of Twin Creek (see TWIN CREEK and WEST TWIN CREEK). 29, 152

ECHO ROCK (7,100'); MT. STEEL (5G). While yelling at it from the Anderson Glacier, an echo results. 140, 169, 184.5

EEL GLACIER; MT. STEEL (5G). Rudo L. Fromme, U.S. Forest Service Supervisor, named this glacier in the summer of 1920. Why?

I proposed this name to a campfire audience the evening following a Mountaineer's Club climb, which I accompanied, to the top of the Middle Peak [now referred to as Mt. Anderson] of Mt. Anderson, the summer of 1920. I explained that this was to honor our guide, Fairman Lee. His name was spelled backward, I jokingly said, because he had no idea where he was going, merely leading us dupes, or dopes, on a scouting trip. I added, the Geographic Board would not approve the correct spelling, because he wasn't quite dead yet.

Fairman B. Lee led the first ascent of Mt. Anderson with a party of 13 Mountaineers on August 5, 1920. 22, 68, 120, 184.5, 207.5

EIGHT STREAM; MT. STEEL (5D). This was the site of Camp Number Eight for the 1890 O'Neil Expedition (see INTRODUCTION). The O'Neil Expedition did not actually name the stream. Explorers in later years, however, in deference to the O'Neil connection, referred to it as Camp Number Eight Stream. It was later shortened to Eight Stream. 208

ELBOW CREEK; SPRUCE MTN. (7E). The creek has a sharp elbow-like bend in it, which accounts for the name. 152

ELEVEN BULL BASIN; MT. OLYMPUS (5D). Herb and Lois Crisler built a shelter here in the fall of 1943. They remained at the site for weeks, observing and filming a herd of elk which, at one observation, included eleven bulls. The film they gathered was later edited and used to produce the Disney Studios popular movie *The Olympic Elk*. Because of the presence of the eleven bulls, Crisler affixed that name to his campsite. 95

ELIP CREEK; MT. CHRISTIE (3D). The name is Chinook for "the first," "the foremost," or "the best." Kimta Creek, not far up river, is "the lesser of the two." (See ALCKEE CREEK.) The name was applied by the U.S. Forest Service, not by Natives (see KIMTA CAMP). 90, 120

ELIZABETH FALLS; MT. CHRISTIE (7G). The 1889-90 Press Expedition named the falls for one of their members' friends or relatives. (See INTRODUCTION.) 120

ELK CREEK; MT. STEEL (6A).

ELK CREEK; LAKE OZETTE (5C). Many herds of elk roamed this area during early settlement times; thus the name. 63, 103

ELKHORN RANGER STATION; MT. ANGELES (2D).

ELK LAKE; MT. OLYMPUS (3D). In the 1920s, early settlers referred to this body of water as Beaver Lake for the furry creatures therein. Common, local usage, however, brought about the name Elk Lake for the obvious reason that herds of these animals frequented the immediate vicinity. 131, 152

ELK LICK CREEK, MOUNT (6,517'); MT. STEEL (8F). There are several points along the Duckabush and Dosewallips Rivers where sulphur (mineral) water comes to the surface. At such "elk licks," deer and elk gather and stand in the water, drinking copiously. There is such a spot here, a fact which accounts for the name of both the mountain and the stream. 53, 152

ELK MOUNTAIN (6,764'); MT. ANGELES (5F). It is ironic that today there are no elk in this area. At one time, however, elk in greater numbers roamed the entire region. A story is told that in 1890, William Wooding, a local homesteader, along with some friends, slaughtered 15-20 elk at this spot, leaving their carcasses to decay in the woods. Upon

Left: ELWHA SNOW FINGER. SEATTLE MOUNTAIN-EERS ON THE MARCH IN THE OLYMPICS 1913. Many landmarks were named by the Seattle Mountaineers during their early Annual Outings. (Clallam County Historical Society Collection)

Below: ELKHORN RANGER STATION. Located in the upper reaches of the Elwha this ranger station is now a national historic site. The old station is still standing to the right in this 1930s vintage photograph. (Olympic National Park Collection)

returning to civilization, Wooding made the mistake of bragging about the episode. He and his friends were promptly ordered by the authorities to return to the site and carry out the dead elk. It is not known whether any other penalties were imposed. 136

ELWHA BASIN, CAMPGROUND, RIVER, RANGE, RANGER STATION, SNOWFINGER (see SNOWFINGER, ELWHA); MT. ANGELES (2B), MT. CHRISTIE (7G), JOYCE (5B), MT. OLYMPUS (6A), MT. STEEL (1G). There are several theories as to the origin of the name "Elwha" all of them dealing with Native legends passed down through the ages.

The name may be a corruption of the Quileute word "e ilth quath," pronounced "a ilth'q-uatt," a place name with no known English translation. The more popular theory is that the name is a corruption of a Klallam Indian word meaning "elk," from "ilkwah."

Another account says that "Elwha" means "deep-voiced people," referring to a Klallam Indian legend about a family whose members all had deep voices. In fact, their voices were so loud that the sound hurt listeners' ears.

A third version, perhaps most plausible, relates to a Klallam village along the banks of the river, circa 1853. The name of the village was "Elwha," from which the present name of the river evolved.

The river itself was discovered by white men (Manuel Quimper and his crew) in 1790. However, it was not until Henry Kellet's 1846 map that it first appeared on paper as the "R. Elwha." The Elwha trail to the Quinault River was completed in 1910. 50, 93, 120, 155, 195

ENCHANTED VALLEY, CHALET; MT. STEEL (5F). According to early Native legends from the Quinault, Chehalis and Cowlitz tribes, it was in this wide, level valley, surrounded by mountains, that peoples of all the Indian nations gathered in peace to trade and enjoy games.

Seatco, chief of all evil spirits, was taller than the tallest trees, his voice louder than the roar of the ocean, and his face more terrible to see than the fiercest wild beast. He could travel by land, air or water and was able to tear up trees by their roots. Moreover, he could heap rocks into mountains, and by merely blowing, could change the course of rivers.

Once, as tribal members gathered at Enchanted Valley (earlier referred to by local trappers as "The Valley of a Thousand Waterfalls"), so the legend goes, Seatco became angry with them for no apparent reason. Therefore, he caused a great trembling of the earth and a rumbling of the mountains surrounding the valley, which swallowed up most of the people gathered there. The few who escaped told the story and the tribes never returned.

Indian agents Michael T. Simmons and Benjamin F. Shaw claim to have crossed the Olympics in 1855, thus recording the first documented non-native exploration of the Enchanted Valley area.

In August 1890, the O'Neil Expedition passed thorough Enchanted Valley, heading west.

Other white men who explored the Valley in the 19th Century were Samuel C. Gilman and Charles Andrew Gilman, who ascended the Main Fork of the Quinault River to the base of Mt. Anderson via Enchanted Valley in October, 1889.

Fred W. Cleator, forester, camped in the Valley in 1928 as he examined the recreational potential of the Olympic forests. Cleator is credited with being the man who suggested the name "Enchanted Valley," and his description of the area is worth noting: "Hundreds of small waterfalls…shoot, trickle, cascade, or otherwise pour over these cliffs into a scenic masterpiece."

The chalet was begun in 1930 and completed August 6, 1931. (See SKYLINE TRAIL, HALFWAY HOUSE AND LOW DIVIDE.) 39, 72, 207.5

ENNIS CREEK; PORT ANGELES (3B). Ennis is a derivation of the word "I-enn-nas" which was the name of the Klallam Village at the mouth of this creek east of downtown Port Angeles.

Lt. Joseph O'Neil noted in his log that he entered the upper valley of Ennis Creek on August 16, 1889, during his Olympic Mountain trek. 86, 114, 120

ERICKSON'S BAY, CAMPGROUND; LAKE OZETTE (3D). This area is named for Norwegian pioneer Ole Erickson, who built a cabin on the site in 1890. 58, 108, 120, 156

EVERETT PEAK (5,275'); MT. OLYMPUS (2F). Named in honor of William "Billy" Everett (1868-1950), one of the Olympic Peninsula's most famous early explorers.

Billy Everett, of both Native and Caucasian heritage, earned the nickname "Mowich Man" (Chinook Jargon meaning "deer man" or "mighty hunter") for his many Olympic backcountry exploits. He was one of the first white men to reach the Cream Lake area (hiking there in 1885) and one of the first to traverse the Bailey Range. Often, he would hike

50 wilderness miles or more in a single day, then casually curl up to sleep inside a small canvas he carried with him.

The "Mowich Man" enjoyed exploring the Olympic Peninsula's backcountry with local dentist and close friend Dr. Thompson. Together, with little or no food to sustain them, they would set out for destinations located deep in the forest, certain they could live off the land, and they did, killing deer, elk, and smaller animals for food. On at least one occasion, the men were known to have killed a grouse with a thrown rock! Nevertheless, Everett freely admitted that he had experienced many close calls during his years in the Olympics. Once, he related, he nearly died of hypothermia.

Photographer Herb Crisler's wife, Lois, tells of another Billy Everett brush with death. Billy, she recalls, "was supple and lithe…(and a man who) had the power of being happy." She remembers Billy in his latter years, telling her and Herb the now-famous story of how he had killed a black bear in the Olympic backcountry years earlier using only a knife! Billy "lunged…leaped back…must have jumped backward four or five feet! It was to save his dog that he had done that bold and dangerous thing."

Billy Everett is thought to be the first person to have climbed Everett Peak, later bringing to public attention the Olympic Hot Springs located near the top of that mountain. The tough, old mountain man retained a seemingly boundless wellspring of energy into his advanced years. It is known that even with a broken hand and numerous other ailments, he crossed the Bailey Range when he was more than 70 years of age.

In his declining years, this remarkable explorer settled down and opened a resort at Olympic Hot Springs. Later he became part owner of the site on which the Springs are located. 44, 94, 120, 169, 173

EVERGREEN; SALMON RIVER (4C). John Banta and S. Price Sharpe led more than 100 settlers into the Queets River area during a two-year span, 1890-91, establishing a colony there known as Evergreen. All of the settlers paid Banta and Sharpe $50.00 per family for transportation, and were, in effect, availing themselves of the 1860 Homestead Act, which offered each citizen or head of a family 160 acres of public land free of charge. (See HIBBARD CREEK.)

Originally known as "Banta's Place," the bustling Queets River colony boasted 64 separate homesteads at its peak, each one ranging from 5-40 cleared acres. It lasted for a full 50 years, or until 1940, when President Franklin Delano Roosevelt added the lower Queets River Valley strip into the newly-formed Olympic National Park. President Harry S. Truman made the designation official in 1953. 1, 133, 160, 167, 198, 203

FAIRCHILD CREEK, MOUNT WILLIAM FAIRCHILD (6,950'); MT. OLYMPUS (5E). Named in honor of bush pilot, William R. Fairchild, who engineered a plane capable of landing on the Snow Dome and supplying the research hut on Panic Peak. He was killed in a tragic plane accident at the Port Angeles airport that bears his name (Fairchild International Airport). The names given these two geographic Park landmarks were officially accepted in 1975 by the U.S. Board of Geographic Names. 141, 152

FAIRHOLME CAMPGROUND; LAKE CRESCENT (3C). The first white settler at the west end of Lake Crescent, circa 1890, was W. V. Wilson. Following shortly thereafter (1891), Caroline (Carrie) Jones homesteaded here, calling the place "Fairholme" because, in her judgment, it represented a "fair home." Carrie married Theodore Rixon in 1899 and later moved to Teahwhit Head near La Push. (See MOUNT CARRIE)

Yet another tale, however, relates that the name Fairholme was given the place by postmaster Mrs. George E. Machelle, on October 1, 1891 when the post office there needed a name.

It is noteworthy that manganese was mined throughout this area for several years in the early twentieth-century. The valuable mineral was discovered by Olympic Hot Springs owner, Charley Anderson, whose partners in the subsequent mining venture were well-known settlers Chris Morgenroth and Carrie Jones' husband, Theodore Rixon. 8, 111, 153.5, 160, 179, 183

FALLS CREEK; LAKE CRESCENT (7B). As this stream descends from the high Olympics toward Lake Crescent, three waterfalls are to be found along its route. The best known with hikers and tourists among these is the beautiful Marymere Falls, which can be reached after a short, 3/4-mile walk from the Ranger Station near Lake Crescent Lodge. 120, 152

FALLS CREEK; LA PUSH (8C). A 40' waterfall near its mouth accounts for the name of this stream although the source of the name is unknown. 120, 152

FALLS CREEK; MT. OLYMPUS (1D). Several picturesque waterfalls found along the length of this stream account for this name. 120, 152

FALSE SUMMIT (7,900'); MT. OLYMPUS (2B). Slightly east of the true peak of Mount Olympus, this pinnacle is sometimes confused with Olympus' true summit. It is sometimes called Five Fingers, because of the five spires located there. False Summit offers an unobstructed view of the highest point of the Olympics, the West Peak of Mt. Olympus. 152, 169, 184.5

FATHER AND SON; LAKE OZETTE and CAPE FLATTERY (2G). The original Makah Indian name for this geographic feature was "d wi-qs is iki," pronounced "doo weegs ish i-ki," meaning "father and son." There is a big rock and little rock here from which the name derives. With a little imagination they can be perceived as father and son out for a walk. The Makah name for the big rock is "suc-suc'apt," pronounced "schuch-shu-c'apt," which means "tree-topped rock." 121

FIFTEENMILE CAMP; SPRUCE MOUNTAIN (7E). The shelter is only 14.4 miles from the trailhead, but the trailhead has been moved up river perhaps twice since the shelter was built by the U.S. Forest Service in the late 1920s, Somewhere along this continuum, an unknown hiker evidently made a subjective decision that this camp was close enough to the mark to have the name applied.. 64.5, 152

THE FIN (5,500'); MT. STEEL (6B). A wafer-thin pinnacle on Sawtooth Ridge shaped like a fin on a fish's back. The Fin was probably named during the 1939 first ascent by Don Dooley and Ruth Carlow. 146.5, 152, 169, 184.5

FINLEY CREEK, PEAK (3,419'); KLOOCHMAN ROCK (8C). The Finley family, for whom these two features were named, were Quinault area pioneers. Atop the peak, climbers will find the remains of a cabin, complete with stove top, trail, and mining tools. Today, hikers will find only remnants of trails continuing six miles south toward the Quinault River, and three miles north to Three Lakes. 94, 152

FIRST BEACH; LA PUSH (4E). First Beach is so named because it is just that. It is the first stretch of Pacific Beach found south of the Indian Village of La Push. It is separated from Second and Third Beaches by impassable headlands. 59, 152

FIRST DIVIDE; MT. STEEL (6D). This was the first pass, or divide, reached by the 1890 O'Neil Expedition (see INTRODUCTION). 208

FIRST TOP (5,510'); PORT ANGELES (2A). Leaving Heather Park via the trail located there, this is the first "top" or summit encountered. 94

FITZHENRY CREEK, MOUNT (6,050'); MT. OLYMPUS (4E). These two landmarks were named in honor of Edward A. Fitzhenry, who was Clallam County Surveyor from 1892-1900. The name of the peak was assigned - by parties unknown - sometime between 1900 and 1910., 94, 120, 169, 179, 195

FIVE FINGERS (7,900'); (see FALSE SUMMIT).

FIVEMILE CAMP; THE BROTHERS (4F). This name came into common usage with early trail crews working in the area. The camp, which formerly boasted a shelter, is located five miles up the valley from where the Duckabush Trail formerly began. 74

FIVE STREAM, RIDGE PEAKS (5,072'); MT. STEEL (4B). Five Stream (with peaks to the south) was the site of the 1890 O'Neil Expedition's Camp Number Five. Though expedition members themselves referred to the creek as the "South Branch of the Skokomish River," local settlers and trappers identified it with the number of the campsite. It therefore became known locally as Camp Number Five Stream, a cumbersome title that later was shortened to the simpler "Five Stream."

In a somewhat humorous aside, it can also be noted that O'Neil's men jokingly dubbed the spot "Jumbo's Leap," in deference to a heroic feat performed by one of their companions. It seems that the expedition's resident hound, Jumbo, anxious to follow a scouting party he felt had deserted him, actually jumped 80 feet into the boiling water below, swam the river, then climbed the steep bank on the opposite side to catch up with the men. 120, 208

FLAPJACK CAMP; SPRUCE MTN. (5D). On this site in the 1920s, Henry Huelsdonk and his U.S. Forest Service crew (the land was then under U.S.F.S. jurisdiction) constructed a shelter.

Early trail crews, working an area known as "Flapjack Bar," usually found it difficult to locate good, reliable camp cooks. Therein lies the tale of how Flapjack Camp received its name.

One of the Huelsdonk crew cooks, not famed for his planning ability, made flapjacks late one evening, expecting to sleep late the next morning,yet still have "breakfast" ready for the hungry trail crew. Unfortunately, he left the cakes in the Dutch oven overnight. Bleary-eyed workers discovered to their dismay the next morning that their flapjacks were the consistency of Douglas fir planks. They were so stiff, in fact, that the camp dog, while biting into one, was actually lifted off the ground by a crew member hoisting the flapjack into the air. The pancake itself remained intact and eyewitnesses swore that it was hardly damaged! Then and there, the surrounding area was dubbed Flapjack Bar and the kitchen area named Flapjack Shelter, because of its proximity to the site. The shelter no longer exists. Flapjack was one of about 25 U.S. Forest Service Guard Stations. 29, 64.5, 125

FLAPJACK LAKES; MT. STEEL (6B). Though nobody can be certain, it is most likely that the name of these two lakes evolved because of their appearance. They look much like round flapjacks, especially when viewed from nearby mountains. 27, 53, 186

FLATTERY ROCKS, NATIONAL WILDLIFE REFUGE; LAKE OZETTE (2D). These rock formations off Cape Alava were named by Captain George Vancouver during his journey to this area, 1790-1795. He did so to differentiate them from the entrance to the Strait of Juan de Fuca, earlier referred to as Cape Flattery by Captain James Cook (in 1778).

The refuge (also called Washington Islands National Wildlife Refuge) includes all offshore islands from Cape Flattery to Cedar Creek, southwest of Ozette Lake. 155, 156

FLYPAPER PASS; MT. STEEL (6G). Climbers ascending to this pass on the Anderson Glacier appear from a distance to be "clinging to a vertical wall," much like flies on flypaper. 152, 209

THE FORKS; MT. OLYMPUS (5G). Boulder Creek and the Elwha River formerly joined at this point in "fork" fashion. The name came into common usage among early settlers circa 1890. We know that it was called "The Forks" that year when Press Expedition (see INTRODUCTION) members passed through the region enroute to the Quinault. The entire area known as "The Forks" now lies beneath the waters of man-made Lake Mills. 152, 207

FOUR STREAM; MT. STEEL (5A). The confluence of Four Stream and the North Fork Skokomish River is the site of the1890 O'Neil Expedition's fourth camp. Although not actually named by expedition members, local settlers and trappers began calling it Camp Number Four Stream shortly thereafter; the creek's name was ultimately shortened to "Four Stream." 120, 208

FRAKER CREEK; SPRUCE MTN. (5D). Although he never lived in this area, timber cruiser Jack Fraker toured the Bogachiel Valley region in 1912, examining it for its logging potential. The area is now named in his honor, and today many of his descendants still live in the Hoh and Bogachiel River areas. 29, 79, 120

FRANCIS CREEK; MT. CHRISTIE (4E). This area of the North Fork Quinault was originally dubbed the "Chester Valley" by members of the 1889-90 Press Expedition (see INTRODUCTION). The stream located here, a tributary of the North Fork Quinault River, is named in honor of Frank Milward's daughter, Francis. Milward, who worked for the Aloha Lumber Company in Aloha, Washington, often camped alongside this stream with his children. Because of his daughter's fondness for the site, he simply nailed a sign on a nearby tree "naming" it Francis Creek. U.S. Forest Service trail locaters who found the sign honored it, and the name thus achieved official status. 120, 156

FREEMAN CREEK; JOYCE (5B). Early homesteader Denny Freeman settled on 160 acres near the present-day Elwha Ranger Station. His son Al settled on 40 acres where Freeman Creek enters the Elwha River. In 1926, the entire area was purchased by Dr. Durant and a Mr. Bailey, who later sold the entire package to Dewitt Sisson. The entire area is now located within the boundaries of Olympic National Park. Moreover, Freeman Creek along its entire length is now inside Park boundaries. 179

FRIGGA (5,300'); MT. OLYMPUS (1A). In Norse mythology, Frigg, the wife of Odin, is the goddess of marriage, love, and fertility. The word "Friday" derives from her name.

The first ascent of this peak was made in 1970 by R. Beckett, D. Haley, G. Kelsey, M. Lennox, D. Michael, H. Pinsch, D. Stevens, and R. Yekel. The name Frigga was probably assigned to this peak by Glenn Kelsey and Harold Pinsch. 69, 140, 169, 184.5, 207.5

FROG LAKE; MT. ANGELES (4B). The term "Frog Lake" is a misnomer, for the body of water located at this spot is not really a lake at all. Frog Lake is merely a pond, which, during summer months, is inhabited by huge numbers of amphibious critters. 141

THE GALLERY; MT. ANGELES (2C). This beautiful vista point was discovered by Press Expedition members Christie and Barnes on April 18, 1890. They named it "The Gallery" because of its inspiring view southward toward the Elwha and Goldie Rivers, which look much like twin silver ribbons at the foot of massive Mt. Dana. This picturesque spot is located at the southwest corner of Semple Plateau (see SEMPLE PLATEAU). 207

GARDEN ISLAND; LAKE OZETTE (4D). Early Scandinavian settlers planted exotic flowers all over this island, as well as nearby Tivoli Island, circa 1900. It is not known who first applied the name. 147

GARDEN OF THE GODS; MT. OLYMPUS (5B). Bernard Bretherton, of the 1890 Lt. Joseph O'Neil Expedition, named this spot in Queets Basin. About the site he observed: *...(we) emerged upon a beautiful level plateau of about one hundred acres. Great pinnacles of rock were scattered over it, and huckleberries were found in great profusion. On every hand immense fields of ice sparkled in the sun, and in the midst of all the air was filled with the twitter of song birds. It was an inspiration and we called it the "Garden of the Gods."* 30, 120

GEODETIC HILL (3,018'); SPRUCE MTN. (5D). The location was once used as a survey station by the U.S. Coast and Geodetic Survey team. During World War II, the U.S. Army maintained an enemy aircraft spotting station on the site. 120

GEODUCK CREEK; MT. CHRISTIE (7E). Rudo L. Fromme, who was Forest Supervisor of Olympic National Forest between 1913 and 1926, named this creek sometime during his tenure. A man with a sense of humor Fromme highlighted the gesture with the following comments:

...the proper spelling for the name of this prized clam was evoking quite a lot or argument around Olympia at that time. It was actually pronounced "gooeyduck," or sometimes "Gweduck," but the self-ordained, more highly-educated element advocated and apparently won the spelling "Geoduck." They argued that this spelling identified this particular clam with geology, since it was prone to dig deeper into the earth when pursued than any other clam. This always appealed to me as an idiotic claim for this clam's behavior, particularly in view of the long-used pronunciation (sic). 68, 120

GERI-FREKI GLACIER; MT. OLYMPUS (1A). Relating as it does to Norse mythology, this glacier's naming by Harold Pinsch and Glenn Kelsey in 1970 is most appropriate. The ice mass is situated at the foot of Woden Peak (6,038'). Woden (Old English for Odin) was a primary god in Norse myth, a one-eyed warrior who was fond of feeding his two pet wolves, Geri (Greedy) and Freki (Gobbler), table scraps as they lay at his feet. (See THE VALHALLAS and WODEN.) 69, 78, 120, 140, 169, 184.5

GEYSER VALLEY (BASIN); MT. OLYMPUS (6F). Press Expedition members, when passing through this area in March 1890, thought the unusual sounds they heard in the nearby forest came from a geyser. Not having time to thoroughly investigate the noises, they nevertheless (and arbitrarily) assigned the name "Geyser Valley" to the area. It is now a commonly accepted theory that what expedition members actually heard that day was the "drumming" of a ruffed grouse. As they described the incident: "...the sounds lasted exactly eight seconds, beginning slowly like the clicking of a ratchet on a cog-wheel, gradually increasing in rapidity, and at the end becoming too rapid for the ear to distinguish, and ceasing abruptly at the end of a few seconds."

One would think that the cumulative knowledge of such a distinguished group of woodsmen would have permitted them to make a clear distinction between the sounds of a bird and a geyser. Nevertheless, no other plausible

Above: GEYSER VALLEY HOUSE AND APIARY. Dubbed by the Seattle Mountaineers *The Honey Ranch*, Dr. Ludden's way station on the Elwha was famous for its hospitality and honey from bees that frequented the high Olympic meadows. Pictured here is a group from the Port Angeles Klahhane Club circa 1920. (Clallam County Historical Society Collection)

Below: GLINES CANYON DAM. (Upper Elwha River Dam). This is a 1926 photograph of the dam project. Dam construction on the Elwha proved to be deadly for workers as well as fish. (Peterson Collection)

explanation has been set forth nor have any hot springs or geysers ever been found in the vicinity!

It is interesting to the hiker that Geyser Valley is situated on a very distinct fault line. Perhaps because of this, many travelers in the area have detected the pungent odor of hydrogen sulfide emanating from what seems to be the valley floor. 12, 17, 207

GIANTS GRAVEYARD; LA PUSH (6C). Well-known as a tourist attraction, "Giants Graveyard" is a craggy piece of offshore real estate near the Quileute Village of La Push. Comprised of about a dozen sea stacks and rock islands, the landmark was first charted in May 1887 by coastal surveyor John Francis Pratt. 120

GLACIER CREEK; MT. OLYMPUS (2C). The creek was named in 1911 by a U.S. Forest Service survey party because it drains the Blue, White, and Black Glaciers. 120, 152

GLACIER MEADOWS; MT. OLYMPUS (3C). Glacier Meadows is a subalpine area located below the terminus of Blue Glacier. The area includes large meadows near the terminal moraine (glacier deposits), obviously the source of the name. However, it is not known who first applied the name to this region. 152

GLACIER PASS; MT. OLYMPUS (3B). Robert Wood named this pass between the Blue and Hoh Glaciers on Mt. Olympus in 1958. It was previously called Hoh-Blue Pass and, incorrectly, Blizzard Pass. 152, 207.5

GLADYS DIVIDE, MOUNT (5,600'); MT. STEEL (6C). In 1913 this mountain was named by a party of campers in honor of Gladys Easterbrook, a member of the group.

The reader should be aware that this peak is marked incorrectly on the 1947 Mt. Steel quadrangle. There it is shown as a 6,104' peak somewhat southeast of its actual location. That particular location, in fact, is actually the site of Mt. Cruiser, a fact which is made clear on other maps available to the public.

Mount Gladys was the site of the Black & White Mine, which produced some gold, manganese, and copper from 1907 through the 1940s. 120, 131

GLADYS LAKE; MT. ANGELES (5D). Named by then-Clallam County Sheriff's Deputy Fred Rice for his wife Gladys (Long) Rice. When he christened this body of water (thought to have occurred during the 1920s), Rice was accompanied by his friend Joe Keeler (see MOOSE LAKE). Fred Rice was the first person to place "eyed" (fertile) trout eggs in Gladys Lake, thus establishing a thriving trout population there. Gladys Rice, later Gladys Rivett, was still living in Port Angeles, Washington, when this book first went to press in 1984. 34, 59, 77, 94, 106.5

GLINES CANYON, CANYON DAM; JOYCE (5A). Both the canyon and dam were named for Mr. George A. Glines, a Winnipeg, Canada, capitalist, who together with well-known Port Angeles promoter Thomas T. Aldwell, organized the Olympic Power and Development Company. Lower Elwha Dam was constructed in 1912 through 1914, and Glines Canyon Dam was constructed in 1927, bringing the first cheap electric power to the North Olympic Peninsula. Construction of the dam in Glines Canyon cost the lives of eight men. 12, 64.5, 96, 120, 181

GOBLINS CANYON, GATE; MT. OLYMPUS (6F). One of the Park's most extraordinary landmarks, "Goblin Gates" was named by the 1889-90 Seattle Press Expedition. Mapmakers later altered the spelling to "Goblins Gate." Here the Elwha River swerves at a severe right angle and tumbles into a narrow cliffside opening. Resembling two large gates such as might have been found on a medieval castle, the rock portals appear to reach out and suck the waters of the Elwha into their grasp, only to send them plummeting down a precipitous canyon in a headlong rush to sea level.

It is the eeriness of Goblins Gate, however, that is noteworthy. Perpendicular canyon walls usually immersed in shadows somehow combine to fire one's imagination. Many visitors to Goblins Gate are able to squint their eyes and easily visualize demons, goblins, and various other monsters lurking within the rock-strewn canyon.

Press Expedition member Charles Barnes described it thus: "...like the throat of a monster, silently sucking away the water" and as a "multitude of faces...with tortured expressions." Numerous visitors have described a wide variety of animals they have been able to "see" along the walls at Goblins Gate, ranging from rats and buffalo to elephants and apes.

In a confusing chronology, there have been two bridges which crossed the 20-foot chasm at this point. Bob Haggery and Bill Anderson are said to have constructed the first bridge over the chasm in 1903, using an existing foot log. One bridge was washed away in high water around the turn of the century. Another became a weather-beaten hazard and had to be removed by a Ranger (Chris Morgenroth or Sanford Floe) in 1935. The power of water in the Olympics has always exerted a strong influence on the lives of its residents. Pioneers Isaac Anderson, Herman and John Huelsdonk, Chris Morgenroth, Fred Fletcher, Pete Brandeberry, Pete Willoughby and others often spent days away from home waiting out rain storms and flood waters at a neighbor's cabin or even the hollow of a stump until waters receded and they could ford a river and return home. 12, 64.5, 195, 207, 207.5

GODKIN CREEK; MT. ANGELES (2A). This stream received its name in 1890 during the Press Expedition's journey through the area. Members of the expedition named it for E.L. Godkin, editor of the *New York Post*. The Press party originally referred to it as Godkin River. 207

GOLDIE RIVER; MT. ANGELES (1C), MT. OLYMPUS (7B). This stream may have been called Higley Creek on the 1890 Gilman National Geographic map. Nevertheless, the name "Goldie" was applied in 1890 by members of the Seattle Press Expedition (see INTRODUCTION). One story asserts that the name Goldie belonged to a relative of one of the expedition's members. A more official-sounding version, however, suggests that the river was named in honor of R.H. Goldie of Seattle, whose name may have been selected from the list provided them by their sponsor, the *Seattle Press*. 73, 114, 207, 207.5

GOODMAN CREEK; FORKS (1C), LA PUSH (8C). It is not known who applied this name or what year it was done, but Goodman Creek is named in honor of a man who worked on a township survey team in 1890. The Goodman Creek gorge empties into the Pacific Ocean near La Push, Washington, squeezed between steep, 100-foot cliffs. The 1896 Gilman National Geographic map originally listed the creek as "Keh-chen-whitt," so-called by local Quileute tribesmen. Yet another Quileute name for this narrow, swift-running stream is "tsa dis qualth qu," meaning "mouth is narrow and overhanging with branches and brush." 73, 113, 120, 131, 180

GOVANS HILL; LAKE CRESCENT (8C). The hill at the east end of Lake Crescent was named for Hugh Govan, who constructed the 1921-1922 portion of road from Lake Crescent's east end (top of grade) nearly a mile west on US 101. In 1909-1920, for less than $100,000, he also built the Sol Duc Hot Springs road from Fairholme to the hot springs for Michael Earles. 64.5

GRAND CANYON; MT. OLYMPUS (7F). Seattle Press Expedition members (see INTRODUCTION) camped here early in April 1890. An awe-inspiring sight, the deep, hollowed-out gorge appears to be the result of tremendous landslides at unknown points in prehistoric time. Press Expedition members had been told of several Native legends describing a great catastrophe that occurred here. One member wrote: ...*The convulsion of nature or catastrophe which has overwhelmed the Indians while attending the last pow-wow in the mountains, in which the "Spirit of the Mountains" shook the earth, opened great chasms and swallowed up the returning bands.*

While camping in the area expedition members dubbed it "Convulsion Canyon." The name has since been changed by unknown parties to Grand Canyon because of the beauty of its steep canyon walls and its resemblance to the famous Grand Canyon in Arizona. 120, 152, 207, 209

GRAND CREEK, LAKE, PASS, VALLEY; MT. ANGELES (6E). Amos B. Cameron, an early (1889) settler in Clallam County, Washington, and one of the first white men to visit this area, named the valley "Grand Valley" because of its scenic setting-then christened the largest body of water here "Moose Lake" (see MOOSE LAKE). Because it is the largest of the three lakes in the valley, the name was changed, by sources unknown, to the more appropriate Grand Lake. Early trail crews blazing their way up the slopes out of Cameron Valley often referred to the mountain pass located at this point as "Mankiller Pass," a descriptive title the author found to be nearly accurate, as did outfitter Minnie Peterson who had four pack horses go overboard here in August of 1965. 12, 31, 46, 94, 120, 153.25

GRAVES CREEK, CAMPGROUND, RANGER STATION; MT. CHRISTIE (6C). Originally known as Success Creek (it is not known who named it so), this stream became Graves Creek in 1915, being thus christened by Rudo Fromme, then U.S. Forest Service Supervisor. Fromme apparently thought the new title more appropriate after he and a few other adventuresome woodsmen shared an experience along its banks that year. According to his account:

This was originally known as "Success Creek" all the way to the E. Fork Quinault, or main river, but after the Chief

Forester, Henry S. Graves, spent a rainy night sitting up, huddled under a large old Douglas fir, I thought it appropriate to commemorate the ordeal by changing "Success" to "Graves." However, Mr. Graves wasn't alone under that dripping would-be shelter. He had the grumbling company of District Forester George H. Cecil of Portland and Mining Promoter F.H. Stannard of Seattle and Forest Supervisor Rudo L. Fromme of Olympia.

We had no bedding, wet or otherwise, to wrap around our shivering bodies, having expected to reach the main river that evening where District Ranger E.R. Paull would be waiting with horses, bedding, and a prepared evening meal. (Incidentally, when we did reach the main river in misty daylight the next morning, there was no ranger, horses, or hot coffee or anything. Paull had misread the instructions and come three days before. 67, 68

GRAY WOLF PASS, RIDGE (7,218'), **RIVER**; MT. ANGELES (7C). Grey wolves once roamed the entire area now known as Olympic National Park. However, as man continued to encroach upon their territory, the animals were forced out or killed. The specific territory around what is now known as Gray Wolf Valley was one of the last abodes of this magnificent animal on the Olympic Peninsula.

It appears this entire area was called Graywolf because some local residents believed the last of the species living on the Peninsula had been killed here by local settler Amos B. Cameron. Though that story is incorrect since Cameron actually killed the "last" wolf a few miles to the northwest along Cameron Creek, the name remains today. The peak was first climbed in 1928 by Leigh B. Lint. 34, 94, 120, 179, 184.5

GRAYS HARBOR COUNTY. The southwestern portion of Olympic National Park is situated within Grays Harbor County. The name of the county was taken from the name of the bay located here, Grays Harbor. Covering an area of 1,910 square miles, Grays Harbor County was called Chehalis County from the time it was formed by Washington's Territorial Legislature (April 14, 1854) until June 9, 1915.

Shipmaster Robert Gray of Rhode Island, former officer in the United States Continental Navy and a member of the crew which first carried an American flag around the world, discovered this bay on May 7, 1792, while sailing aboard the *Columbia Rediviva*. Gray christened it Bullfinch's Harbor, after Charles Bullfinch, one of the ship's owners. Later, during his own five-year voyage through Pacific Northwest waters, British Sea Captain George Vancouver sent one of his officers, Lt. Joseph Whidbey, to survey the harbor discovered by Gray. Whidbey changed the name to Grays Harbor during that visit.

Grays Harbor is the second largest bay between Cape Disappointment and Cape Flattery. 89, 120, 131, 199

THE GREAT STONE ARROW; (see LOST ARROW PASS).

GREEN MOUNTAIN (5,622'); MT. ANGELES (7F). It is not known who applied the name Green Mountain to this landmark or when it was done. Nevertheless, this mountaintop is mostly free of trees or any precipitous cliffs and during summer months is predominantly green. Often, the color is enhanced by the large, subalpine meadow expanses located nearby. 94, 136

GREEN PEAK (4,720'); MT. TOM (5E). The source of this name is unknown. The mountain itself is green and remarkably prominent. Its summit, though nearly at timberline, is forested clear to the top. 63

GRIFF CREEK, PEAK (5,120'); JOYCE (8A). Named for Jeremiah "Griff" Griffiths, known by local residents as a "little old Welshman" who homesteaded beside the stream, circa 1895. Griffiths' homestead was located near present-day Elwha Ranger Station at Griff Creek. 12, 39, 114, 179

GUNSIGHT PASS; TYLER PEAK (2B). The source of this name is unknown, but the reason for it is quite easy to observe. When the pass is viewed from Del Monte Ridge, one can imagine looking straight down the barrel of a rifle, using as "gun sights" the twin cliffs of Mt. Mystery and Little Mystery (see MOUNT MYSTERY and LITTLE MYSTERY). 152

GWIN FIELD; SALMON RIVER (6D). Named for the Gwin family, six members strong, who occupied this area from 1918 to 1944. The area had been originally homesteaded by earlier settlers named Glover, then Sorenson, circa 1890.

The land was used for hay and pasture, a 1/2-acre vegetable garden, and an orchard (including apple, plum, and prune trees). Animals raised on the property included 50 Galloway cattle (sold after 1928 and replaced by 200 sheep), one milk cow, several pigs, 12 to 20 chickens, and 100 geese. These areas have returned to a natural state. 203

HADES CREEK; SPRUCE MTN. (4D). The source of this name is unknown. Hades Creek drains a wet, north-facing slope and is heavily overgrown with the spiny plant known as Devil's Club. In point of fact, it is worth noting that this entire area is overgrown with the same jagged plant. Nearby creeks such as Cultus (Chinook for "worthless" or "good-for-nothing") and Devil Club reflect the difficulties encountered by early explorers traveling cross country. 63

HAGEN LAKE; MT. STEEL (7D). Originally applied to what is now called Scout Lake, this section of Olympic National Park is named for Mr. Hagen, scientist and employee of the Washington Department of Fisheries around the turn of the century. 94

HAGGERTY CREEK; MT. OLYMPUS (6F). Named for Mr. Robert (Bob) Haggerty who settled in the Elwha River Valley on a section of land between Cat Creek and Geyser Valley, not far down river from Billy Anderson's Field prior to 1895. Though it is known that Haggerty resided here during the economic panic of the early 1890s, he never finished "proving up" his land and never did establish a permanent residence at the site. However, while there he helped Anderson construct the only bridge over Goblin's Gate in about 1903, using an existing foot log. 12, 64.5, 120, 156, 173, 179

HALF-ACRE ROCK; THE BROTHERS (4G). This landmark is an immense stone shattered into pieces and lying near the Lake Constance Trail. A "guillotine-like" rock feature can be found inside the broken stone formation. Frank O. Shaw named this during his first trip to Lake Constance around 1927. It previously was called "Hell's Half Acre" by the Lloyd B. Hunt family of Gig Harbor. 207.5, 209

HALFWAY HOUSE; MT. CHRISTIE (4D). Named for its excellent location approximately halfway between the North Fork Graves Creek Road junction (once the North Fork trailhead) and Low Divide. It is also known as Ninemile Camp. In the early 1930s, this was the site of a chalet which provided accommodations to weary travelers. Today there exists only an excellent campsite on the river at this location. Nothing is left of the chalet. (See SKYLINE TRAIL, ENCHANTED VALLEY, LOW DIVIDE.) 58.5, 106, 182

HALFWAY ROCK (2,000'); PORT ANGELES (2B). Halfway Rock is the first high point a hiker encounters traveling from Heart of the Hills to Heather Park (4.1 miles) or Heather Pass (4.6 miles). Located 2.2 miles beyond Heart of the Hills, this is a large rock formation and is the first moderately good viewpoint one finds on a trail noted for its dense mantle of forest cover (see HEART OF THE HILLS CAMPGROUND). 115, 152

HAMMER CREEK, CABIN; MT. STEEL (5C). An early miner, Chris Hammer, mined in this area, circa 1910, and the stream and cabin both carry his name. When this book first went to press, remnants of the cabin could still be found though in a state of collapse. While there, the author found parts of an iron stove within the rubble. 58.5, 74, 94, 159

HANDSOME JACK SLIDE; MT. STEEL (2G). In 1944 District Ranger Jack Nattinger, astride his horse Handsome Jack and leading a string of pack horses, was enroute to repair a bridge spanning the Elwha River near Buckinghorse Creek. As the story was told by Nattinger later, both he and Handsome Jack were sleepy and somehow the animal fell sideways off a puncheon bridge into a steep ravine. Both the Ranger and the horse awoke to find themselves plummeting down the incline toward the Elwha River. Luckily enough (and comically enough), the bewildered pair landed on the riverbed with Handsome Jack upside down and Nattinger straddling his belly! Neither was injured, so they returned to the top of the hill and resumed their journey.

Shortly thereafter, well-known local resident Emil O. "Cougar Mike" Michael (see MICHAELS CABIN) heard of the incident and commemorated it with a sign at the spot, dubbing it "Handsome Jack Slide," as it is called today. 141

HANGING GLACIER; MT. STEEL (6G). Hemmed in by cliffs that virtually surround it, this huge glob of ice appears to be dangling, or "hanging" from their ridges, thus the name. There may actually be two hanging glaciers here. According to former Ranger Jack Nattinger, the glacier may be mislabeled on maps. It is possible that the real "Hanging Glacier" feeds Anderson Creek (to the west). 74, 141, 152, 184.5

HAPPY FOUR CAMP; MT. TOM (6D). At the request of District U.S. Forest Service Ranger Sanford "Sandy" Floe, a pre-1938 Forest Service crew comprised of Charles Anderson, Bob Anderson, H.O. Melbourne, and Otto Kestner constructed a shelter at this site. (Some reports claim that a fifth party, Bobby Locke, also worked on this project. That story, however, cannot be validated.) Apparently the four members of the crew were not exactly friends by the time the project was finished. In fact, the men grew to dislike each other more each day. Shortly after being thrown together to work on this shelter, they reached a point where they didn't even speak to one another! It appears that the name "Happy Four Camp" was applied by Sanford Floe as a joke. 43, 64.5, 79, 117

HAPPY LAKE, CREEK, RIDGE; JOYCE (3A). Happy Lake is located at the head of Happy Creek, while Happy Ridge slopes east-west at a point just south of the body of water. An early trapper by the name of Thomas "Slim" Farrell named the lake. Farrell had moved here from the Midwest, built a log cabin at the lake and trapped on Baldy and Happy Lake Ridge.

A somewhat legendary Mountain Man, Farrell left this area in approximately 1913, leaving behind him the Happy Lake name(s) as his legacy. The ridge and creek are named for proximity to the lake (see OLYMPIC HOT SPRINGS). 9, 120

HARLOW CREEK, LOWER LAKE, UPPER LAKE; KLOOCHMAN ROCK (4F). Named in honor of the Harlows, a prominent Native family (it is not known if they were Quinault or Queets) who lived near the boundaries of the Quinault Indian Reservation circa 1900. Another Harlow Creek enters the Queets River further downstream. The origins of the names are probably related, but this is not known for certain. 167, 178

HART (Heart) LAKE, PASS; MT. STEEL (5E). Several stories are told, all purporting to explain how Hart Lake received its name. Frank S. Hart made a notarized statement on December 17, 1953 that it honored his uncle, William Hart, a North Olympic Peninsula pioneer who died in 1890. He had spent years prospecting throughout the upper Duckabush area.

Harry Fisher and Nelson Linsley, members of Lt. Joseph O'Neil's Expedition (see INTRODUCTION) are claimed to have previously named this beautiful body of water "hearts lake" because of its unusual shape. This event took place in 1890. Mapmakers later altered the name to Hart based on the claim in the above paragraph. Fisher named the peak north of O'Neil Pass "Heart's Peak," because of its proximity to the lake he had recently christened. Lt. O'Neil, in his official report, referred to a body of water in the vicinity as "Lake John."

The author leans heavily toward the explanation in paragraph two above. 12, 19, 81, 106, 207.5, 208

HAYDEN PASS; MT. ANGELES (5B). This pass is possibly named in honor of Ferdinand V. Hayden, who, in 1867, was appointed geologist-in-charge of the U.S. geological and geographic survey of the territories. Hayden led expeditions to survey the western territories. It was common practice at that time for survey topographic parties to name geographic landmarks as they traveled throughout wilderness areas of the United States. Perhaps Hayden Pass was christened in this fashion, even though Mr. Hayden never actually visited this site. Since 1916 there has been a trail to the pass. 94, 120, 207.5

HAYES RIVER, GUARD STATION; MT. ANGELES (2B). Named in honor of Christopher O'Connell Hayes, who at age 22 was the youngest member of the 1889-90 Seattle Press Expedition (see INTRODUCTION). Hayes was the grandson of a famous Irish patriot, Daniel O'Connell, and before joining the Press Expedition worked as a cowboy in Washington's Yakima Valley.

This river was mistakenly listed as the Elwha River on the 1896 Gilman National Geographic map, even though the Press Expedition members had already named it during their journey through the Olympics. The earlier name prevailed.

HEART LAKE; MT. OLYMPUS (2E). The source of this name is unknown. Obviously, though, the lake was named for its valentine heart shape. (See also HART LAKE.) 94

HEART OF THE HILLS CAMPGROUND, RANGER STATION; PORT ANGELES (3B). A deeply wooded setting nestled among the gently rolling foothills, this area was given its name in 1921 by Eloise Nelson who, with her husband Oscar, operated a fruit and dairy farm on the site, circa 1918.

Local residents recall that a previous resident at Heart of the Hills was the well-known, colorful mountaineer Jack Fisher. 58.5, 115

HEATHER CREEK; TYLER PEAK (3B).

HEATHER PARK, PASS; PORT ANGELES (2A). Open, subalpine meadows are featured at Heather Park, providing a sharp contrast to the dense forest one must negotiate to arrive at the spot. A quantity of mountain heather carpets the area, providing the logical name. Nevertheless, the source of that name is unknown.

Heather Pass was called Tombstone Pass by early trail crews because of the number of tombstone-shaped rocks strewn about. It is a feature which seems to create a noticeably somber atmosphere in the pass area. 46, 152

HEE HAW CREEK, PASS; MT. CHRISTIE (3G). Though the actual source of this name cannot be verified, it probably relates in some way to Chinook Jargon. A nearby stream, Hee Hee Creek, is said to be Chinook for "will always laugh," "happy," (see ALCKEE CREEK). The term "Hee Haw" is quite possibly an Americanized version of the Chinook term. The author has in his possession a letter from a descendant of early homesteader George Shaube. Shaube, who lived at Smith Place in 1919 (see SMITH PLACE), wrote that the major creek encountered above Alta Creek on the Queets River was named "Hee Haw," and the second "Hee Hee." The two names have been inexplicably reversed on today's maps.

The pass at the creek's head was named by Robert L. Wood on August 21, 1964. 152, 167, 207.5, 209

HEE HEE CREEK; MT. CHRISTIE (2F). Probably named by Rudo Fromme, the words "Hee Hee" (see HEE HAW CREEK) are part of the Chinook Jargon and mean "laugh," "joke," "amusement," "fun," and "happy." (See ALCKEE CREEK) The christening was probably meant to record a humorous event occurring in the vicinity, or capture the "spirit" of the creek as it cascades merrily down the canyon into the Queets Valley. 90, 120, 156

HELL CREEK; MT. OLYMPUS (3G).

HERMES (6,860'); MT. OLYMPUS (3B). The name of this peak has its basis in Greek mythology in which Hermes played a dual role as both the Greek god of fertility- and messenger for the other deities. Hermes' counterpart in Roman mythology is the god Mercury. The first ascent of this peak, which is westernmost of two adjacent pinnacles, was made in 1955 by Richard Hubley and Edward LaChapelle. They named it following the theme previously established for the Mt. Olympus massif, mythological "Home of the Gods." 69, 140, 169, 184.5

HIBBARD CREEK; SALMON RIVER (2B). Henry Hibbard was among the 55 passengers aboard the *Lucy Lowe* sailing out of Tacoma to the Queets area on May 1, 1891. Hibbard and most of the other passengers aboard the ship were among the vanguard of those seeking to establish the settlement know as Evergreen (see EVERGREEN), founded that year by S. Price Sharpe. Hibbard homesteaded along the creek on the north side of the Queets River in the northwest section of Section 26 and southwest corner of Section 23; his entire spread accounted for 154 and 95/100 acres. 1, 63, 64.5, 203

HIDDEN CREEK; MT. ANGELES (8A).

HIDDEN LAKE; MT. TOM (6F). The source of this name is unknown. Today it is a popular fishing spot about 1,000 feet above the Sol Duc Valley. The term "hidden" seems to be appropriate, inasmuch as this body of water between Mink and Deer Lakes is well concealed and there is no cleared trail leading to it. 94

HIGH DIVIDE; MT. OLYMPUS (2E), MT. TOM (8E). The source of the name is unknown, but it is, nevertheless, most descriptive of this picturesque, 5,000-foot ridge which divides the Hoh and Sol Duc Valleys. 152

HIGLEY CREEK, PEAK (3,025'); KLOOCHMAN ROCK (4A), QUINAULT LAKE (4G). Alfred V. Higley and his son, Orte L. Higley, crossed the Olympics from Hoodsport to Quinault Lake in the footsteps of the O'Neil Expedition (see INTRODUCTION) during the fall of 1890.

They entered the Quinault Valley area and soon thereafter Higley Sr. opened a sawmill. Both Higleys stayed, becoming permanent settlers on the north shore of the lake.

Alfred Higley was a popular lakeside resident and became well-known locally as a guide, homespun philosopher, and companion to lonely travelers. Some years after his arrival (date is unknown), he opened a general store near the lake's shoreline.

In 1901, Orte Higley began delivering mail weekly to the Evergreen settlement group (see EVERGREEN), located

OSCAR PETERSON JR. ON HIGH DIVIDE. This 1945 photograph of outfitter Minnie Peterson's son was taken within months of his return from Germany after WWII.
(Peterson Collection)

Above: HEART LAKE. Some names evolve naturally as is the case with Heart Lake on the High Divide. (Olympic National Park Collection)

Below: CROSSING THE HAYES RIVER. The Cleveland Museum of Natural History Expedition pack string crosses the Hayes River in the summer of 1931. (Peterson Collection)

Above: JACKSON RANGER STATION. Settler on the Hoh River, Pete Brandeberry and his dog Ring are pictured here at Jackson Ranger Station (the present site of the Hoh Rainforest Visitor Center). Ring was honored by the naming of Ring Lake in the Bogachiel Valley. Photograph is circa 1920. (Peterson Collection)

Left: HOH LAKE. This area provides spectacular views of Mt Olympus as well as the Hoh Valley. (Olympic National Park Collection)

Above: HOH GLACIER. The ice of this glacier marks the terminus of the Hoh Valley on the Northeast flank of Mt. Olympus. Photograph circa 1920. (Marilyn Lewis Collection)

Left: HOH RIVER ICE BRIDGE. Avalanches from the High Divide and the Mt. Olympus massif form bridges across the Upper Hoh River. Photograph circa 1925. (Olympic National Park Collection)

on the shore of the Queets River, a distance of 24 miles. Needless to say, even on horseback, the journey was difficult in good weather. When it rained as it does most of the year in this area, Orte was forced to walk across damp, swampy areas on end-to-end fallen logs, a path he called his own personal "elevated railway." Understandably, when Orte resigned as a mail carrier, nobody else ever applied for the job!

The name Higley Peak was suggested by Joseph Fulton (U.S. Forest Service Ranger) shortly after the mountaintop was cleared to establish a lookout station there in 1932.

At one time there was a fine trail leading to the Higley Peak from Lake Quinault, but today it is overgrown and difficult to find. Remnants of the old lookout station's foundation still remain at the top; the building itself no longer stands. There is, nevertheless, a splendid view of Lake Quinault and the mountains to the south. 1, 40, 59, 89, 94, 123, 162, 208

HIGLEY FIELD; SALMON RIVER (3B). The area now known as Higley Field was first occupied by the James Donaldson family who arrived in the Queets Valley from Scotland by way of Tacoma in September, 1892.

Higley Field's name stems from its occupancy between 1930-1944 by one or more members of the Ransom and Maggie Higley family; Anne Higley Slater and her husband Ralph homesteaded here from 1933 to 1937 and later developed a thriving, 21-acre ranch on the site. 203

HOH CAMPGROUND, CREEK, GLACIER, HEAD, INDIAN RESERVATION, LAKE, PEAK (5,572'), RANGER STATION, RIVER, SOUTH FORK RIVER; DESTRUCTION ISLAND (3G), MT. OLYMPUS (3B). There is little doubt that the word "Hoh" derives from the language of an Indian tribe located on the Olympic Peninsula. However, which tribe and what the exact meaning is to each of the local tongues are unknown.

It is thought by several sources contacted that the word "Hoh" is from a Quileute Indian word "Ohalet," which has also been spelled "hooch," "holes," "huch" and Hooh," thought to mean "fast white water" or "snow water."

Another explanation is that the word is a corruption of the Quinault Indian word "qu," meaning "that place" or "boundary." In this version, the Quinault name for the river is "ch'la qu," pronounced "ch q la qh," meaning "can speak ch la (the Quinault language) to that place." Yet another version says that "Hoh" means "man with quarreling wives."

Hoh Head first appeared on John Francis Pratt's charts May 28 to June 1, 1887. The Hoh Reservation was established by presidential decree on September 11, 1893. The earliest recorded exploration of the upper Hoh River was in August of 1894, when D.W. Starrett, A.M. Godfrey and W. Daggett climbed Cameron Creek, went up the Elwha River to Dodwell-Rixon Pass, and descended the Hoh River.

Forty-four foot deep Hoh Lake is drained by Hoh Creek, historically called Lake Creek by settlers. The Hoh Ranger Station in earlier times was called Jackson Ranger Station after Native American Andrew Jackson who settled near the site. 101, 117.5, 120, 131, 155, 156, 171, 180, 207, 209

HOLE IN THE WALL; LA PUSH (4F). The source of this name is unknown. Referred to by early white settlers as "Tunnel Rock," the landmark now called "Hole in the Wall" is a natural wave-carved arch in a large shoreline rock monolith. Local tribesmen say that many years ago the Quileute tribe was badly defeated here in a retaliatory raid by the Nitinat tribe of Vancouver Island. 120, 152

HOLMES RANGE; TYLER PEAK (2C). The Press Expedition of 1889-90 named the range and the peak (Mount Holmes, now Mt. Deception) for John H. Holmes, editor of the *Boston Herald*. The Holmes Range may have referred to what is now named the Needles. 169, 184.5, 207

HOME CREEK, LAKE; TYLER PEAK (4B).

HOME SWEET HOME CAMP; MT. STEEL (6E).It is thought that Tom and Lon Rule, two trappers who worked the North Fork Skokomish Peak area from 1890-1910, named this remote outpost. It was their base of summer operations as they tended their trap lines, and was located in a pleasant, subalpine meadow with a clear-flowing brook nearby. The author personally recommends this site as an overnight camp. 74

HONEYMOON MEADOWS; MT. STEEL (6F). At least two couples have spent their honeymoon at this spot. Frank Maranville states that A.E. and Bertha Smith camped here during a twelve-day honeymoon trip in 1925 when they christened the meadow with a carved sign.

Mr. and Mrs. Edward Diamond were married on Christmas Day, 1885 at the age of 18 and are also said to have spent their honeymoon here. (See DIAMOND MEADOW.) 20, 57.5, 94, 186, 207.5

THE HORN (5,500'); MT. STEEL (6B). Members of the first party of climbers to ascend this 5,500-foot peak on Sawtooth Ridge in 1939 dubbed it "The Horn" because its shape has been found similar to an animal's horn. This peak has also been called "The Mouse" after an unknown hiker imagined its "nose" (the peak) touching the "green cheese" moon.

The first ascent was comprised of Don Dooley, Elvin R. Johnson and others whose names are not known. 140, 169, 184.5, 186

HOWE CREEK; MT. CHRISTIE (4B).

HUBERT GLACIER; MT. OLYMPUS (2B). Named in honor of Seattle Mountaineer Anna Hubert, of Johns Hopkins University, Baltimore, MD. She was the only woman participant in the 1907 first ascent of Mt. Olympus and the first woman to climb the Middle and West Peaks.

Queets Basin is a vast area rimmed by snow and glacier-capped peaks. In order for them to reach the Humes Glacier, Anna Hubert first had to descend via steep animal trails to the valley bottom and then climb cliffs to the Humes Glacier. When her party reached the massif later in the day, they could see this glacier in the distance below and named it for the lone lady in the group.

Olympia photographer Joseph Jeffers died on the Hubert Glacier, rather than on the Jeffers Glacier, which bears his name. 96, 120, 142, 153.5

HUGHES CREEK; JOYCE (5B).The source of this stream's name is unknown. It was christened in honor of a homesteader named Hughes who settled in this area in the very early 1900s. 80

HUGIN (5,990'); MT. CHRISTIE (1G). The author was not able to determine with certainly who actually christened this peak and its nearby companion, Munin (see MUNIN). Hugin may have been named by Glenn Kelsey and Harold Pinsch of Bremerton in 1970.

The appellation Hugin is consistent with the "Home of the Gods" theme established earlier and refers to one of two ravens found in Norse mythology. Hugin (Thought) and Munin (Memory), according to legend, sat on the shoulders of the great god Woden (see WODEN), whispering into his ear pertinent news they had gathered during their round-the-world flights. In this part of the mountain range, Hugin is presumed to be sitting on one of the shoulders of Woden. 78, 169, 184.5

HUMES GLACIER, RANCH; MT. OLYMPUS (4B, 7F). Named in honor of William E. "Bill" Humes who first explored the glacier, circa 1907. The men credited with honoring him are Professor Herschel C. Parker, Walter G. Clark, Belmore H. Browne, and Dewitt C. Sisson who ascended Humes Glacier in July 1907 during their attempt at a first ascent of Mt. Olympus.

Bill Humes remained on the Olympic Peninsula until 1914 when he left for New England. His brother, the well-known Grant Humes, maintained the 120-acre homestead and fruit orchard nearby and made his living for most of his life by hunting cougar. He also was known to lead many hiking and climbing parties into the backwoods of the Olympics; he also made his living as a hunting guide and cabin builder. Grant had a certain flair for poetry and attempted to capture the atmosphere of a balmy summer day on the ranch when he wrote:

> Now then -
> As from toil you rest,
> And upon field and plain
> the noonday sun is shimmering.
> Take pen and pad,
> Seek a shady nook
> And let your thought go glimmering.

The Humes Ranch is now a national historic site. 12, 54, 64.5, 67, 94, 95, 98, 100, 120, 152, 170, 179, 185, 195, 204

Above: HOH RAINFOREST. Clarence Albrecht, a naturalist from the Chicago Field Museum, began his explorations in the Olympics in 1914 and continued to return for decades. Clarence is seen here with his new movie camera in the wilds of the Hoh circa 1925. (Peterson Collection)

Left: HOLE IN THE WALL. This wave-carved, eye-catching landmark was referred to as "Tunnel Rock" by early settlers. Today it is one of the more popular places to visit on the Olympic National Park coastal strip. Fanny Taylor of Mora who captured this image, recorded important historical images of Native life in turn-of-the-century La Push. This photograph is circa 1910. (Olympic National Park Collection)

HUNGRY CREEK; THE BROTHERS (2F).

HUNGRY GUT HILL; MT. ANGELES (6B). When Marian Taylor was a teenager helping her stepfather Frank Vincent pack travelers into the Dose Meadows area of the Olympic Mountains (circa 1915; see BADER VALLEY), Vincent dubbed this formidable, 1,000-foot, four-mile uphill grind "Hungry Gut Hill." Because of the very real hunger pangs many climbers and hikers have subsequently suffered trudging their way up the torturous, monotonous slope, the colorful appellation caught on permanently and remains today. 190

HURRICANE CREEK, HILL (5,757'), **RIDGE**; MT. OLYMPUS (7G). Lt. Joseph O'Neil and Norman Smith (son of the founder of Port Angeles, Washington, and later mayor of that city) were the first white men known to visit Hurricane Ridge; they arrived there on July 27, 1885, and camped in a deserted bear's den with only a blanket each for warmth. Shortly thereafter, O'Neil and his Army Expedition members (see INTRODUCTION) established a main camp at the site.

Four years later, during the 1889-90 Seattle Press Expedition (see INTRODUCTION), one of the peaks - known today as Hurricane Hill - was named "Mt. Eldridge" in honor of journalist William C. Eldridge of Washington D.C. The present name of that mountain, Hurricane Hill, derives from the term "Old Hurricane" as the peak was affectionately called by local settlers. Once prevailing winds (from the southwest) push storm clouds as far as the Bailey Range, the next obstruction is Hurricane Ridge, seven miles northeast. Winds up to 100 miles-per-hour, hurricane force, scream over these subalpine meadows, chiefly during winter blizzards.

The mountain was dubbed Hurricane Hill by prospector W.A. Hall, who climbed it from the southwest, or Elwha, side of the mountain on an extremely windy day in 1897. Years later, during World War II, there appeared to be an imminent threat of a Japanese invasion of the Pacific Northwest and Hurricane Hill was designated to be an observation point. A 13'-by-13' lookout tower was erected on the mountain and was occupied during the entire winter of 1942-43 by famous wildlife photographer Herb Crisler and his wife Lois. 95, 114, 120, 131, 152

HYAK CREEK; MT. TOM (2E). Hyak is Chinook Jargon for "rapid," "swift," or "hurry," which describes the creek's movement down a precipitous ravine. The name was probably applied by U.S. Forest Service officials rather than Natives. (See ALCKEE CREEK.) 93, 120

HYDE'S CREEK; LAKE CRESCENT (6B). Named in honor of Dr. Frederick Hyde who built a home alongside the lake, circa 1930. 141

ICARUS (6,200'); MT. OLYMPUS (4B). A double-spined peak on the south edge of Humes Glacier, Icarus was first climbed in 1966 by B. West and M. West. Its name most likely was applied by Hubley and LaChapelle in preparation for the 1957-58 International Geophysical Year. Following the naming of Mt. Olympus with its reference to Greek mythology, most smaller peaks on the massif are named for aspects of Greek or Roman mythology.

In Greek mythology, Daedalus' son Icarus used artificial wings to fly near the sun. The intense heat melted the wax which Icarus had used to fasten the feathers to his wings, causing him to fall into the sea and drown. 69, 140, 169, 207.5

ICE RIVER, GLACIER; MT. OLYMPUS (4C). Though both features are named most logically, the actual source of those names remains unknown. Ice River itself drains the glacier and its flow siphons off huge, boulder-size hunks of frozen water. 152

ICEBERG LAKES; MT. STEEL (5G). Situated at the 6,000-foot elevation, these relatively small bodies of water freeze solid during the winter months and retain large chunks of ice, both in the lakes and around their edges, long into summer. 152, 206

ICICLE LAKE; MT. OLYMPUS (4C). William Fairchild (see FAIRCHILD CREEK and MT. WILLIAM FAIRCHILD) and Jack Nattinger (see HANDSOME JACK SLIDE) named the lake in 1951-52 due to its location below a glacier. 42

IDAHO CAMP, CREEK; MT. OLYMPUS (7F). Bill and Martin Humes (see HUMES GLACIER, RANCH for further information on Bill Humes) arrived on the banks of the Elwha River in 1897. Though Bill Humes remained at this site for many years, brother Martin relocated to Idaho where he later died. It is thought that Idaho Creek and Idaho Camp were named by Bill Humes in honor of his brother.

Though it is not known exactly when the names were applied, an early Humes letter indicates that the creek must have been named prior to March 6, 1898 (See PRESCOTT CREEK.) 87, 94, 100

IGNAR CREEK; MT. STEEL (3D).This somewhat unusual little stream was named in honor of Ignar Olson, long-time resident of the Quinault Valley. However, there are two accounts as to how it came to be called Ignar Creek.

One source contacted by the author alleges that Ignar Olson, twice-married father of 17 children, frequently hired himself out as a guide and packer for climbing and surveyor parties in the region. One such party trekked up the Quinault River in 1906, camping alongside a different creek each night. The good-natured men began naming each watercourse they encountered for a different member of the group, and according to this story, Ignar's turn came on the fourth night out while they were camped near this streamlet. A sign proudly proclaiming it to be "Ignar Creek" was nailed to a nearby tree.

Another account, however, paints a different picture. As noted, Ignar Olson earned a living packing for groups wishing to enter the Olympics. On one of those journeys, while accompanying a U.S. Geological Survey team, he led the party into Enchanted Valley. And while there, a couple of the men made note of the fact that no landmarks anywhere had yet been named for their popular guide. This version asserts that the surveyors scanned several existing maps of the area, spotted one as-yet-named stream, and promptly christened it Ignar Creek on the spot. It is noteworthy that if this story is true, the christening was quite possibly made in jest. As surveyors of the terrain, the men undoubtedly knew that during the dry summer months this stream does not maintain enough volume even to make it all the way to the Quinault River. Rather, it sinks underground some 300-400 feet from the river bank!

Many stories are told about the fun-loving, imaginative Ignar Olson. Once, it is reliably reported, his leg was broken in a backwoods scuffle with a black bear, yet the diminutive fellow was on his feet in a matter of days, hobbling through his beloved Olympics.

One of the author's favorite tales though, was related by John Olson, Jr., a son. (It should be noted that Olson did *not* vouch for its authenticity!) It seems that Ignar Olson and his brother were out with their dogs one day, busily setting trap lines. Because the Olson's trained hounds had recently died of old age, the two men had been forced to take along several young, inexperienced pups. In short, they were most unsatisfactory, so Ignar's brother set out for town to try to buy a few already-trained dogs. For some unknown reason, however, he returned to camp a few days later with a *parrot*! Needless to say, Ignar was not impressed with the flying squawk box. Nevertheless, according to son John, the two carried the noisy, talkative bird with them along their trapline.

At this point in the story, the imaginative side of Ignar's personality takes over. As he told the story to his son - apparently with a straight face - the dogs soon picked up the scent of an elk and the parrot began circling overhead yelling encouraging words such as "Sickem Tag! Sickem Tag!" And then, to what we are told was the utter amazement of the Olson brothers, the bird flew back to where they were standing and screeched "This way, Ignar! This way, Ignar!" There is no record available concerning the fate of the elk. 59, 63, 72, 74, 146

THE INCISOR (7,350'); TYLER PEAK (1C). Named by Heathershaw and Spencer and first climbed in 1958 by K. Heathershaw and B. McKee, the difficult-to-climb pinnacle is shaped precisely like an incisor (tooth). 140, 184.5

INDIAN CREEK, PASS; SPRUCE MOUNTAIN (3E). Though it cannot be proven, it is thought the name Indian Creek is derived from the usage of the low pass by Natives - tribe unknown - for hunting access from 1908 to about 1928. Their living quarters were situated at the point where this stream enters the Bogachiel River. A Ranger Station was once located at this spot, known as Indian Guard Station. A WW II lookout was located on a side ridge not far from the pass. At the age of 17, Wirth Brandeberry helped construct a trail up to it and packed equipment to supply it. 29, 64.5, 154

INFINITY TOWER (6,900'); TYLER PEAK (5B). Though it is not known when this peak was named, we do know that the term "Infinity Tower" was first used by Arnold Bloomer of Bremerton (see HONEYMOON MEADOWS) on a first ascent in 1968. Bloomer noted later that he felt this peak's ascent posed "infinite" problems. When D. Muntz and R. Olson, Jr. ascended Infinity Tower, they are said to have thrown a cod line over the 150-foot summit so that they could make a prusik ascent. 140, 169, 184.5, 207.5

INNER CONSTANCE (7,670'); TYLER PEAK (4B).It is thought that the name originated with the late George W. Martin, a Bremerton, Washington, resident, but we do not know when this occurred.

Once known as the "West Peak of Mt. Constance," Inner Constance does indeed stand separate from the Mt. Constance massif, and one source speculates that Martin applied this name to give the peak some individuality.

"C-141 Peak" (7,339'), one mile northwest of Lake Constance along the Inner Constance ridge, refers to an Air Force C-141 which crashed there on March 25, 1975. The plane smashed into the northwest face of Inner Constance (see INNER CONSTANCE), killing 16 crew members.169, 184.5

IRELY CREEK, LAKE; MT. CHRISTIE (3C). Named in honor of Jacob Irely (a.k.a. Eyerly) an early homesteader in the Olympics. Irely was inadvertently responsible for a tremendous forest fire in the summer of 1891 when he attempted a controlled burn on a patch of cedar trees near his home so that he could plant blackberries. The slash fire he started blazed out of control, destroyed 2,500-3,000 acres of forest and burned for a full two weeks! Later it acquired a measure of fame, being referred to as the "Quinault Burn of 1891." 40, 120

JACKASS LAKE; see OBSTRUCTION LAKE.

JACKSON CREEK; LA PUSH (7C). This stream is named in honor of Peter Jackson, an Indian (tribe unknown), who lived at Toleak Point in 1893. 63, 120

JACKSON CREEK; MT. TOM (4C). There exist two possibilities as to the source of this name. One story asserts that it was named in 1911 for a timber cruiser named Jackson who worked in the area. The other explanation, told by pioneer Lena Huelsdonk Fletcher and corroborated by other locals, asserts that the name honors Native American settler on the Upper Hoh, and neighbor of the Huelsdonks, Andrew Jackson. Jackson's cabin was located off what is now "C" loop in the Hoh Rainforest Campground. The earlier name for the Hoh Ranger Station, Jackson Ranger Station, as well as the Snider-Jackson Trail (the southern-most part now called the Hoh-Bogachiel trail) is also thought to be named for Andrew Jackson by most locals and old timers. 43, 79, 117.5, 120

JAGGED ISLAND; LA PUSH (2G). William Dawson described it in 1905 as "a long ridge of fantastically eroded sandstone ...200 yards long, about 50 yards wide, 68 feet high. Swept by severe storms and entirely destitute of vegetation."

The description is fitting, as the island does indeed have a saw-tooth edge. Incidentally, the island is actually four sea stacks, not one, as it first appears from shore. Jagged Island is also a sea lion rookery.

In *Exploring Washington*, by Harry M. Majors, this island is called "Wishaloolth Island." In 1906 ornithologist William Dawson is said to have seen nearly 3,000 glacous-winged gulls here and described it as "a mountain range in miniature, and one of the most weirdly picturesque of the Olympiades." Majors puts Jagged Island 1.5 miles west (254°) of its actual location. 120, 152, 209

JAMES ISLAND; LA PUSH (4E). There are two different stories of how James Island got its name (1840-1895). The island was originally called "Ah-kah-laht," "Akolot," or "Alekislet," meaning "way up there." Now favored by Natives is "A-Ka-lat." Historically, when the Quileute Indians were attacked they retreated up the only trail to the protection of this island's 200-foot cliffs. From there they could easily dump rocks and boiling water on enemy braves.

Early historian and explorer Judge James G. Swan tells a different story. Swan was the first white man to extensively record life during the early days at the Quileute settlement of La Push. In this journal he wrote: "Believe F. (Francis) W. James, of Port Townsend, to be the first white man to climb Alekislet, so I therefore named it James Island." This provided a name more easily pronounced by white men. Accompanied by Major John F. Sewell and Thomas Brackett, F. W. James traveled from Port Townsend to James Island in 1855 to remove mail from the wreckage of the steamer S.S. Southerner. 34.5, 92, 120, 153, 167, 190

JANE CREEK; see WINDFALL CREEK.

JEFFERS GLACIER; MT. OLYMPUS (3B). The name Jeffers Glacier was applied by U.S. Forest Service Supervisor Rudo Fromme in honor of Joseph C. Jeffers, prominent Olympia, Washington photographer, who was legendary for his daring. Joe's luck ran out on a rock wall above Hubert Glacier while attempting a decent into South Fork of Hoh Valley. In the midst of a pendulum move on a short rope Joe dislodged a hail of boulders that sent him tumbling into the moat

Above: GRANT HUMES ON CABIN FLAT. This photograph is circa 1910. (Olympic National Park Collection).

Left: GRANT HUMES WITH BYNG. Humes and his dog Byng are headed out on a cougar hunt in this early photograph. (Olympic National Park Collection)

Left: HUMES RANCH. This was the Elwha Valley home of Grant Humes, outfitter guide and explorer of the Olympic Wilderness. In this March 1926 photograph he is pictured with friends from Port Angeles, left to right; Chet Howser, Margie Walton, Grant Humes and Phyllis Walton. (Olympic National Park Collection)

Below:JAMES ISLAND. In addition to the island note Rialto Beach (upper left) and First Beach at La Push (middle right) in this aerial view. (Olympic National Park Collection)

between the rock wall and Hubert Glacier ice. Joe's teenage climbing partner and son, Vibert retraced their route across Mt. Olympus. Late Sunday night on August 24, 1924 Vibert stumbled into Olympus Guard Station, (Lewis Meadow) where Charley Lewis was on duty. That night Lewis assembled a rescue team that included among others Henry Huelsdonk (brother of the Iron Man-John and engineer of the first Hi Hoh Bridge). With Vibert they returned Monday, August 25 to the accident scene. Risking life and limb, Charley descended part way into the bergschrund, and then retreated with his team off the mountain.

Wednesday, August 27, Vibert was driven back to Olympia from Sol Duc by family friend, Felix Donges. On Thursday, Hans Fuhrer, an experienced Mt. Rainer guide and others left Olympia for the Olympics. At Forks the expedition which now numbered in excess of a dozen, met packer Oscar Peterson. The next three days of travel took the team first to Spruce on the Upper Hoh, then up the South Fork through both of its canyons to a base camp at the Boulder Field (nestled beneath the peaks of the Valhallas at the mouth of Valkyrie Creek). Climbers in the group probed the hazardous and steep upper margins of Hubert glacier for several days without success. According to Oscar Peterson's day book the men returned to Forks on September 5th. Rumor has it that Joseph Jeffers in his earlier history declared that he hoped Mt. Olympus would be his sepulcher. On August 24, 1924 Joseph's wish was granted.

To add to the abundance of confusion surrounding this event, Supervisor Fromme, who named Jeffers Glacier, and his subordinate Chris Morgenroth wrongly assumed in their memoirs Jeffers died in Jeffers Glacier.

It is possible that Jeffers Glacier was previously called University Glacier. Roy Muncaster (see MUNCASTER MOUNTAIN) and another unnamed University of Washington student explored the upper Queets Valley in 1914, ascending Mt. Olympus via the glacier. A year later, when Muncaster was traveling to Europe on the Lusitania, the ship was sunk by a German U-Boat. The glacier may have been named for his alma mater. Confusion persists however, as to whether University Glacier was the earlier name for Jeffers Glacier or for a spider-shaped glacial mass at the head of the West Fork of Paull Creek. 67, 68, 94, 96.5, 117, 120, 153.75, 154.5, 185

JEFFERSON COUNTY. The county encompasses a major portion of the central Olympic Peninsula. It was created on December 22, 1852, by the Oregon legislature (prior to establishment of Washington Territory); the name honored President Thomas Jefferson. 199

JEFFERSON COVE; FORKS (2A). This bay was named by Captain George Vancouver on April 29, 1792, during his detailed, five-year exploration of the Northwest. It is not known why he assigned this particular name to it.

The Jefferson Oil Company (presumably naming itself after the cove) began drilling for oil in 1913. Oil Company workers navigated into the cove aboard a scow, then, using a steam-driven donkey engine, laboriously hauled their drilling equipment a quarter-mile up the steep banks on a skid road. Two test oil wells were drilled each going about 1,100 feet deep but both were "dry" and the oil boom abruptly terminated. 63

JEMROD CREEK; MT. OLYMPUS (2C).

JERSTED POINT; OZETTE LAKE (4D). Named in honor of Severn (spelling uncertain) Jersted, who lived here as an early homesteader. 193

JULY CREEK, CAMPGROUND; QUINAULT LAKE (5G).

JUMBO'S LEAP; see FIVE STREAM.

JUNE 10TH PEAK (6,019'); MT. STEEL (2E). The present name of this mountain derives from its first ascent by several Seattle residents, Dr. Julian Ansell, Eiichi Fukushima, Curtis Howard, and Robert McConnell on June 10, 1963. Originally, June 10th Peak was referred to as "Capitol Mountain," so labeled by Harry Fisher of the 1890 O'Neil Expedition (see INTRODUCTION) because he thought it resembled the "domed" silhouettes of the Capitol Building when viewed from the east. 120, 169, 207.5

KAHKWA CREEK; SPRUCE MTN. (1E). When settlement of the North Olympic Peninsula first began Chinook was a commonly-used trade language, a sort of "pidgin" jargon that was an effective means of communication between Natives and white men (see ALCKEE CREEK). The word "Kahkwa" is taken from the Chinook language and means "like" or "equal." 120

KALALOCH, CAMPGROUND, CREEK, RANGER STATION, ROCKS; DESTRUCTION ISLAND (4D). The word "kalaloch" is a corruption of an original Quinault term "k' E le ok," pronounced "Kq a la ok" and meaning "a good place to land," "canoe launch and landing," or "sheltered landing." Kalaloch was one of the few safe landing sites for dugout canoes between the Quinault and Hoh River mouths. Other translations of this word, less substantiated than those previously listed, are "land of plenty," "easy living," or "lots of clams."

On March 21, 1928, Charles W. Becker became the first postmaster of Kalaloch. Then, during World War II (on September 22, 1944) the site of the Kalaloch Post Office was relocated to a building the dimensions of which totaled only six-and-one-half square feet. It was so tiny that it received a great deal of publicity, being billed as "The Smallest Post Office in the United States." The U.S. Postal authorities discontinued its operations in that building on March 23, 1956. Kalaloch Creek was previously called Duncan Creek on the 1896 Gilman National Geographic map. 73, 155, 160, 180, 189

KAYOSTLA BEACH; LAKE OZETTE (3B).

KELLY FIELD; SALMON RIVER (7D). This area was homesteaded by the three-member Killea family (who called it "Killea Field") from 1889-1917. In 1917 William Killea sold his acreage to M.M. Kelly and the latter's brother-in-law, a man named Ferguson. Later the Kellys purchased adjacent properties and accumulated a spread known as "The Kelly Ranch." Here they originally raised Hereford cattle, later replacing those animals with horses used for packing to and from civilization. Famed Western novel author Zane Grey was a guest at the Kelly Ranch for several summers and used the Queets as a setting for one of his novels. 58.5, 203

KERR CREEK; SALMON RIVER (1B). This stream was named in honor of Dave Kerr, an Irishman who maintained a ranch along the Clearwater River during the latter years of the nineteenth-century. When his home on the alder flat was flooded, he moved to the abandoned Glover home.

Kerr's home was quite isolated from civilization. One day when returning from a hunting trip with his boat, laden with deer and elk meat, the boat suddenly filled with water and sank. It took two days for him and the men to reach civilization through the thick vegetation. Thus was life in the Queets at the turn of the century. 1, 56, 63

KESTNER CREEK; KLOOCHMAN ROCK (6A). Named for the Anton Kestner family, who established a permanent homestead just a few miles above Lake Quinault in 1891. Anton Kestner was a former violinmaker in Austria, and in fact, possessed a piano at his wilderness home. The Kestners' son Joseph joined the U.S. Forest Service in 1916.

Mrs. Kestner was very likely the first white woman settler in this area, and from all accounts, was a formidable person. While her husband worked in logging camps to earn a living for his brood, the strong-willed Mrs. Kestner stayed busy raising the children and "chopping down the brush and shooting cougars."

Once, she said, she spotted a big cat near her home, took a shot at it, but missed. Again she took careful aim and "hit him in the same place." The third slug, according to this hardy pioneer, was the charm, and she bagged the animal. One of her favorite afternoons, she said, was when she gave birth to a baby - and still had enough energy to milk seven cows! 40, 59, 124, 162

KILKELLY CREEK; MT. CHRISTIE (2G).The National Park Service dubbed this creek in honor of Johnny Kilkelly, an early Queets Valley settler who lived on the west side of the mouth of Sam's River Inlet. The name is frequently misspelled "Killkelly." 76, 167

KIMTA CAMP, NORTH FORK CREEK, PEAK (5,399'), SOUTH FORK CREEK; MT. CHRISTIE (3F). The Seattle Press Expedition (see INTRODUCTION) in 1890 called the stream flowing here "The Lost Chord" and according to existing records, may have christened the peak "Mt. Frazier," for S.R. Frazier, editor of the *Seattle Press*.

The present name, Kimta, was applied by the U.S. Forest Service and is a Chinook word meaning "behind," "since," "last," "after," or "the lesser of the two." Elip Creek (Chinook for "first" or "foremost") is reached before Kimta Creek when ascending the North Fork Quinault River Valley. (See ELIP CREEK.)

Kimta Camp (also known as Par Camp) is near the south end of the basin and at the base of Kimta Peak. It is situated on a rocky, tree-adorned knoll and was the sixth camp established by wildlife photographer Herb Crisler. It was the farthest south of many such camps he set up in the Olympics strung southward from the Humes Ranch along the Bailey Range and Skyline Ridge. Kimta Camp was well-covered with rocks and branches when he left the area; he

SOUTH KIMTA BASIN. The Cleveland Museum of Natural History Olympic Expedition on the move. On foot is Frank Hibben, on horseback is packer Oscar Peterson Sr. Photograph by Pat Bole dated July 26, 1931. (Peterson Collection)

BASIN OF THE LILLIAN. The Seattle Press Expedition (1889-1990) applied the name Lillian to the river flowing from this high basin. (Olympic National Park Collection)

KLAHHANE LODGE. The Klahhane Club was organized by Port Angeles outdoor men and women in the spring of 1915. Members are pictured here in the midst of lodge construction in the Olympic foothills South of Port Angeles circa 1920.

(Clallam County Historical Society Collection)

would then construct a tarpaulin lean-to when returning to visit the site. Some of the footage Crisler shot at Kimta found its way into Disney Studios' famous movie "Olympic Elk." 12, 95, 120, 169

KLAHHANE RIDGE; MT. ANGELES (2G). "Klahhane" is a Chinook term meaning "out of doors," "without," "outside," " good times in the mountains," "good times out of doors." (See ALCKEE CREEK.) The name applied to the Ridge by late-19th-century settlers was officially placed on maps in 1961 and was also adopted as the official name of a popular Port Angeles, Washington, hiking club.

On August 5, 1885, Lt. Joseph O'Neil and three members of the Chambers family of Port Angeles climbed Peak 6,101 on Klahhane Ridge. During this trek, Lt. O'Neil named the lower western portion of the ridge "Victor Pass," in honor of Victor Smith, the founder of nearby Port Angeles. 12, 19, 50, 88, 120, 180

KLOOCHMAN ROCK (3,356'); KLOOCHMAN ROCK (2E). "Kloochman" is said by some to be a term from the Chinook Jargon meaning "woman," "wife," "Indian woman married to white man, or female." (See ALCKEE CREEK.)

According to Queets Indian legend, Queets tribesmen traveled up the river in the fall of each year in their dugout canoes. There they would hunt deer, elk, and fish for salmon, smoking the meat in the alder flats, then return to their homes along the Pacific Ocean. On one such hunting foray, many long years ago, an old "squaw" (known as a "klooch") accompanied the hunters. During the hunt, the old woman wandered off from camp onto the hillside of this peak. Soon thereafter a cold, heavy snowstorm swept in and searching tribesmen were unable to find her. When the storm abated they looked up to the top of the mountain (where today a lookout platform rests on the sharp rock spire) and imagined they could see the outline of her body. Anxious to continue on their journey homeward, they concluded that the old woman must have become lost, climbed to the top of the hill for a better view of the valley below, and froze to death while doing so. Before leaving, they named the mountain after their "klooch." The second syllable of the word "kloochman" was a much later addition and was applied by European settlers.

Wilbur Northup, a Queets settler descendent, flattened the peak of Kloochman Rock off and helped construct a lookout there in 1932. The following summer he hired on as its first lookout and took his bride, Louise, up there for the season on their honeymoon. In more recent times, local folks who have attempted to climb Kloochman Rock have been known to refer to it as "Boulder Hill," a particularly descriptive term. 12, 56, 64.5, 73, 153.5, 167, 169, 205

KLOSHE CREEK; SPRUCE MTN. (4D). It is thought that Rudo Fromme, former U.S. Forest Supervisor, applied the name to this creek based on a Chinook language (see ALCKEE CREEK) term meaning "beautiful," "kindly," or "good." The actual christening by Fromme could not be verified, but if he did indeed name the stream, it would have had to occur between 1913 and 1926. 90

KNERR CREEK; MT. ANGELES (6B).

KRAUSE BOTTOM; MT. OLYMPUS (6F). It is not known who affixed the name to this bottomland but we know it was christened in honor of Ernest and Meta Krause, who settled here, circa 1895. Some claim that the Krause family did not settle on this precise spot, but rather homesteaded in the area now lying beneath the waters of man-made Lake Mills a few miles away. However, fruit trees still on the bench above Krause Bottom in 2004 may have been part of the Krause homestead.

The acreage now called Krause Bottom was the site of a major camp established in March 1890 by the Seattle Press Expedition (see INTRODUCTION) as they tramped across the Olympic Range. 58.5, 64.5, 94, 114, 120, 156, 195

KURTZ LAKE; MT. CHRISTIE (2D). Named in honor of David A. Kurtz of Aloha, Washington. It is not known who assigned the name or when this was done. 91

LAFALLETTE FALLS; LAKE CRESCENT (2C). Miss (first name unknown) LaFallette was a resident of this area who maintained a land claim quite near Fairholme Resort (see FAIRHOLM CAMPGROUND). It is said that the fair-skinned Miss LaFallette, a dressmaker, had a skin disorder which required that she carry a parasol when traveling outdoors. 111, 157

LAKE ANGELES, MOUNT (6,454'); MT. ANGELES (2G, PORT ANGELES (3A). The names of these geographical landmarks all derive from their proximity to the city of Port Angeles, Washington.

Lt. Joseph O'Neil, during his first expedition (1885 - see INTRODUCTION) originally called the mountain "Mt. Sherman" in honor of United States Senator John Sherman or (some claim) the Senator's famous brother, General William Tecumseh Sherman. However, Lt. O'Neil muddied the waters somewhat insofar as this name is concerned, by referring to the peak in his official notes as "Sister Peaks" - with the nearby ridge now known as Klahhane (see KLAHHANE RIDGE) being listed as the other "sister." The pass between these two was dubbed by O'Neil as "Victor Pass" (see VICTOR PASS).

Despite O'Neil's efforts on behalf of the famous Shermans, Port Angeles settlers were routinely calling the mountain Mount Angeles by the year 1890. 70, 156, 207.5, 208

LAKE BEAUTY; see CAMP BEAUTY.

LAKE BLACKWOOD; see BLACKWOOD CREEK.

LAKE CONNIE; MT. CHRISTIE (5B). In the early 1900s the John Olson family named this body of water for Connie Egge, an employee at the Quinault Lake Hotel. Connie Egge's family were early pioneers here and Connie herself became a well-known trail camp cook. Prior to her service at the Quinault Hotel she had been an employee of Ignar Olson (see IGNAR CREEK) at the mine he operated between Howe and Litchy Creeks. Connie (Egge) Brandt is known to have visited her namesake at least once and was still living when this book first went to press. 120, 146

LAKE CONSTANCE; see CONSTANCE CREEK.

LAKE CREEK; PORT ANGELES (4B). The source of the name is unknown; this stream drains Lake Angeles (see LAKE ANGELES). 152

LAKE CREEK; see HOH CREEK.

LAKE CRESCENT, RANGER STATION; LAKE CRESCENT (6B). It is not known with any great certainty whether the name of this 624-foot-deep lake emanates from its natural crescent shape or because of its nearness to nearby Crescent Bay, named by Captain Henry Kellett in 1846.

Two Canadian trappers, John Sutherland, and John Everett forged their way inland in 1849, probably from Crescent Bay, and affixed their names to the two lakes encountered in their path, just south of the Strait of Juan de Fuca.

Everett was a larger man than Sutherland, so the larger lake (now Lake Crescent) was originally called Lake Everett. Approximately 20 years later, Lake Everett's name was changed to Lake Crescent. It has also been called "Big Lake" and "Elk Lake." (See MOUNT STORM KING for legend concerning formation of the lake.) 12, 34, 90, 120, 155, 173

LAKE LACROSSE, MOUNT (6,417'), **PASS**; MT. STEEL (6F). Two members of the 1890 Lt. Joseph O'Neil Expedition, Fisher and Linsley (see LINSLEY GLACIER), named this body of water the "Lake of the Holy Cross" in August 1890. At that time, according to the two men, a large moss-covered tree stood guard over the lake, its trunk and right-angle branches forming a cross. All of it reflected spectacularly in the calm waters below. In the months and years that followed, the lake underwent a number of name "changes" as it was described in print and was even renamed by another group of explorers. Prominent Seattle newspaperman Portus Baxter called it "Maltese Cross Lake" in an 1899 article. But Lt. O'Neil in his official report referred to it as "Lake Francis." And yet another group, the Banner Exploring Party had named it "Lake Darrell" (for reasons unknown) when they visited the lake 10 days before Fisher and Linsley. Nevertheless, it was an article in 1900 by Bernard Bretherton, also a member of the O'Neil expedition which took hold. Bretherton referred to it as "Lake of the Cross" a term which subsequently was shortened to Lake LaCrosse. 120, 208

LAKE LILLIAN; see LILLIAN GLACIER.

LAKE MARGARET; MT. CHRISTIE (7G). This body of water was named by the six-man Seattle Press Expedition (see INTRODUCTION) as they journeyed through the Olympics in 1889-90. Some observers believe the lake was christened

LAKE CRESCENT AND PYRAMID MOUNTAIN. This is a location of beautiful sights easily spotted from U.S. Highway 101 in the Olympic National Park. (Olympic National Park Collection)

LOW DIVIDE CHALET. On horseback is Oscar Peterson Sr., packer for the Cleveland Museum of Natural History Expedition. 1931 photograph by Pat Bole. (Peterson Collection)

in honor of Expedition member John Crumback's mother, Margaret Crumback.

By way of further identification, it was at this point that the men of the Press Expedition shot and killed a bear. According to their notes, the group was near starvation at the time and actually managed to skin and dress the animal and have it in a frying pan - *in 15 minutes*! 12, 179, 187, 207, 207.5

L

LAKE MARY; MT. CHRISTIE (7G). Lake Mary was named by the six-man Seattle Press Expedition (see INTRODUCTION) while they camped there early in May 1890. Records do not clarify why it was so named, though historians have speculated that "Mary" was no doubt a sweetheart or close friend of one of the explorers. 12, 187, 207

LAKE MILLS; JOYCE (5A). This body of water is named in honor of E.M. Mills, one of the founders of the Olympic Forest Products Company, forerunner of today's giant ITT/Rayonier, Inc.; however, it is not known who applied the name. Mills played a leading role in the development of the power dam(s) located on the Elwha River which produced this 200-foot-deep man-made lake. 12, 120

LAKE NO. EIGHT; MT. OLYMPUS (1E). The actual source of this name is unknown. The prevailing theory though, declares that when Seven Lakes Basin (where this body of water is located) was named, it was because of the number of lakes found therein. Apparently when yet another lake was discovered nearby, logic and a sense of humor prevailed; thus the term "Lake No. Eight" was applied. 94

LAKE SARAH; MT. ANGELES (6C). Amos B. Cameron, early Clallam County hunter and explorer, christened this lake in honor of his wife, Sarah. It is not known with any certainty when this occurred, only that it was sometime prior to the year 1940. 31, 34

LAKE SHARON; MT. TOM (7F). Olympic National Park employee Gary Kish spotted this lake from Boulder Peak in 1955. After bushwhacking his way to it, he christened the lake, the larger of the two in this basin, in honor of his girlfriend Sharon Headrick, whom he later married. Kish even erected a National Park Service sign to this effect at Lake Sharon. 112

LA POEL, CREEK; LAKE CRESCENT (5B). Rudo Fromme, Olympic National Forest Supervisor, apparently named this creek sometime between the years 1913 and 1926. For some reason, it had previously been called "Pancake Point," and in trying to maintain the spirit of the original title, yet apply a more phonetic, charming name to it, Fromme gleaned the words La Poel from the prevailing Chinook Jargon of that day. The Chinook dictionary describes a "frying pan" as "la poel." The lilting phrase obviously derives from the French language, which in turn, is part of the fabric of Chinook's "pidgin" English. (See ALCKEE CREEK.) The original Native name for this picturesque roadside rest was "Sapool."

La Poel, once a bustling truck stop with a general store, cabins, and tavern, is now a quiet picnic area. La Poel Creek flows into Lake Crescent just west of the point. 12, 64.5, 68, 156, 157, 205

LA PUSH, ROAD; LA PUSH (4E). There are two versions as to the origin of this name. One claims that it stems from a French word appropriate to its location. La Push is a perverted version of the French phrase "la bouche" (pronounced La boos), which means "the mouth" in Chinook. (see ALCKEE CREEK) This term accurately describes its geographic location at the mouth of the Quillayute River. According to this version, the site was so named January 29, 1883, by Postmaster Dan Pullen shortly after the original post office (Quileute) was moved inland by the U.S. Postal Service.

Prior to the settlement of the area by the white man, the Makah name for this area was "Kwidi-yt' atx," pronounced "Kwi-deey-tatx."

Others claim that the name for this area derived strictly from the Chinook Jargon term "la pesh," which means "a pole." Such a phrase would refer to a setting pole used by Natives when steering their canoes.

No doubt one of the two versions described above relative to the etymology of the term La Push is the correct one, but the author is not prepared to state with any conviction which one. 12, 50, 96, 121, 155, 160, 180

LAMATA CREEK; MT. STEEL (4E).

LEITHA CREEK; MT. ANGELES (3A).

LENA CREEK, MOUNT (5,995'), **UPPER LAKE**; THE BROTHERS (3D). Topographers Arthur Dodwell and Theodore Rixon discovered this 140-foot-deep lake in 1898. Later, sometime between 1900-1923, unknown parties affixed the name "Lena" to the topographic features in this area, including a Lower Lena Lake outside the Park. 74, 120, 152, 184.5

LEWIS MEADOW; MT. OLYMPUS (1D). This landmark carries the surname of a native Missourian who came west in the early 1900s. During World War I Charley Lewis found employment in the Bremerton Shipyards. After the war, Charley was hired by Chris Morgenroth for work in the Snider area, then assigned to Olympus Guard Station (located in what became known as Lewis Meadow). Shortly after his arrival (around 1919) Charley expanded his station, dug a well and developed a clearing for horses. In 1924 Charley was on duty when Vibert Jeffers came down from Mt. Olympus looking for help (see Jeffers Glacier). In 1926 Olympus Guard Station was moved to its present location and Charley continued there as forest guard. In the mid-twenties Charley bought into Fred Fisher's Will-go-for Fur farm, eventually buying Fred out and acquiring much of what is now Lewis Ranch on the Upper Hoh at the Park boundary. In 1927 Charley married Marie, John (Iron Man) Huelsdonk's youngest daughter. Charley's exploits as a ranger, hunter, trapper and rancher eventually created a legend that surrounds his name to this day. 43, 59, 64, 117, 117.5, 153.25

LILLIAN GLACIER, LAKE, RIVER; MT. ANGELES (4D). Though we do not know the person for whom these landmarks were named, we do know that the term "Lillian" was first applied to the river by the six-man Seattle Press Expedition (see INTRODUCTION) on that group's 1889-90 journey through the Olympics.

It was at Lillian River in May 1915 that Forest Ranger Chris Morgenroth reported being hunted and then attacked by two wolves. The incident occurred, he declared, where the Elwha Trail crosses the river. Morgenroth said he quickly scrambled up a snag and decided to wait out the hungry animals, but later changed his mind, descended and fought them off with a club and rocks his only weapons. No doubt the harrowing episode left a deep impression on Morgenroth for soon thereafter he rescinded his long-standing order that rangers couldn't carry weapons with them in the backwoods! 12, 64.5, 114, 120, 141, 207

LINCOLN CREEK, GUARD STATION (see STAIRCASE RANGER STATION), **MOUNT** (5,868'); MT. STEEL (6A). It is not known who actually christened Lincoln Creek, Mt. Lincoln, and Lincoln Guard Station although it is probable the peak's name was assigned first. First ascent was in 1932 by K. Soult and E.S. Harmon. It is assumed that the name was intended to honor President Abraham Lincoln, in keeping with the Presidential theme so prevalent in this section of the Olympic Peninsula. During his tenure in office, Lincoln signed an Executive Order which designated the town site of Port Angeles as the "Second National City," and federal funds were granted for the establishment and maintenance of a military reservation at the town site.

It should be noted that the Lincoln Guard Station is now known as Staircase Ranger Station (see STAIRCASE RAPIDS, RANGER STATION). 94, 146.5, 152

LINSLEY GLACIER; MT. STEEL (5G). This glacier was first referred to as Linsley Glacier by members of the Lt. Joseph O'Neil Expedition (see INTRODUCTION) on August 12, 1890. It was so designated in honor of mineralogist Nelson E. Linsley (1842-1925), who accompanied Lt. O'Neil on his second excursion through the Olympics.

It should be noted that, unofficially, many people call Linsley Glacier Quinault Glacier because of the river flowing from it. 146, 162, 207.5, 208

LITCHY CREEK; MT. CHRISTIE (6B). According to Quinault resident John Olson, Litchy was an army officer (rank unknown) who led a small-scale expedition into this area sometime after the 1890 O'Neil Expedition had completed its work. Records do not support this, unless the officer's name was subsequently misspelled. 146, 162, 207.5

LITTLE DIVIDE; MT. TOM (5F). The low portion of High Divide (see HIGH DIVIDE), Little Divide, is a ridge running roughly east-west, dividing the Sol Duc from the Bogachiel drainage. The ridge is 4,000' high, which is approximately 1,000' lower than High Divide. It is sometimes referred to as Bogachiel Divide or more uncommonly, Low Divide. 94

LITTLE MYSTERY (6,941'); TYLER PEAK (2B). The source of this peak's name is unknown. The rationale, though, is its proximity to and smaller size than Mt. Mystery. 152, 210

LITTLE RIVER, SOUTH BRANCH; PORT ANGELES (1B). Little River, which feeds the mighty Elwha, was probably named subsequent to a reference in the notes of James Christie, co-leader of the Seattle Press Expedition in 1889-90 (see INTRODUCTION). Christie's exact statement: "McDonald's claim, where we are at present camped, is situated on the south branch of the little river on the east side of the Elwha..." The name Little River took hold throughout the region shortly thereafter and was in formal use by 1892. 109, 120, 207, 207.5

LITTLE SIBERIA; see ANDERSON PASS.

LIZARD HEAD PEAK (5,300'); JOYCE (2A). It is thought that Lizard Head Peak was once called Mt. McClure, in honor of Colonel A.K. McClure of the *Philadelphia Times*. Though their notes are unclear on the matter, Seattle Press Expedition members (see INTRODUCTION) apparently named it so in 1890.

Actually, a smaller, nearby peak had originally been dubbed "Lizard Head Peak," because it appeared to be "lizard-like" in profile. Later, the name itself was shifted to its present location. 94, 207

LOKI SPIRE (5,700'); MT. OLYMPUS (1A). The first ascent of the 300-foot pinnacle was in 1971 by R. Beckett, D. Haley, G. Kelsey, M. Lennox, D. Michael, D. Stevens, and R. Yekel. It is thought that the naming of the spire was by H. Pinsch and G. Kelsey. The peak is named in keeping with the Norse god theme already established in the Valhallas. According to Norse mythology, Loki is the evil god known for creating disorder and mischief and for bringing disaster and embarrassment to the other gods. Loki is described in Norse verse as "handsome... but inside, the soul of spite and completely fickle... " Further, he is said to have "...a talent and skill in slyness which leaves everybody else far behind, knowing a trick for every occasion."

As described in mythology, the Loki Spire in this mountain range, appropriately, sits behind Wodin (Odin - see WODEN) which it "deceives." 69, 140, 152, 169, 184.5

LOLO CREEK; MT. TOM (2F). "Lolo" is a Chinook Jargon term (see ALCKEE CREEK) meaning "to carry." 63

LONE TREE; MT. OLYMPUS (6C). The source of this name is unknown. Here a mountain hemlock tree stands entirely alone in an otherwise tundra-like ridge top, windswept and barren. This "pass" is a favored camp spot on the Bailey Range. 152

LONG CREEK, RIDGE; MT. OLYMPUS (7E). For reasons unknown, Long Creek was christened "Belle River" by the 1889-90 Seattle Press Expedition (see INTRODUCTION). Notes from the Expedition relate that Charles Barnes, historian and co-leader of the group, had what he termed a close brush with a cougar here as he journeyed up the stream alone March 29-31, 1890. After sleeping all night beside a fire, he said, he arose in the morning to find the tracks of a large cougar quite near his bedroll.

The permanent name for Long Creek derives from the activities of Frank Long. Long lived in the Elwha Valley, circa 1890, probably near what is now U.S. Highway 101. Perhaps his claim was nearer the Anderson Homestead, close to the mouth of Long Creek.

As with so many early settlers, there are but few written references to Frank Long in existence. However, if we may judge from the comments of traveler Ward Sanders, who came through this area in 1898, Long was apparently a cordial host. In a letter Sanders described a December visit he had with "settler Frank Long," during which he ate dinner with the Elwha Valley man. According to Sanders the two enjoyed a repast of "potatoes, coffee, bread and butter, milk and cream, honey and pear preserves..." 94, 120

LONG LAKE; MT. TOM (7F). The source of this name is unknown, but most observers believe that the elongated shape of the lake is responsible for it. 94

LOOKOUT ROCK; PORT ANGELES (5A). The source of this name is unknown. Located on a steep, rocky mountainside along the Hurricane Ridge Road, it is popular with tourists. Drivers can pull their cars over, get out and stretch their legs, and gaze at the picturesque valley below. In the distance, the Strait of Juan de Fuca, Dungeness Spit, Mt. Baker, and Glacier Peak offer a spectacular view. Lookout Rock is located just prior to entering the first of three tunnels on the Ridge Road. 152

Above: LONG RIDGE TRAIL CONSTRUCTION. Trail building was tough everywhere in the Olympics but nigh impossible on Long Ridge where Civilian Conservation Corps workers blasted and picked their way through ribs of slate. Photograph circa 1939. (Olympic National Park Collection)

Left: DOC LUDDEN. This flamboyant "doctor" from Tacoma settled the banks of the Elwha River around 1908. This photograph is circa 1926. (Olympic National Park Collection)

LOS FRAYLES; LA PUSH (4D). Sea explorer Bruno Heceta affixed the name to these islands on July 12, 1775, because of their resemblance to the appearance of monks or friars. 91

LOST ARROW PASS; MT. STEEL (7D). Many years ago, an unnamed hunter or trapper, using available stones, created a distinct arrow-shaped form on the ground at this spot. It points west in the general direction of Mt. Hopper and still was in existence, and quite visible, when the author hiked through this area in 1983. Hikers also refer to Lost Arrow Pass as "The Great Stone Arrow." 27, 140

LOST CABIN MOUNTAIN (3,900'); MT. OLYMPUS (8F). Name possibly derived from observations of members of the 1885 Lt. Joseph O'Neil Expedition (see INTRODUCTION). At that time O'Neil's men found a little old log cabin on the mountain and assumed it had been erected for use by hunters while they stayed in the area. However, the existence of the cabin has never since been verified and, indeed, it is not known with certainty whether it was actually on this mountain to begin with. Five years later, the Seattle Press Expedition (see INTRODUCTION) affixed the name Mt. Brown to this peak, in honor of Amos Brown of Seattle. That title was later dropped in favor of the present appellation. 57, 207, 207.5, 208

LOST PASS, PEAK (6,515'), **RIVER**; MT. ANGELES (5B). The source of this name is unknown, but the riverside is difficult and confusing enough that Jack Hughes, seasoned Olympic Ranger, once described it as "a good place to get lost!" 94, 152

LOTLOH CREEK; SPRUCE MTN. (7E). Lotloh comes from the Chinook Jargon (see ALCKEE CREEK) and means "noisy." In the author's opinion the term aptly describes this creek's nature. 120, 152

LOW DIVIDE, RANGER STATION; MT. CHRISTIE (6G). While camping at this spot May 4-8, 1890, Seattle Press Expedition members called the this the "Elwha Pass." It is the lowest divide (3,650') in the Olympic heartland.
   The first Low Divide cabin was constructed privately in the late 1920s. Herb Crisler broke into it in 1930 on the last leg of his 30-day survival trip across the Olympics to win a $500 bet. From the early 1930s to 1938 a chalet (perhaps the same, improved cabin) was located here, featuring flush toilets and hot showers. It should be noted that the new Ranger Station located here has neither. (See SKYLINE TRAIL, HALFWAY HOUSE, and ENCHANTED VALLEY.) 64.5, 94, 152, 163, 182

LOW MOUNTAIN (4,654'); MT. OLYMPUS (7B). Low Mountain was first climbed and subsequently described by 1889-90 Press Expedition (see INTRODUCTION) member Charles Barnes on April 29, 1890. It is at the low end of a ridge east of the Goldie River that culminates with Mt. Wilder (5,928'). Tabletop Mountain (also described by Barnes for its shape), which does not appear on today's maps either, is 1.7 miles to the south. 120, 152, 207.5

LOWER TWIN CREEK; TYLER PEAK (2A). The source of this name is unknown. The creek is just downstream or "lower" than Upper Twin Creek by less than 1/4 mile, where the two meet the Dosewallips River. 63

LUCKY CAMP; MT. OLYMPUS (8C). This April 26, 1890 camp of the Seattle Press Expedition (see INTRODUCTION) was a "lucky find." Charles Barnes described the incident in his journal:
   All day long we traveled without seeing a bare spot large enough to camp on, and we expected to have to make our beds in the snow bank again. But just as we were about to camp we discovered a little bench above the [game] trail, 15 by 20 feet in dimensions, enclosed by the hillside behind two jutting rocks. Sunny and warm and bare of snow it was the coziest little camping place imaginable...It was the best camp that we had had. The boys wished that they could pack it along with us...We named this Lucky Camp. 207

LUDDEN PEAK (5,828'); MT. OLYMPUS (7D). Originally named Mt. Squire by the Seattle Press Expedition (see INTRODUCTION) in honor of Washington State Senator Watson C. Squire, this peak was later renamed for early Clallam County, Washington, pioneer Addison "Doc" Ludden.
   For several years, circa 1908, "Doc" Ludden was, technically speaking, a squatter on the banks of the Elwha River. Nobody who knew him while he lived in Clallam County was ever certain of Ludden's occupation prior to moving here. Certainly his nickname gave no hint whatsoever, for in those days the term "Doc" - the only name people around here

ever called him - was a casual form of greeting to physicians, dentists, and even barbers. To further compound the uncertainty, it was also rumored that he had previously been a streetcar conductor - and various Tacoma, Washington, telephone directories listed Ludden as a policeman, a day jailer, and (circa 1905) a photographer and prospector. Obviously, the good "Doctor" was a man of many talents or a very fast talker!

Over the course of several summers prior to building a home in the Elwha Valley, "Doc" Ludden maintained a mining claim and cabin near the peak and was known to camp alongside the river. Later, circa 1909, it is thought that he leased some land from the U.S. Forest Service near a section of Elwha Valley referred to as Geyser Valley; (see GEYSER VALLEY) and proceeded to construct a residence befitting his bohemian lifestyle. Visitors to "Doc's" abode said they were genuinely startled by prominent signs festooning the outside of his home—he liked to call it "Geyser House"—advertising "Honey, "Bread," "Vegetables" and "Stereoscopic Views."

"Doc" Ludden, along with being a colorful personality, was remarkably self-sufficient. He raised bees for their honey and took a mule load of the goods to Port Angeles biannually to sell. His property was heavily planted with trees offering apples, quince, prunes, plums, and pears. Then too, there were wheat stalks, grapevines (for wine, of course), raspberries, and loganberries. Ludden even sewed his own clothing - from deer and elk hides.

As for the naming of the peak (he was fond of referring to it as "My lump"), "Doc" was not impressed with (or perhaps not cognizant of) the Press Expedition's title, Mt. Squire. Therefore, in his typically direct way, he simply renamed it by erecting a large, bold "Ludden Peak" sign on his property pointing toward the mountain!

A raconteur through and through, "Doc" Ludden liked nothing better than to find an audience - any size would do - and spin yarns for them about gold mines and other "secrets." It is said he could keep his listeners fascinated for hours. After his death (November 8, 1927), rumors surfaced that "Doc" had somehow been involved with the development of the world-famous Luden's cough drops. Nobody has ever been able to verify such a claim.

About five years later (June 13, 1933), Mr. E.O. "Cougar" Michael moved into the ostentatious old homestead and the place quickly became known as "Michael's Cabin" (see MICHAEL'S CABIN), thus turning a new page in the history of the Elwha Valley.

Nevertheless, Ludden and his genuine love for the Valley had made a permanent impact on the place, quite beyond the mere "naming" of a mountain peak. Some of his wondrous tales were so popular with listeners that he took time to compose them into verse - later found among his belongings. One of the author's favorites is the following quote, the fifth stanza of one of his compositions:

> Trampin' yer man-made royas
> Dreamin' of home sweet home;
> Thinkin' of Ol' mountain zephyrs,
> Back whar I love to roam.
> There's somethin' up thar' at's callin'
> Callin' in tones that thrills;
> 'Come to the wide free open
> Back in the Geyser Hlls.

12, 51, 54, 64.5, 80, 98, 169, 195, 207

LUNCH LAKE; MT. TOM (7E). Lunch Lake is the first of seven such bodies of water a hiker encounters while dropping into the Seven Lakes Basin (see SEVEN LAKES BASIN). Its popularity as a good spot to eat lunch while resting from the downward climb to the Basin no doubt accounts for its name. Nevertheless, the actual source of that name remains unknown. 94

LUNCH ROCKS; MT. ANGELES (7G). During 1965-1968 when winter patrol rangers skied up the Deer Park Road from the Olympic National Park boundary, Lunch Rocks, at the 14 1/4-mile point, was an excellent place to stop for lunch. It featured appropriate-size rocks to lean against if one were weary, and, perhaps because of such weariness, always seemed to be a warm and pleasant site. After lunch, Park rangers would ski up to Deer Park, passing "Whistler Point" on the way. Whistler Point is a term originated by road crew foreman Bill Heckman, circa 1956, because of the large colony of marmots located there. (Marmots are popularly known as "whistlers" due to their habit of emitting sharp, piercing whistles when threatened.) It is the first place on Deer Park Road where a skier or hiker can catch a glimpse of "The Needles" - the sharp, almost needle-like series of peaks on the horizon (see THE NEEDLES).

Old timers will recall another popular resting place along Deer Park Road, "Waterbarrel Point." It was situated about 3/4-mile down the road from Lunch Rocks toward the town of Port Angeles and was used to fill radiators more frequently than is the case with today's machines. 94, 152

LYMAN RAPIDS; SALMON RIVER (3C). H.B. Lyman was one of seven people who were led into the Queets River country by John Banta on June 10, 1890. D.H. Lyman, a relative, was one of 56 people taken there onboard the *Lucy Lowe* on May 1, 1891, for the purpose of settling the "Evergreen Colony." (See EVERGREEN.) One (or both) of the Lymans homesteaded at the mouth of a creek near these rapids. 1, 63

LYRE RIVER; LAKE CRESCENT (6D). Named by British Admiralty Surveyor Henry Kellett in 1846 or 1847 (accounts differ), the Lyre River is the outlet for Lake Crescent. The Lyre River's mouth - where it empties into the Strait of Juan de Fuca - was discovered July 17, 1790, by Spanish explorer Manuel Quimper, who called it "Rio de cuesta," meaning "river from hill." On some old, outdated maps, such as the 1896 Gilman National Geographic map, this stream was labeled the "Lyle" River. 19, 50, 73, 120

MADELINE CREEK; MT. STEEL (5B). This creek was christened by Roland and Stanley Hopper for their sister, Madeline Hopper. The Hopper Brothers were heirs to the Singer Sewing Machine Company fortune (see MOUNT HOPPER), but it is not known when they bestowed Madeline's name on the creek. 159

MADISON CREEK; JOYCE (7B). There have been at least seven different owners of the homestead first established here by a Mr. Madison, whose name was permanently affixed to the nearby stream. Madison (the name may have been spelled "Matson") first settled here in the early 1890s and drove a mine shaft into the hillside adjacent to what is now Bridal Veil Falls (sometimes referred to as Madison, or Matson Falls.)

The 40-acre site where Madison homesteaded (but did not own) was later occupied by a settler named Schmitt (approximately 1892) and later by the man who ultimately bought the land, a Mr. Bowman. Subsequent owners were Lester Sweet, Mr. Myren, and finally, the U.S. Government. (Olympic National Park.)

The mine shaft originally driven by homesteader Madison can still be found and, in fact, was still being "explored" by adventurous hikers 30 years ago. One of these amateur spelunkers, Elmer Kelly, related to the author that he and some friends once entered the shaft, took a wrong turn at an "intersection," and nearly didn't return! Another, Oscar Hanson, reports that he explored the shaft with some friends, their only light a candle. He said the experience, though successful, was somewhat harrowing - he termed it "eerie" - after dripping water doused their light, leaving the would-be adventurers "in the dark." 80, 109, 179

MAGGIES CORNER; MT. ANGELES (2G). Maggie's Corner is a section of roadway located about 0.8 miles below "The Slot" on Hurricane Ridge road, where drivers on their way to the top may first spot the Bailey Range. During winter months, blizzards frequently bombard this stretch of road with incredibly deep snows, and huge plows must literally create a "slot" through the drifts created here.

During the winter of 1956, U.S. Senator Henry "Scoop" Jackson was scheduled to attend the dedication of the winter ski season—the first year for public skiing on Hurricane Ridge. Lovell "Maggie" McGoff was a snowplow operator doggedly trying to clear the road so that Senator Jackson and his entourage could get through to the Lodge the next day. The snowstorm was so intense that McGoff, driving one of the old gas-rotary plows, floundered his way into deep drifts and blowing snow and was unable to free himself. Hopelessly imbedded too far up the road for fellow workers to help him—he was forced to spend a chilly, scary night right there in the cab of the plow. Soon thereafter the National Park Service crew began referring to the gently curving stretch of road as "Maggie's Corner." 94, 152

MAIDEN CREEK, LAKE, PEAK (6,434'); MT. ANGELES (6F). As with so many other landmarks in Olympic National Park, there are two stories, both purporting to be correct, concerning the naming of this stream.

According to "Billy the Cook," (real name not known), Maiden Lake received its name in approximately 1913 when a group of young men and women camped along its shores for a short time during the summer months. The young folks were allegedly fond of "skinny dipping," and Billy claims that at least one of these "maidens" was later found to be "in a family way."

Another story claims that the area was named for sentimental or glamorous reasons by an early party of hikers who came through this area from Lake Cushman. 92, 114

MANNY'S PRAIRIE; LAKE OZETTE (3F). Manny's Prairie, located 1.6 miles from Lake Ozette, is one-half mile long and ranges from 0.1 to 0.4 miles wide. It carries the name of a Danish family, early homesteaders in the area. A rather unique berry, the white cranberry, can be found at Manny's Prairie. 193, 196

MAPLE POINT; LAKE CRESCENT (6B). Fifty or more years ago, big leaf maple trees could be found growing throughout this area. Ecological succession, however, has shifted the balance away from these lovely trees and there are now proportionately more alders, fir, and hemlocks than there are the stately trees for which this site is named. 138, 152, 175, 205

MARMOT LAKE; MT. STEEL (5E). Messrs. Fisher and Linsley, members of the 1890 O'Neil Expedition (see INTRODUCTION) named this lake on August 12, 1890, probably because of their many sightings of Olympic marmots here. The furry little creatures are native to the Olympic range and are quite at home in this subalpine setting. 208

MARTIN CREEK; MT. OLYMPUS (3D).

MARTIN PEAK (7,575'); TYLER PEAK (2C). George W. Martin (1901-1970) along with Elvin R. Johnson made the first ascent of this peak in 1940. While the name has been used locally, it has never been approved officially by the Board of Geographic Names. 120, 140, 169, 184.5

MARTINS LAKES, PARK; MT. CHRISTIE (7F). It is thought that the name applied to these landmarks honors Martin Humes, the eldest brother of well-known Olympic pioneer Grant Humes. Proof of Martin's activity in this area is the fact that he and another brother, Will, had constructed a cabin near the Lillian River (though the site cannot be pinpointed today with any degree of certainty).

There is a 1907 photograph in Park files which carries a caption written by Grant W. Humes. The caption seems to support the claim that these places were named for Martin Humes. It reads: "...'lake' in 'Martins Park' named for Martin Humes - a pretty and seldom visited park-like meadow where he once shot a bear, 30 miles from Humes Ranch."

Though other versions of the christening of this area have surfaced over the years (some say it was named for a former Governor of Washington named Martin; others have called them the "Surprise Lakes") it is the author's opinion that the Humes account is authentic (see PRESCOTT CREEK for further information concerning Martin Humes). 51, 97, 185, 195, 204, 206

MARYMERE FALLS; LAKE CRESCENT (7B). There are several accounts extant as to how the name "Marymere" came to be applied to this beautiful, accessible waterfall located about one-half mile south of the Lake Crescent Ranger Station. The passage of time and unclear records make it all but impossible to determine which of the stories is the correct one. All have the ring of authenticity, and any of them might be the true version.

One account says that Marymere Falls was first discovered in 1895 by a Seattle patent attorney, Pierre Barnes, and his brothers, members of a family who pioneered in this area. Pierre Barnes and one of his brothers, Edward, (other brothers were Charles, Paul, and Horace) apparently entered into a friendly dispute with their mother, Sarah P. Barnes, over the christening. The boys wanted to name it after her, but she in turn wanted the falls named after Mary (Barnes) Eldridge, her daughter and the sister to Pierre and Edward. According to this story, all parties compromised, settling on the name Marymere ("Mary" for the sister, the "mere" being a French term meaning "mother.")

The second story relative to the designation of the word "Marymere" involves members of the same Barnes family. In this version, the word "Mary" is applied in honor of the same sister Mary Alice (Barnes) Eldridge and the "mere" stems from the Scottish word "lake."

The third account says that the word "Marymere" derived from the first name of Mary Daum, who owned and operated nearby Rosemary Inn (with co-owner Rose Littleton); here again, the "mere" emanates from the Scottish word for "body of water." 120, 126, 156, 207.5, 209

MARY('S) FALLS, CAMP; MT. ANGELES (1E). Sanford Floe, U.S. Forest Service Ranger (at Snider Ranger Station) and his wife had two daughters, one of whom was said to be named Mary. In point of fact, their two daughters were named Maxine and Dorothy. He purportedly named the falls located at this site in Mary's honor. The camp previously had been given another title by members of the 1889-90 Seattle Press Expedition. Member Charles Barnes described the site in his notes of April 4, 1890, this way:

Logs, snow and debris of the woods lay so heavy and deep toward the bottom that it was extraordinary how Dollie (one of the mules) ever got through. A rough and headlong tumble and roll would carry her down 100 feet and land her over head and pack in the snow drift. We would dig her out - fortunately we had the shovel to do it with - and another tumble would put her down a little farther, until at last we reached bottom with a level space to camp, but such a camp for April! Snow waist deep and no feed for Dollie after her exhaustive struggle.

For this reason, the Seattle Press Expedition dubbed this area "Deep Snow Camp." 75, 128, 153.5, 207

MASON COUNTY; MT. STEEL. The county (in the southeast corner of the Olympic Peninsula, 962 square miles) is named for Charles H. Mason, first Secretary of Washington Territory, who often undertook the duties of Acting Governor. Mason died in 1859 at the age of 32. The bill for creation of this county was introduced March 13, 1854; it passed on April 15, 1854. At first, the county was referred to as "Sawamish County," meaning "drifting, not permanent people," but in 1864 the name was changed by the legislature to Mason County. 66, 120, 131, 199

McCARTNEY CREEK, PEAK (6,499'); MT. ANGELES (4D). The story of how McCartney Peak actually received its name is somewhat convoluted, due primarily to mapping errors made by early surveyors and topographers.

Pat Fox, whose grandfather was Marvin H. McCartney, shares that McCartney used to guide the USGS and others around the Olympic Mountains when they were creating the maps and naming the mountains. Thus they named one after him. Around 1966-68, Pat, her father (Marvin M. McCartney), uncle (Dennis McCartney), and friend Dennis Tucker climbed various peaks, including McCartney, leaving a Band-Aid can with their names in it buried at the summit, a peak they said had the Lillian Glacier nestled on its side.

The summit we now know as McCartney Peak was, in the late 19th Century, referred to as "Lillian Peak." Another account related that a trapper known as "Old Man McCartney" used to frequent the area. Somebody (unknown) named a nearby peak known today as "Windfall," for the old trapper, and for a few years the two mountains standing side-by-side were shown on maps as McCartney and Lillian Peaks, respectively.

A major mapping error then occurred. Somehow, "Lillian Peak" vanished from the scene, and McCartney's name was shifted to that location. The "vacated" summit previously bearing the old woodsman's name suddenly became Windfall Peak and remains so today.

The stream located here somehow retained McCartney's name, even though it drains Windfall Peak! 64.75, 114

McCORMICK CREEK; QUINAULT LAKE (4G).McCormick Creek was named in honor of a homesteader here, circa 1890. 146

McGRAVEY LAKE(S); MT. STEEL (1B). One of 12 children, John F. McReavy was born in Northfield, Maine, in 1840. A farmer and logger in his youth, McReavy traveled extensively through Mexico and ultimately worked his way to California while, so the story goes, looking for a lost brother. It was only years later that he discovered the boy had died before McReavy's search for him had even begun.

McReavy's travels eventually brought him to Puget Sound where he became a timber faller at Point No Point. An accident involving his right arm caused him to look for a more sedentary occupation, so he became a cook. One source, referring to John's prowess in the kitchen, smilingly recalled that "John got more flour in his whiskers than in the bread."

McReavy was a large man with a persuasive voice and, as it turned out, was also a natural promoter. He finally found his niche in life in 1876 when he purchased the Puget Mill Company in Mason County for a $7,000.00 price tag although he reportedly had no cash when he bought it. McReavy's Puget Mill Company was one of the earliest logging operations in Mason County and became a rousing success. In 1883, flush with new-found prosperity, McReavy moved his firm to Union, Washington, where he renamed it the Union River Logging and Railroad Company. His business and fortune grew and shortly thereafter he met and married beautiful, petite (97 lbs.) Fannie Dow Gove.

McGravey Lake (actually there are two, but one is so small it doesn't show up on maps) was named in honor of the clever, lovable promoter after he accompanied the "Lake Cushman College Boys" on a journey through the Olympics in the 1890s. (The guides carrying the Lake Cushman nickname might possibly have been the Hopper brothers - see MOUNT HOPPER - but this fact could not be verified.) The spelling of the McReavy's name has been corrupted over the years, to its present "McGravey."

John F. McReavy died in Union City, Washington, September 18, 1918, at the age of 78. 5, 52, 66, 207.5, 208

McKINNON CREEK; SALMON RIVER (2C). N.A. McKinnon and his wife were among 55 colonists led by John Banta and S. Price Sharpe to the Queets Valley area in approximately 1890. Traveling out of Tacoma aboard the *Lucy Lowe* captained by a man named McDonald (first name unknown), the group established what later became known as The Evergreen Colony (see EVERGREEN).

The McKinnons' first residence was constructed alongside the creek now bearing his name, but in 1895 because of heavy flooding at the low level where the home was situated, McKinnon moved his family to a nearby bluff. Their riverside home was then used as a schoolhouse and was known for years as the "Old McKinnon House." McKinnon officially filed his original claim on the 163 and 35/100 acres in the year 1907. Later the land passed to subsequent owners, two gentlemen named Erikson and Anderson. 1, 56, 104, 203

MELDRIM POINT; LAKE CRESCENT (4B).

MERCURY (6,950'); MT. OLYMPUS (3C). Richard Hubley was reportedly the first to ascend this nearly 7,000-foot peak along with glaciologist, Dr. Edward LaChapelle, who dubbed it "Mercury" in keeping with the "Home of the Gods" theme previously established in affixing other names within the Mt. Olympus massif. The event coincided with formal preparation of the 1957-58 International Geophysical Year.

In Roman mythology, Mercury was the god of commerce, eloquence, and skill - as well as the patron of travelers, merchants, and thieves. His duties included rather mundane chores, such as being messenger for the other gods. Mercury's Greek mythology counterpart is Hermes (see HERMES). 69, 140, 168, 169, 184.5, 207.5

MICHAELS CABIN; MT. OLYMPUS (7F). Emil O. Michael was a hermit-like homesteader who apparently resided near the acknowledged showplace of the Elwha Valley, the "Doc" Ludden homestead, during the 1920s and 1930s (see LUDDEN PEAK). Available records suggest that Michael was the famous Elwha Valley character known as "Cougar Mike," but this fact could not be verified.

The building referred to as Michaels Cabin was one of several structures on the Ludden property and it was here that Michael moved following the death of "Doc" Ludden. The cabin now found at this site is situated about 100 meters from the clearing where the original Ludden home had been. 54, 58.5, 94, 186

MIDDLE PEAK, MT. OLYMPUS (7,930'); MT. OLYMPUS (2B). This is the middle of three spires located high on the Olympus massif. The Olympus massif was originally called Mt. Bennett by the 1889-90 Seattle Press Expedition (see INTRODUCTION) for James G. Bennett of the *New York Herald*. The name Middle Peak (the designation for the middle of the three highest peaks) fell into common usage by explorers and climbers over the course of several decades. Barnes was the only member of the Press Expedition to see this peak during the 1889-90 trek; it was obscured from the view of the other explorers by the presence of Mt. Noyes. First ascent in 1907 by B, H. Browne, W. G. Clarke, G. W. Humes, H. C. Parker, and H. Sisson. 146.5, 152, 207, 184.5, 207.5

MIDDLE ROCK; DESTRUCTION ISLAND (2G). Located offshore from the mouth of the Hoh River, this is the middle of three prominent rock formations in the area. The two which surround Middle Rock are known as North Rock and South Rock (see NORTH ROCK and SOUTH ROCK). 152

MILK LAKE; THE BROTHERS (2D).This lake was discovered by surveyors Arthur Dodwell and Theodore Rixon in 1898. Its name most likely stems from the milky color of the water, or reflected color from snowfields located on the north slope of Mt. Bretherton. 120, 152

MIMIR (5,400'); MT. OLYMPUS (1A). The christening of this peak for Mimir, the Norse myth symbol of wisdom, reflects its location among the Valhallas, mountains named for other characters found in Norse mythology. Mimir was the guardian of a magic well, the waters of which proffered wisdom on all who drank from it. It bubbled from beneath Yggrasil, an exceptional ash with but three roots: one leading to the gods themselves; one to the well and nearby frost giants; and one over Niflheim. Chief god Odin pledged one of his eyes to Mimir in return for a draught of wisdom from the magic well. Mimir was eventually beheaded but continued to provide wisdom to Odin, who sang spells over the wise guardian's severed head. Jim White, Mike Lonac, Jim King, Mike Merchant, Rich Steward, Frank Stinchfield, and Bill Larson likely named the peak during their first ascent in 1978 of Mimir's 120-foot summit spire. (See WODEN and VALHALLAS.) 69, 78, 120, 140, 146.5,169, 184.5

MINERAL CREEK; MT. TOM (4D). The area near this stream has an unpleasant hydrogen sulfide odor, indicative of mineral water upwelling. The author did not personally detect this odor when there in 1983. Who named the creek or when this was done is unknown, but it may have been dubbed because of one-time odorous circumstances of the region.

It is thought by many people that consumption of mineral water is conducive to good health. The lengths to which some people will go to drink such liquids and the self-deception that is possible, is dramatized by the "true" story of a trail crew working the Mineral Creek area early in this century.

One day in the spring, the crew opened a new trail to the stream. A sulphuric odor emanating from the water convinced the health-conscious young men that mineral content in the stream was quite high and must therefore be unusually wholesome. Beginning then and continuing through the rest of their summer tour, they drank from the stream, filling canteens from its flow each and every day. Toward the end of their stay, one of the crewmen lay on his belly taking an unusually long gulp from these "special" waters, when, to his disgust, a maggot floated by on top of the water, quite near the tip of his nose. More than a little nonplussed, he walked upstream a short distance and there, lying in the stream before his disbelieving eyes, lay a rotting elk carcass...the real source of the "mineral" in their favorite mineral stream! 63, 79, 209

MINK LAKE; MT. TOM (5F). This lake was so designated by Glenn (Micky) Merchant, Olympic National Park employee, close friend and assistant to packer Minnie Peterson, and fisherman of considerable reputation. Micky was a direct descendant of S'Klallam Chief Ha-que-nilth, fourth son of the seven sons in the house of the great S'Klallam Chief Ste-tee-thlum. Micky made the suggestion because it was his feeling that other lakes and streams in the Olympic Range bore the names of animals indigenous to the area (Elk Lake, Deer Lake, etc.) but there were no landmarks honoring minks. His proposal was accepted by the U.S. Board of Geographic Names. 153.75, 154

MINNIE CREEK; see CEDAR CREEK.

MINNIE'S CAMP, RIDGE; MT. TOM (6E). This site is named for outfitter Minnie Peterson who maintained a camp and cabin on this ridge near the High Divide during the 1930s and 40s. Though the cabin was built in 1932 and destroyed by fire in the late 40s, old timers still use the term Minnie's Camp. Minnie packed visitors into the Olympic backwoods from her headquarters at Sol Duc Hot Springs in the early days (1927-1962). Later in her career she headquartered at her Hoh River Ranch, retiring in 1977. 153.75

MISERY PEAK (3,700'); MT. TOM (3E).

MOOSE LAKE; MT. ANGELES (5D). Moose Lake is one in a chain of three lakes located in Grand Valley near the upper branches of the Dungeness River. In 1905, Amos B. Cameron, famous early Clallam County settler, named the lower of the three lakes in honor of his friend and hunting partner, Frank Moose. (Subsequently, the name "Moose" was somehow shifted by mapmakers to the next or middle lake, in the valley.)

Cameron was an obvious admirer of the man for whom he dubbed this body of water, for among his papers can be found, in his own rough grammar, this description of Frank Moose:

Frank Moose was a native neighbor of mine in Penna (Pennsylvania). A wood man par excellence. Farmer. Timber man. Dam Builder in Log Driving Days. A student of all Nature. Loved to Hunt & Fish. Loved our mts. and had a host of friends. To know him was to admire his traits and love him.

Frank died at his "Penna" farm in February, 1928. His two sons and a daughter still lived in Port Angeles as recently as 1949.

In the past there has been some confusion regarding the names applied to these three lakes. Joseph Keeler, who herded sheep in this area, applied a few names of his own to them which obviously clouded the issue for some travelers through the valley. Nevertheless, Moose Lake, as named by Amos B. Cameron, remains as a permanent landmark and is affixed to all pertinent maps of this area. Certainly we know that it was named for Frank Moose and not a four-legged animal. There are no moose in the Olympics, nor have there ever been. 12, 31, 32, 77. 94, 120, 156

MORA CAMPGROUND, RANGER STATION, ROAD; LA PUSH (5E). This area was first settled in 1872 by Frank T. Balch. Almost 19 years later, after a sufficient number of settlers had moved in to warrant official designation as a Post Office, Balch, store owner and well-known merchant in the area, was appointed to the first Postmaster's position

Above: MINNIE PETERSON ON HIGH DIVIDE. This site with the Hoh Valley in the foreground and Mt. Olympus in the background was one of outfitter Minnie Peterson's favorite places. Minnie guided the Olympic backcountry for the 50 years between 1927 and 1977. This photograph is circa 1940. (Olympic National Park Collection)

Left: MINNIE'S CABIN. Olympic outfitters Minnie and Oscar Peterson built this cabin above Deer Lake on what became known as Minnie Peterson Ridge in the summer of 1932. This photograph is circa 1935. (Peterson Collection)

Above: BOSTON ON THE QUILLAYUTE. This location was settled by Frank Balch in 1872 and later acquired by K.O. Erickson. Photograph is circa 1900. (Clallam County Historical Society Collection)

HOTEL MORA. Owner J.E.L. James is pictured here in front of his hotel. James, a tavern owner in Seattle, was put out of business by Prohibition and moved to Mora. (Clallam County Historical Society Collection)

on February 12, 1891. For reasons that are today unclear, he christened his post office and the entire area around it "Boston," creating confusion in the Postal Service, since there already was a city in Massachusetts by that name.

Apparently Frank Balch was a swindler of sorts. Elizabeth "Missy" Barlow (age 86), Hoh River third generation Huelsdonk and daughter of Fred and Lena Fletcher, told Stan Fouts that she recalled a song that as a child she and others skipped rope to. Part of it went like this:

> I bought a hen for 50 cents
> From Balch, from Balch
> The gosh darn thing flew over the fence
> To Balch, to Balch

Later, well-known Clallam County businessman Kron O. Erickson, then a settler in Balch's "Boston," purchased the postmaster's store and also became the postmaster. He promptly renamed it "Mora" (on December 5, 1900) in honor of his birthplace in Sweden, the parish (county) of Mora, and by so doing erased the confusion of the earlier name. 58, 58.5, 64.5, 96, 120, 155, 160

MORGENROTH LAKE, CREEK; MT. TOM (8E). Chris Morgenroth came to the United States from Germany and homesteaded in 1890 along the banks of the Bogachiel River. A hard worker, Morgenroth constructed a log house and with his Quileute wife, Suzanne, developed an enviable spread which boasted apple, plum, and cherry trees. All the while he continued to explore and come increasingly under the spell of the Olympic backcountry. Chris joined the ranks of the Reserve Rangers June 25, 1903 (under the Department of the Interior). On Feb. 1, 1905 President Theodore Roosevelt signed a bill moving the reserve to the Department of Agriculture and on April 1, 1905 Chris was sworn in as a U. S. Forest Ranger.

After completing a short course in forestry at the University of Washington in the fall of 1909 Chris was promoted to the post of District Ranger. Headquarters offices for the 600,000 acre District 1 were located in Port Angeles where Chris moved with his second wife, Katherine Spease.

There are two versions told as to how Morgenroth Lake was named. Either could be accurate, for the principals involved certainly were men of character; each probably believed his account to be the correct one. The first involves Theodore Rixon.

During the 1898-1900 Dodwell-Rixon survey of the Olympics, Morgenroth frequently traveled with his old friend Rixon on trips which often combined work and pleasure. Often they hiked into the Seven Lakes Basin together. In later years Morgenroth spoke fondly of the evenings the two men spent sitting around a campfire together, Chris lighting his pipe from a coal (never a match) as the conversation flowed. On one such journey, when Rixon was both surveying and assigning names to lakes and other landmarks, the famous surveyor suggested renaming Lewis Lake after his friend and colleague Morgenroth. It is reported that the good-natured Chris didn't put up an argument, so the lake and an adjacent stream were properly christened Morgenroth.

The popular Jack Henson, Port Angeles journalist (known best by his pseudonym, "The Wandering Scribe"), later (September 1941) published his version of how Morgenroth Lake came to be named. As Henson recalls:

...On the other side was the Seven Lakes Basin, with its scores of gem-like lakes whose shores were studded with mountain flowers and picture-book alpine trees. One of those lakes, perhaps the most beautiful of all we promptly named Morgenroth Lake, in honor of the man who was our guide on the trips. It was Chris Morgenroth on each of these trips, who stood entranced at the changing scenes of beauty and who was eloquent as he expressed his love for the area. Two years ago Chris Morgenroth died. He said that before he died he wanted to go back to the High Divide and that he wished his ashes could be scattered over the waters of the three rivers, to be carried down through their pleasant waters to the ocean and the strait. Last week Chris Morgenroth's ashes were carried to the High Divide by his son John. They were scattered to the four winds to reach the three rivers...

Chris Morgenroth retired from the U.S. Forest Service in 1926, moved to the Lake Crescent area and continued to actively support the creation of Olympic National Park. Twelve years later such action was taken at the federal level and the Park was born. 62.5, 67, 84, 117, 120, 138, 162, 191

MORSE CREEK; PORT ANGELES (5A), MT. ANGELES (4G). Originally called Chambers Creek for early settler Frank Chambers, Sr., this stream which empties into the Strait of Juan de Fuca just a few miles east of downtown Port Angeles, now carries the name of the two men who homesteaded there in 1863, Eben Gay Morse and his brother,

Davis W. Morse. The men came to Port Angeles that year from Nova Scotia, began buying property, and soon owned all of what is now the 80-acre Four Seasons Ranch, a residential area with a nine-hole, par-three golf course. 12, 139, 208

M

MOSQUITO CREEK; FORKS (2B). The source of this name is unknown, but its designation is most appropriate to its character. Flowing through an isolated section of the Olympic coastline and an area that experiences heavy rainfall almost year-'round, much of the terrain on either side of the stream is quite swampy, a first-rate breeding ground for mosquitoes. First mentioned officially by Coastal Surveyor John Francis Pratt in May 1887, Mosquito Creek was for a time referred to as the Chalatt, or Cha-latt River, because it was so depicted on the 1896 Gilman National Geographic map. A False Mosquito Creek and campsite are located down river of Mosquito Creek on the Bogachiel. 64.5, 73, 120, 152

MOSQUITO CREEK; SPRUCE MTN. (2E). The source of this name is unknown. No doubt early explorers and settlers commonly referred to it as Mosquito Creek because of the infestation of the creek-bed area by these pests. 29, 94

MOUNT ANDERSON (7,321'); see ANDERSON CREEK.

MOUNT ANGELES (6,454'); see LAKE ANGELES

MOUNT APPLETON (6,000'), **PASS**; MT. OLYMPUS (1F). It is not known who applied the Appleton name to this mountain and mountain pass or when it was done. We do know, however, that the designation was intended to honor Dr. T.J. Appleton, who moved to Port Angeles, Washington, from the state of Michigan, circa 1897.

Dr. Appleton was a conscientious physician, who often made house calls in some of the most rural, unsettled parts of Clallam County. Frequently, Appleton related, he had to ford the Elwha River in his horse and buggy in order to treat patients too sick to travel. Moreover, he was the first white physician in this area to treat the local Native population.

Doctor Appleton's introduction to Port Angeles was a bit rocky. While still living in Michigan, but knowing he was going to move to Clallam County, Appleton purchased two lots located in what was then the "downtown" section of Port Angeles. Only when he arrived in Port Angeles weeks later did he realize that the land he bought lay under water at high tide! Undaunted, the resourceful physician merely built a house on stilts at the site, later moving it to higher ground. Appleton was an eloquent speaker and noted author, and in 1930 wrote and had published a philosophical treatise on matter entitled "Basis of All Life and Subsidiary Articles." Later, the public-spirited physician became a three-term mayor of Port Angeles. Dr. T.J. Appleton died in 1942. 24, 195

MOUNT BALDY (4,680'), **RIDGE**; JOYCE (4B). Seattle Press Expedition member Charles Barnes (see INTRODUCTION) mapped "Mt. Sutherland" during the 1889-90 journey across the Olympics. Its name reflects the lake it dominates, Lake Sutherland. The mountain's present name - no doubt a result of common local usage - is clearly indicative of the lack of trees at the peak's summit area. 94, 152, 207, 207.5

MOUNT BALDY (6,797'); TYLER PEAK (3E). The source of this name is unknown. We can reasonably assume that it is so christened because of the contrast of its forested lower slopes to the open-meadow summit area. 94, 152

MOUNT BARNES (5,993'); MT. OLYMPUS (6B). It appears that Press Expedition members applied the permanent name to this peak, naming it in honor of Captain Charles Adams Barnes, U.S. Revenue Marine, historian and co-leader of the Expedition (see INTRODUCTION). It originally may have been dubbed Mt. Childs by Press Expedition members, but later there was some confusion amongst historians as to which mountain was intended to have that name. Some thought it referred to a 6,041' peak one mile southeast of this site. Nevertheless, the 5,993' peak is now officially designated Mount Barnes on all current maps. 17, 120, 169, 202, 207, 207.5

MOUNT BELVEDERE (7,528'); see MOUNT CLARK.

MOUNT BRETHERTON (5,960'); THE BROTHERS (2D). Named for Bernard Joseph Bretherton, a member of the 1890 Joseph O'Neil Expedition (see INTRODUCTION). A zoologist and member of the Oregon Alpine Club (for further information about this group, see MOUNT STEEL), Bretherton agreed to accompany the expedition on O'Neil's' second (the first was in 1885) mountain trek. Highly regarded by the expedition leader, Bretherton was selected by O'Neil to be a part of the group he appointed to climb Mt. Olympus.

Above: **MORGENROTH HOMESTEAD ON BOGACHIEL RIVER.** Ranger Chris Morgenroth on left and Charley Lewis at what had become by the time of this photograph (mid- 1920s), the U.S. Forest Service Bogachiel Ranger Station. A lake in the Seven Lake Basin is named for this early pioneer and first District Ranger of District 1 of the Olympic National Forest. Morgenroth was also a force behind the Olympic National Park movement.

(Marilyn Lewis Collection)

Left: **MT ANDERSON.** In the summer of 1885 explorer Lt. Joseph O'Neil named this peak for this for his commanding officer Major-General Thomas H. Anderson. The identity of the sleeping hiker in this 1906 photo is unknown. (Olympic National Park Collection)

Above: MT CARRIE. Theodore Rixon named this peak for his homesteader, frontier woman, artist, musician wife-Carrie Jones. (Olympic National Park Collection)

Below: SUMMIT OF MT. DANA. It has been generally accepted that this peak was first climbed by a USGS party in 1928. Contrary evidence is provided by this photograph from the Olympic National Park's Humes file. The photo is dated 1910. (Olympic National Park Collection)

Unfortunately, the men assigned the task of climbing Olympus made what might be considered in some circles a colossal blunder: *They climbed the wrong summit!* Some think the climbers ascended Athena II, but nobody is certain. Nevertheless, the ascent was an accomplishment of some note and in doing so, Bretherton and his colleague became the first men ever to climb a 7,000-foot-plus peak in the Olympic Mountains. Upon their return, the group claimed they had placed a copper box, containing pertinent information of the day, at the summit of the conquered peak. Many climbers have sought this box over the years, but it has not yet been located.

Bretherton's reports on the trans-Olympic Expedition ran as a series of articles in the *Seattle Post-Intelligencer* from July to September 1890. 70, 120, 152, 169, 207.5

MOUNT CAMERON (7,192'); see CAMERON BASIN.

MOUNT CARRIE (6,995'), **GLACIER**; MT. OLYMPUS (4E). Named by famous surveyor and mapmaker Theodore Rixon for his wife Caroline "Carrie" (Jones) Rixon.

In 1893, "Carrie" Jones lived on a 160-acre homestead at the west end of Lake Crescent, a place she called Fairholme (see FAIRHOLME RESORT). A noted artist, painter and singer, Carrie also taught music to the children of local settlers. Later, when the Ovington Post Office was opened, she became postmistress (see OVINGTON), serving lakeside settlers and residents of the Sol Duc Valley.

One day in 1899, Theodore Rixon, in the midst of a three-year survey of the Olympics, entered the Sol Duc Valley trail and spotted Carrie Jones chopping wood. He made her acquaintance while helping her fill her wood box and it turned out to be an important event in both their lives. They fell in love and were married the same year.

Rixon was fond of relating an anecdote about his wife's soft heart especially toward animals. Once, he said, a pet chicken turned up with a broken leg, probably from a barnyard altercation. The injury surely seemed to dictate the butchering of the bird. Instead, Carrie promptly splinted the injured fowl's leg and it survived quite nicely.

Because Rixon was a surveyor and mapmaker he found himself in a unique position to immortalize his wife by naming a mountain after her—and he did just that. Mt. Carrie was in 1899 one of the last major unnamed peaks of the Olympics.

The Rixons lived at Fairholme until moving to Teahwhit Head (see TEAHWHIT HEAD). Carrie Jones Rixon died May 20, 1946. 17, 94, 96, 111, 120, 153.75, 169, 207.5

MOUNT CHILDS (6,205'); MT. OLYMPUS (6C). From their vantage point near Deception Divide, Seattle Press Expedition (see INTRODUCTION) members Christie and Barnes named this peak in honor of George Washington Childs, owner of the *Philadelphia Ledger*. This was done on April 29, 1890. 120, 207

MOUNT CHRISTIE (6,179'); MT. CHRISTIE (7F). This stately, glacier-coated peak was named by the 1889-90 Seattle Press Expedition (see INTRODUCTION) in honor of the group's leader, James Halbold Christie. Christie himself, accompanied by Charles Barnes, comprised a two-man scouting party on April 29, 1890, which first sighted this mountain. It is interesting to note that, unlike other peaks scattered through this region, Mount Christie stands aloof from the others, as befits a leader.

James Christie was born in Moray County, Scotland in 1854 and was, from all accounts, an adventurer down to his bone marrow. Indian fighter, Canadian Arctic explorer and fresh from exploring the wild Mackenzie, Peace, and Liard Rivers in Canada, Christie was enroute to Africa in 1889 when he stopped in North Yakima, Washington, to visit with friends. There he spotted an article in the *Seattle Press* newspaper calling for experienced men to explore the wild and virtually unmapped Olympic Mountains. In his letter of application for one of the positions, he described himself as "...no ambitious, untried youth.... but a man tried in all the vicissitudes of mountain, forest and plain life, schooled in the great plain of the northwest territories."

Christie's background was so unique and so impressed the editors that he was promptly named leader of the expedition.

After Christie and his colleagues finished the famed Olympic traverse, he continued on his bold, adventuresome way, living out his later years in British Columbia as a Canadian citizen. Writer Robert Hitchman recalled Christie in his old age as "testy and stubborn. Pretty much of a remittance man [a person from a wealthy family, supported in his endeavors by family money] too, I think."

The first recorded ascent of Mount Christie was made on August 5, 1907, by photographer Asahel Curtis and 11 other mountaineers. 18, 45, 73, 90, 91, 169, 207, 207.5

MOUNT CLARK (7,528'); TYLER PEAK (2C). This mountain was named for Irving Clark, Sr., Seattle conservationist and a leader in the movement to create Olympic National Park.

Mt. Clark had previously been dubbed Mt. Belvedere by George R. Martin and E.R. Johnson, following their first ascent of it on August 21, 1940. Martin and Johnson named it Belvedere by way of oblique reference to the Italian town of Anzio (Antrum), where, during World War II, the 10th Mountain Division of the Italian campaign landed (January 22, 1944). The term "Belvedere" was chosen by the two men because it was among the ruins of the ancient city of Antrum that the famed Apollo Belvedere statue, now housed in the Vatican, was unearthed in the year 1485. (Apollo, in Greek mythology, was the Sun God in residence at Olympus; see MOUNT OLYMPUS and MOUNT MATHIAS.) Today, even though the official name "Mount Clark" appears on most maps, this peak is still commonly referred to by many as Mount Belvedere. 120, 169

MOUNT CLAYWOOD (6,836'); see CLAYWOOD LAKE.

MOUNT CONSTANCE (7,743'); see CONSTANCE CREEK.

MOUNT DANA (6,209'); MT. ANGELES (1B). Named by the 1889-90 Seattle Press Expedition (see INTRODUCTION) for Charles A. Dana, editor and proprietor of the *New York Sun*. Although previously thought to have been first climbed by a U.S. Geological Survey team in 1928, a picture of two couples captioned "Summit Mt. Dana 1910," is located in the Olympic National Park's Humes file. 18, 120, 207

MOUNT DECEPTION (7,788'); see DECEPTION CREEK.

MOUNT DUCKABUSH (6,250'), **RIVER**; THE BROTHERS (1E). The name is a corruption of a Native word "do-hi-a-boos," meaning "reddish face," a term accurately describing the appearance of the mountain bluffs in the region. It also has been said that the word is a Twana tribal name applied to the chief of the mythical Salmon People. The salmon supposedly had a crooked mouth and the river is not named because of the abundance of "Duckabush" or "crooked-mouth salmon" found in its waters. Augustus Case of the Wilkes Expedition noted the delta on his charts in June 1841.

The name of the mountain comes from its proximity to the river headwaters. However, it should be noted that there have been several attempts to change the name of this peak. For awhile it was referred to as Mount Arline in reference to the eldest daughter of the U.S. Army Colonel Thomas M. Anderson, Commander of the 14th Infantry, circa 1890.

In August 1890, a Tacoma Federal jurist, James Wickersham dubbed the mountain Mount Susan in honor of his wife, Deborah Susan Wickersham. Yet, almost simultaneously, two members of Lt. Joseph O'Neil's 1890 Expedition (see INTRODUCTION), Linsley and Fisher (see MARMOT LAKE for more information concerning Linsley and Fisher) began referring to the mountain as "Skookum," a Chinook word meaning "strong." By the early years of the 20th Century, all such titles had succumbed to the name Mount Duckabush. 19, 50, 120, 140, 153.5, 155, 169, 180, 208

MOUNT FERRY (6,157'); MT. OLYMPUS (6C). Named by the 1889-90 Seattle Press Expedition (see INTRODUCTION) in honor of Elisha P. Ferry, first Governor of the State of Washington. Governor Ferry's influence over the christening of a large number of Olympic National Park landmarks is significant, for it was at his urging that the *Seattle Press* newspaper decided to sponsor the 1889-90 Olympic traverse. Ferry had been impressed by a report prepared earlier by former territorial governor Eugene Semple, in which he, Semple, had urged a thorough exploration of the Olympic Range.

A portion of Governor Ferry's public comments, which sparked the newspaper's interest in 1889, is as follows:

Washington has her great unknown land like the interior of Africa. The country shut in by the Olympic Mountain... has never, to the positive knowledge of old residents of the territory, been trodden by the foot of man, white or Indian... investigation of all claims of travelers has invariably proved that they have only traversed its outer edges...There are great discoveries in store for some of Washington's explorers...There is a fine opportunity for some of the hardy citizens of the Sound to acquire fame by unveiling the mystery which wraps the land encircled by the snow-capped Olympic range.

The title "Mount Ferry" originally was affixed to the nearby 6,283 ' peak; however, it was later shifted to this 6,157 ' peak. 90, 120, 169, 202, 207

RODO FROMME. Fromme was an early U.S. Forest Service Supervisor who christened dozens of geographic landmarks in the Olympics. Mt. Fromme is named in his honor. This photograph is circa 1922. (University of Washington Libraries, Special Collection Neg# UW 28240z)

MOUNT FITTEN (5,222'); MT. ANGELES (2E). Named by the 1889-90 Press Expedition (see INTRODUCTION) members for DuBose Fitten of Seattle, this peak is located two miles upriver from "Convulsion Canyon" (now known as Grand Canyon). 120, 207

MOUNT FITZHENRY (6,050'); see FITZHENRY CREEK.

MOUNT FRAZIER (5,428'); MT. CHRISTIE (5G). Named by the 1889-90 Seattle Press Expedition (see INTRODUCTION) in honor of S. R. Frazier, editor of the sponsoring newspaper. 120, 207

MOUNT FROMME (6,675'); MT. ANGELES (4B). This peak was christened by the Seattle Mountaineers for Rudo L. Fromme, long-time Olympic National Forest Supervisor, in gratitude for the help he offered their group during their third summer outing in 1920. (See THREE PRUNE CAMP, CREEK for further information concerning Fromme and the Seattle Mountaineers.) In an amusing set of circumstances, however, 20 years later, the Mountaineers, perhaps forgetful, *renamed the same peak* "Mount Miscellaneous," a play on words honoring prominent Mountaineer member Dr. Gustave Wislicenus. Fromme's reaction to the name change was not recorded for posterity, but knowing of his droll sense of humor, it might fairly be presumed to have been nothing more than wry amusement. In point of fact, the circumstances surrounding the naming of this particular summit as Mount Fromme seemed not to overwhelm him. In a letter he penned to Olympic National Park in 1966, he suggested that the peak was a "...rather insignificant looking... bulge." His exact comments were:

I can't find "Mt. Fromme" indicated on any of the maps you have sent me, but, since The Mountaineer's Club was so generous as to leave a copper cylinder record in a previously unnamed, even though rather insignificant looking mountain bulge, which a group of them climbed near Mt. Claywood in the summer of 1920 and sought to honor my name, I trust that this will endure and perhaps come (that's what might be called a German sentence) more to life after I have passed on. I realize that this answer to your Karraker's request of November 1, has carried more gossip than precise information, but I trust that it will supply some historic value. Need I state that the typing was perpetrated by

Yours Truly

(Sig) Rudo L. Fromme

Rudo L. Fromme was born in Paris, Ohio, in 1882. After obtaining his Masters Degree in Forestry from Yale University, he rose through the ranks of the U.S. Forest Service, becoming Forest Supervisor at Olympic in 1913, a post he held until 1926. Fromme retired to California in the mid-1940s; during his leisure years, he did some work in high schools and colleges throughout the southern part of that state. Rudo Fromme died on August 22, 1973, at the age of 91. 16, 67, 68, 94, 120, 169

MOUNT GLADYS (5,600'); see GLADYS DIVIDE.

MOUNT GRADY (5,401'); see MOUNT LAWSON.

MOUNT HOPPER (6,114'); MT. STEEL (7D). It is not known who actually christened this 6,114' peak or when it was done, but we are certain that it was named in honor of two brothers, Stanley and Roland Hopper. The two men were among the last of the so-called "Remittance Men." The term was used to describe wealthy young fellows who were fortunate enough to be supported and kept out West where they would cause no embarrassment by donations from East Coast relatives.

In the Hoppers' case, they were heirs to the Singer Sewing Machine Company fortune and were known to receive substantial checks each month. This, of course, permitted them to spend their summers deep in the Olympics and, in general, live life as they pleased.

During their summer treks into the backwoods, the Hopper boys often camped for months - until chased away by fall storms - near what is now Mount Hopper and Marmot Lake. Then, at some point during the decade of the 1890s, they homesteaded just above Lake Cushman, becoming well-known hunting guides during their tenure there.

Stanley Hopper was a member of a group headed by W.G. Steel and F.C. Little during an ascent of Mt. Steel (see MOUNT STEEL) on August 24, 1906. 53, 148, 169

MOUNT HOQUIAM (4,909'); MT. CHRISTIE (5A). The word "Hoquiam" is a corruption of a Lower Quinault Indian name "ho qui a bits," or "ho qui ob," pronounced "ho kwee um," meaning "hungry for wood," or "lots of wood." As used by the tribe the term referred to people in the area who depended upon driftwood for fuel.

Because of the unusual, step-like outline of its ridge, the mountain was originally called Mt. Sinai (in reference to the original Mt. Sinai located in Israel) by the early Quinault white settlers. It is not known exactly who renamed it Hoquiam or when this was done. One source contacted by the author asserts that the name was applied to the peak by a Grays Harbor, Washington, outdoor club, the Olympians. Lt. Joseph O'Neil (see INTRODUCTION) named the range, which includes Mt. Hoquiam, "Hoquiam" during his 1890 summer expedition because of the great hospitality shown to his weary men by residents of that town. Residents of Hoquiam, hearing that O'Neil's men were approaching their little coastal town on the shores of Grays Harbor, cut 30 miles of trail eastward into the Quinault Valley to meet them. 40, 120, 166, 169, 180, 207.5

MOUNT HUNT (4,550'); JOYCE (4A). Mount Hunt is the easternmost high point on the Happy Lake Ridge (see HAPPY LAKE CREEK, RIDGE) named by the 1889-90 Seattle Press Expedition (see INTRODUCTION) for Leigh S.J. Hunt, the owner of the *Seattle Post- Intelligencer* newspaper. 120, 169

MOUNT JOHNSON (7,650'); TYLER PEAK (2C). The name "Johnson" honors what was formerly thought to be the first ascent of this peak by Elvin Robert "Swede" Johnson and G. Martin in 1940.

Evidence has become available, however, suggesting that the first ascent of Mount Johnson, the highest in the Needles range, was made by Scott Osborn, Joe Halwax, and John King of Seattle, circa 1935. 120, 140, 169

MOUNT LACROSSE (6,417'); see LAKE LACROSSE.

MOUNT LAWSON (5,401'); MT. CHRISTIE (6E). When the Seattle Press Expedition (see INTRODUCTION) came through this area during its six-month trek in 1889-90, members named two peaks standing within one-and-a-half miles of each other. The first, a 4,810' summit, they christened Mount Lawson in honor of Victor F. Lawson, editor of the *Chicago News*, and the second, standing 5,401' and 1 1/2 miles northeast, was called Mount Grady for Henry W. Grady of the *Atlanta Constitution*.

Over the years, however, the names were altered by mapmakers. Mount Grady, which incidentally had been given yet another name, Jingo Peak, by Samuel Gilman on his 1896 National Geographic map, fell into disuse and the name Mount Lawson somehow was shifted to this 5,401' peak, where it remains today. The 4,810' peak is today shown on maps without a name. 73, 120, 207

MOUNT LENA (5,995'); see LENA CREEK.

MOUNT MATHIAS (7,168'); MT. OLYMPUS (3B). This peak is named in honor of Francis Wayland "Matt" Mathias (1884-1959), mountaineer, naturalist, and Grays Harbor, Washington, civic leader. Matt Mathias was Executive Director of the Grays Harbor Chamber of Commerce for over 20 years and after his death in 1959, an outdoor club, the Grays Harbor Olympians, supported a movement to assign Mathias' name to an Olympic peak. It was their feeling that he deserved such an honor because of his decades of service to both that organization and his community.

This particular peak was recommended by Al Cunningham, a National Park Service employee, who had been contacted by the initiator of the movement, Mathias' daughter Ethel Hendrikson. Cunningham, a friend of Ethel Hendrikson's son, Matt Sayre, conducted some aerial reconnaissance around Olympic National Park and after considerable study, selected this 7,168' peak then known as Mount Apollo. Apollo, incidentally had been a fitting name for this peak, due to the Greek and Roman mythological theme established in the christening of Mt. Olympus area summits. Apollo was the Greek god of music, poetry, prophecy, and medicine. Generally considered the most difficult major peak to climb in the entire Olympic Range, Apollo was first climbed in 1957 by Jim Hawkins and Yves Eriksson.

Armed with Cunningham's recommendation and the endorsement of the Grays Harbor Olympians, Mrs. Hendrikson then approached the U.S. Board of Geographic Names with an official request that Mount Apollo be rechristened Mount Mathias. The request was honored and the name Mathias was rendered permanent on all relevant maps.

Matt Mathias is remembered as a great storyteller and camp humorist. When not entertaining companions with tales about frogs that had fur "inside and out," his conversation was just naturally sprinkled with colorful expressions. A clear night to

Matt was "lousy with stars!" He also was fond of rousing his camp charges by screaming at the top of his lungs "Daylight in the Swamp - Everybody Out!" Once, during the first Mount Olympus ascent by a Portland outing group called The Mazamas, one of the climbers recalled "...long tramp over a fairly level ice field to the famous Blizzard Pass. The monotony of this stretch was broken by "Mat" (sic) Mathias, who won fame by pointing out millions of snow worms for the party to wonder over... " (See MOUNT STEEL.) 2, 46, 69, 120, 169

MOUNT McCLURE (5,470'); JOYCE (3A). The precise location of the peak originally designated Mt. McClure by the six-man 1889-90 Seattle Press Expedition team (see INTRODUCTION) is questionable. The 5,470' mountain labeled Mount McClure in present historical records honors A.K. McClure, owner of the *Philadelphia Times* in 1890. 120, 207

MOUNT MEANY (6,695'); MT. OLYMPUS (5A). Another designation by the 1889-90 Seattle Press Expedition (see INTRODUCTION), this peak was dubbed Mt. Meany in honor of Edmond S. Meany then an employee of the *Seattle Press*, later member (and President) of the Seattle Mountaineers. Tall and dignified, Edmond Meany became a full Professor of History at the University of Washington and a renowned, respected scholar. A true lover of nature, he was fond of writing verse; often he combined the two avocations, as in the following:

> In gleam of the crag or in gloom of the hollow,
> Yea, even in awe when the storm thunders roll,
> Abideth a lure, O, a strange lure to follow,
> For here with your God may you meet your own soul!
> - The Mountaineers, 1914, Vol. 7

Edmond Meany was the closest link between the Seattle Press Expedition's sponsor, (the newspaper) and the men who actually led the trans-Olympic journey. It was he who organized the meeting between *Seattle Press* officials and James Christie in December, 1889 while he (Meany) was still a 27-year-old member of the newspaper's staff.

The Seattle Mountaineers paid tribute to Edmond Meany in the form of a published verse from the pen of Frederick T. Rouse. It is as follows:

> I like a mount that bears a name
> Not false or of far degree,
> But the name of a friend of intimate love,
> That Meany is to me.
>
> I like a mount that stands with its mates,
> Not distant and hard to see,
> But social and kind and fells out states,
> That Meany is to me.

The Mt. Meany-Mt. Queets area was referred to as Mt. Mesachie on the 1896 Gilman National Geographic map. The first recorded ascent of the peak was on August 8, 1907, by Asahel Curtis, L.A. Nelson, and P.M. McGregor. 73, 120, 143, 169, 202, 207

MOUNT MISCELLANEOUS (6,655'); see MOUNT FROMME

MOUNT MYSTERY (7,631'); TYLER PEAK (2B). This unusual name was affixed to this peak by a U.S. Forest Service employee, G.A. Whitehead, circa 1915. Whitehead recorded his admiration for the regal appearance of the mountain, especially on foggy days, and thought the adjective "mystery" a most fitting description of it. 210

MOUNT NORTON (6,319'); MT. ANGELES (3A). Originally called Mount Egan by the 1889-90 Seattle Press Expedition (see INTRODUCTION) for *Seattle Press* Editor John G. Egan, this 6,319' peak was renamed in 1925. Quilcene Forest Ranger G.A. Whitehead (see also MOUNT MYSTERY) christened the mountain Mount Norton in honor of his friend and hunting companion, Ernest Norton. 120, 169

Above: PROFESSOR EDMUND MEANY. Professor Meany and friends council with Quinault Natives in Tahola. Quinault paddlers brought the Seattle Mountaineers down the Quinault River at the conclusion of their 1913 Annual Outing. (Clallam County Historical Society Collection)

Below: MT OLYMPUS MASSIF. This area remains a beautiful but formidable mix of rock and ice. (Olympic National Park Collection)

Above: MT. OLYMPUS. 1913 Seattle Mountaineers Annual Outing. (Clallam County Historical Society Collection)

Left: SEATTLE MOUNTAINEERS 1913 ANNUAL OUTING. The Mountaineers are seen here on the march on the upper slopes of Mount Olympus. (Clallam County Historical Society Collection)

MOUNT NOYES (6,150'); MT. CHRISTIE (6G). Named by the 1889-90 Seattle Press Expedition (see INTRODUCTION) for Crosby S. Noyes of DC's *Washington Evening Star*. 207

MOUNT OLSON (5,289'); MT. STEEL (2C). This peak has undergone three name changes in its known history. Its present and permanent name stems from the occupancy nearby of one John August Olson, who traveled to Lake Quinault (circa 1890) from Minnesota and was later joined by his wife and 13 children. Shortly thereafter in 1893 the Olson family, eventually numbering 16 children, homesteaded about eight miles above Quinault Lake.

M

Available evidence suggests that the mountain carries Olson's name merely because it happened to be the informal dividing line he shared with a neighbor: Olson agreed to hunt only north of the mountain on the Quinault side, while his neighbor (name unknown) hunted south of it. John Olson later was one of the builders of the chalet located in Enchanted Valley (see ENCHANTED VALLEY).

Concurrently with Olson's rather roundabout, casual form of "christening" the peak, Mount Olson was referred to by Samuel and Charles Gilman on their 1896 National Geographic map as Mount Diavolo, for reasons not known. The two topographers had climbed the peak November 7-8, 1889, while they were preparing their map.

Just a few months later Frederic Church, a member of the 1890 Lt. Joseph O'Neil expedition, dubbed it for unknown reasons - Mount Raven. It is apparent that neither the "Diavolo" nor the "Raven" titles were etched in stone, and both were superseded by the name Mount Olson. 59, 63, 72, 120, 162, 208

MOUNT OLYMPUS (7,956'); MT. OLYMPUS (2B). The Quileute Indians called the Mt. Olympus area "o sky," pronounced "o el ski," the meaning of which is unknown. The mountain has also been referred to as "Sun-a-do" by Natives.

Juan Perez, the first Spanish naval officer to visit the northwest coast, sighted this lofty, snowcapped peak from the Pacific Ocean while sailing his ship southward on August 11, 1774. He named it either "El Cero de la Santa Rosalia," meaning "peak of Saint Rosalia: or "Sierra de la Rosalia," meaning "range of Saint Rosalia "(records vary on this matter). The name was intended to commemorate a saint who reportedly lived a hermit-like existence in the year 1180, after fleeing to the mountains at age 14. The "Saint Rosalia" name was superseded, though, only a few years later as British exploration of the coast began.

English Sea Captain John Meares first observed the mountain from the Pacific Ocean on July 4, 1778, and applied the name Mount Olympus. It seemed to him a logical place to serve as the home of the gods. He wrote:

...In the northern quarter it was of great height, and covered with (s)now. This mountain, from its very con(s) picuous (s)ituation, and immen(s)e height, obtained the name of Mt. Olympus.

Fourteen years later, in 1792, the famous Captain George Vancouver, exploring virtually the entire Pacific Northwest in his ship Discovery, adopted Meares' name for the spectacular peak and entered it on his maps. Mount Olympus thus became the first geographic feature within the present confines of the present State of Washington to be given an official name.

Hoping to apply the Presidential theme to this marvelous landmark, two eastern Congressmen, Hall J. Kelley and J. Quinn Thorton, later tried unsuccessfully to change Mount Olympus' name to Mount Van Buren.

A few years later in 1864, because of an editorial campaign by the *Seattle Weekly Gazette*, the entire mountain range was being referred to in some circles as the "Olympus Range", a term that did not gain wide acceptance. Then, during the 1889-90 Seattle Press Expedition's journey through the Olympics, (see INTRODUCTION), Charles Barnes, historian and co-leader of the group, sighted the mountain and described it in his notes as "a notable mountain of a peculiar gothic-like appearance." Barnes, however, was not aware that the peak he was observing was the already-named Mount Olympus. He therefore referred to it in his notes as Mount Bennett in honor of James Gordon Bennett of the *New York Herald*. Barnes and his colleagues all thought the nearby peak we now know as Mount Carrie was Mount Olympus. That is why Barnes felt safe in applying the Bennett name.

Writer George H. Himes reports in the periodical *Steel Points* that B.F. Shaw and H.B. Cook were the first to climb Mount Olympus in 1854. However, Himes was unable to provide any concrete evidence to support such a claim. Then, during Lt. Joseph O'Neil's second expedition through the Olympics in 1890, three members of his party, Bernard J. Bretherton (see MOUNT BRETHERTON AND MOUNT STEEL), Nelson E. Linsley (see LINSLEY GLACIER AND MOUNT STEEL), and John Danton, climbed what may have been the 7,250-foot Athena II (see ATHENA II). Whichever summit it was, the men believed they had reached the top of the Olympus massif. Moreover, they deposited there a copper box containing memorabilia of the day; it was never seen again. While in the area, Linsley and Harry Fisher climbed a subsidiary peak on the Olympus massif, possibly Icarus or Circe. They may have designated what we now know as the Valhallas "Trinity Mountain."

In 1891, John Banta and S. Price Sharpe of Tacoma (who founded the Evergreen settlement on the Queets River; see EVERGREEN), claimed they had climbed Mount Olympus from the Queets side, thus making the first ascent of Olympus. Their claim has never been fully proven or disproved. West Peak, the actual summit of Mount Olympus, was first officially conquered on August 13, 1907, by 11 Mountaineers from Seattle. 1, 58.5, 91, 101, 120, 134, 169, 177, 207, 207.5

MOUNT PULITZER (6,283'); MT. OLYMPUS (6C). This peak was christened by the 1889-90 Seattle Press Expedition (see INTRODUCTION) on behalf of Joseph Pulitzer, publisher of the *New York World*. The mountain is often referred to by a sort of nickname, "Snagtooth," a term which quite accurately describes its appearance. The unusual sobriquet originated with some of the early forest fire-fighting crews stationed at Dodger Point Lookout. 120, 169

MOUNT QUEETS (6,480'); see QUEETS BASIN.

MOUNT SCOTT (5,913'); MT. OLYMPUS (7C). This peak was named by the 1889-90 Seattle Press Expedition (see INTRODUCTION) for James W. Scott of the *Chicago Herald*. 120, 207

MOUNT STEEL (6,233'); MT. STEEL (6E). Mount Steel is named for William G. Steel, well-known publisher (the Portland, Oregon-based periodical Steel Points) and Pacific Northwest mountaineer.

It was William Steel who encouraged the U.S. Army's top brass to permit one of their young officers to lead formal expeditions across the Olympic Mountains. The 1885 and 1890 treks were headed by Army Lieutenant Joseph O'Neil; both journeys accumulated vast amounts of new information about the general topography, key landmarks, and past history of the fabled mountain range, data essential to future generations of Puget Sound residents.

William Steel also performed another invaluable task for O'Neil just prior to his second journey in 1890: He recruited for the young Lieutenant three key members of the Expedition, Bretherton, Henderson, and Linsley, members of the Oregon Alpine Club, which Steel founded. All joined the O'Neil party at Steel's urging and rendered invaluable assistance to their leader. Possibly in gratitude for the publisher's unwavering support, this peak was named in Steel's honor, either during or shortly after the second (1890) O'Neil Expedition. Expedition member Harry Fisher earlier had referred to the peak as "Mt. Irlene." Later in possession of Fisher's manuscript, Steel may have made "corrections."

On its second journey across the Olympic range, the O'Neil Expedition encountered some unusual difficulties in the vicinity of Mount Steel. A swarm of yellow jackets delayed crossing of the north slope at the Skokomish-Duckabush Divide in September 1890. Thinking they knew how to solve this pesky little problem, O'Neil's party set what was to have been a small, controlled fire to destroy the wasps. Things got somewhat frantic, however, for the fire blazed out of control and scorched the eastern base of Mount Steel, further preventing them from crossing the Divide!

Mount Steel was first climbed on July 19, 1897. 120, 169, 207.5, 208

MOUNT STONE (6,612'); MT. STEEL (8D). The official history of this mountain's christening has a rather unusual twist to it. Three members of Lt. Joseph O'Neil's 1890 Expedition, Yates, Fisher, and William Marsh first sighted the peak and named it for the latter, "Marsh Peak." However, it was later revealed that Marsh's real name was William B. Wiser and that he was an army deserter. Wiser had been stationed in Montana three years earlier and one day simply disappeared. For some reason, the man decided to re-enlist and did so later that same year in the State of Ohio, identifying himself as William Marsh.

The story of Marsh-Wiser's desertion did not unfold until after O'Neil's Expedition was completed and the peak had already (unofficially) been named for the fictitious "Marsh." Later, as usage of "Marsh Peak" dwindled, the mountain's name was changed to Mount Stone, perhaps because of the vast amount of exposed rock thereon.

The author, after traversing Mount Stone in August 1981 and ascending it in 1983, can best describe it as a "stone desert," a tremendous, exposed area largely devoid of vegetation. 53, 152, 207.5, 208

MOUNT STORM KING (4,534'); LAKE CRESCENT (8B). According to Native legend thousands of years before the Mayflower brought the Pilgrims to this country, a legendary battle took place between the Clallam and Quileute tribes along a small river where today Lake Crescent is located. After three days of furious fighting, Storm King, the great mountain ruler of the area, became angry at the foolish warriors fighting at his feet. He hurled a huge boulder into the valley, killing all of the tribesmen. The rock was so large that it dammed the river, which backed up the waters until all trace of the battle was lost as Lake Crescent formed. For many years, no Natives went to the place where the warriors had been punished by death.

There is some geologic parallel to this legend. The geologic record tells us that once there was a large landslide from the mountain across the east end of Lake Crescent which increased the depth of the already-existing Lake Crescent.

Because of some unusual climactic conditions existing here, storm clouds frequently gather first around Storm King Peak, rendering its name at once descriptive and logical.

For many years beginning in 1915, the ferry *Storm King* - named for the peak - carried passengers from East Beach on the east end of Lake Crescent to Fairholme Resort (see FAIRHOLME RESORT) at the extreme west end of the lake.

Storm King Mountain also was the site of a significant event in the history of the Olympic National Park. It was here on January 1, 1925, that U.S. Forest Service Ranger Chris Morgenroth released four mountain goats that had been imported from the Canadian Selkirk Mountains. Release of the animals was an experiment designed to test the goats' adaptability to subalpine regions of the Olympic Range. To say the least, the experiment was successful: It was the beginning of a goat herd which ultimately would number 800 and would in fact, create a unique ecological problem, since the animals eventually wreaked havoc on subalpine meadows. Some historians cite Press Expedition and Gilman and Son observations in the late 1800s, over 30 years prior to the release on the Peninsula, as evidence that they were native. 39, 64.5, 96, 120, 175, 179, 187.5

MOUNT STRUVE (5,350'); MT. CHRISTIE (6E). The Seattle Press Expedition of 1889-90 (see INTRODUCTION) named this mountain for Judge H.G. Struve of Seattle. 207

MOUNT TAYLOR (6.024'); MT. STEEL (1F). Originally called Peak 6049 because of its elevation, this summit was renamed Mount Taylor by the 1889 Seattle Press Expedition, in honor of Colonel Charles Taylor of the *Boston Globe*. 120, 207.5

MOUNT TOM (7.048'), **CREEK**; MT. TOM (8B).Two stories exist relative to the naming of this peak.

One asserts that Edmond S. Meany (see MOUNT MEANY), who was then the Commissioner of Scouting in the City of Seattle, led a large group of Boy Scouts through the Olympics in the year 1914. Approaching the summit of this unnamed and unclimbed peak, he promised the boys he would name it for the first Scout who reached the top. As this story is told, 13-year-old Tom Martin, who later became Treasurer of the State of Washington and a gubernatorial candidate, bested his companions and Meany designated the peak Mount Tom. Martin later stated the peak had been named for him.

Another story is that the mountain was named for U.S. Land Office Surveyor Thomas M. Hammond, Jr., sometime prior to 1907. Hammond was active in the west end of the Olympic Peninsula from 1895 to 1904. A party of four (possibly including relatives of the "Iron Man of the Hoh") may have made a first ascent on Sept. 2, 1920 when they signed names atop Mt. Tom.

The Press Expedition had previously named the peak Mt. Reid in 1890 after Whitelaw Reid, editor and proprietor of the *New York Tribune*. 63, 120, 140, 169, 207, 207.5

MOUNT WALKINSHAW (7,378'); TYLER PEAK (1D). Previously called "The Citadel" (in the author's opinion a most appropriate title) by Keith Spencer in 1958, this 7,378' peak was later officially designated Mount Walkinshaw to honor Robert B. Walkinshaw, a Seattle conservationist and a leader in the effort to create Olympic National Park. First ascent was by Joe Munson and Elmer Parolini in 1961. 120, 140, 169, 184.5

MOUNT WATTERSON (6,650'); MT. STEEL (4F). During its famed 1889-90 crossing of the Olympic Mountains, the Seattle Press Expedition (see INTRODUCTION) named this peak for Henry Watterson of the *Louisville Courier Journal*. 120, 169

MOUNT WILDER (5,198'); see CAMP WILDER.

MOUNT WILLIAM FAIRCHILD (6,950'); see FAIRCHILD CREEK.

MOUNT ZINDORF (5,539'); MT. CHRISTIE (4F).This peak was named by the 1889-90 Seattle Press Expedition (see INTRODUCTION) for unspecified reasons. 120, 169

M

MUD CREEK; SALMON RIVER (4C). The source of this name is unknown. It is most likely that the term came into popular use with settlers and surveyors who obviously noticed the muddy state of the water during the floods. 63

MUNDEN CREEK; MT. TOM (4F). This creek was also called "Second Dry Creek" by old timers, since in the summer it was the second dry creek below Sol Duc, the first dry creek being Blackwood Creek. 153.5

MUNCASTER MOUNTAIN (5,910'); MT. CHRISTIE (8E). Originally named Mount DeYoung by the 1889-90 Seattle Press Expedition (see INTRODUCTION) for M.H. DeYoung of the *San Francisco Chronicle*, the permanent name for this peak, Muncaster Mountain, was applied by Rudo Fromme, one-time Supervisor for the Olympic National Forest. Fromme christened the mountain in 1915 to honor a former employee, Forest Guard Roy Muncaster, who died along with more than a thousand others in the tragic sinking of the *Lusitania* by a German U-Boat May 1, 1915.

Fromme spelled out in his memoirs (1962) his exact reason(s) why the peak located here deserved to carry Muncaster's name. Excerpts are as follows:

My suggestion of this name for a previou[s]ly unnamed peak situated between the north and east forks of the Quinault River, was to honor former summer Forest Guard Roy Muncaster, who lost his life from the torpedoed Lusitania, while enroute to France as a soldier in the First World War. His death from life boat drowning was reported in a letter from Everett Harphan, an Olympic forest ranger, who was in the same life boat but was thrown by heavy waves onto the rocky shore of west Ireland. Roy was a tall, muscular member of the U. of W. rowing team.

Further research, however, suggests that perhaps Muncaster was on the *Tuscania*, which was loaded with American troops, whereas the *Lusitania* had all civilian passengers. 67, 68, 94, 120, 169, 184.5

MUNIN (6,000'); MT. CHRISTIE (1G). One source contacted by the author asserts that this peak and its companion, Hugin (see HUGIN) were christened during a 1970 climb by Glenn Kelsey, Harold Pinsch, and Roger Beckett. The names Hugin and Munin were affixed to the peaks consistent with the theme (established earlier) of christening Olympic Mountain landmarks in honor of mythical gods.

Both summits located here appear to sit on the shoulders of Woden (see WODEN), as do the two ravens in Norse mythology. Legend tells us that the mythical birds' (Munin means "memory" and Hugin means "thought") sole responsibility was to fly over the entire world daily, then whisper into Woden's ear all that they had seen and heard. Two mountains situated here almost literally sit on the "shoulders" of Woden. 69, 78, 169, 184.5, 207.5

MURDOCK LAKE; MT. STEEL (6C).

MUSCOTT CREEK, CAMP; THE BROTHERS (3G). A curious by unverified story surrounds Muscott Creek and Muscott Camp.

A certain Mr. Muscott (first name unknown) was a Seattle-area resident, circa 1900, who spent much of his time in this part of the Olympic Mountains. Local climbers and trappers were aware that he often grazed sheep in this sector (where today the Dosewallips Campground is situated), and that he discontinued doing so when Federal protection of this area occurred in 1897.

The tight-lipped Muscott also was alleged to be a successful prospector who would often spend large sums of money in Seattle, go broke, and then ostensibly, return to his mine near this stream. Soon he would be back, so the story goes, with huge quantities of precious minerals to "cash in," easily replenishing his depleted wallet. Many people apparently tried to follow him on his forays into the Olympic backwoods, hoping to discover the mine's location, but Muscott always managed to elude them, somehow vanishing in what is now the Muscott Camp area.

It is said that the sheepherder-miner suffered an unfortunate demise, but one which seemed to heighten the mysterious circumstances surrounding his fabulous "mine." One day, while kneeling by a stream, he was supposedly mistaken for a cougar, and shot in the back! Existing records are fuzzy as to whether the perpetrator was ever prosecuted. Nevertheless, the secret of the Muscott Mine - if there ever was one - died with him. Certainly, the treasure-trove has never been found. 27, 190, 207.5

NEAGLE POINT; LAKE CRESCENT (5C). Named for Harold (first name open to question) Neagle who had a summer home here at the end of the North Shore Road at one time. 157

THE NEEDLE (5,800'); MT. STEEL (6B). The source of this name is unknown. The sharp needle-like spire is located above Needle Pass in the Sawtooth Range. 152, 169

THE NEEDLES; TYLER PEAK (2D). The 1889-90 Seattle Press Expedition (see INTRODUCTION) included these mountains in the Holmes Range. The present name is derived from the very sharp needle-like outline of a portion of the range as viewed from any perspective. 94, 207, 207.5

NINE STREAM; MT. STEEL (5D). This confluence was the site of Camp Number Nine of the O'Neil Expedition (see INTRODUCTION). It later became known as Camp Number Nine Stream and was finally shortened to Nine Stream. The 1890 Expedition spent a week or more at some camps while blazing a trail ahead, finally crossing the rugged mountains and making their way out months later through the Quinault Rain Forest on the west side of the mountain range. 207.5, 208

NONAME CREEK; MT. STEEL (3D).

NO NAME LAKE; MT. TOM (8E).

NORTH FORK BOULDER CREEK; see BOULDER CREEK.

NORTH FORK CAMPGROUND, RANGER STATION; MT. CHRISTIE (4C). These two landmarks owe their names to their proximity to the North Fork Quinault River. 152

NORTH FORK SOL DUC RIVER, CAMP; see SOL DUC

NORTH ROCK; DESTRUCTION ISLAND (2G). Located along a rugged coastline offshore from the mouth of the Hoh River, the northernmost of three prominent sea stacks in this area. This particular rock is about 100' wide, 40' across and 200' high. In the past it was an outstanding place for seabirds; in fact, noted ornithologist William Dawson observed over 400 nesting cormorants on this sea stack in 1906. (See MIDDLE ROCK and SOUTH ROCK.) 120, 152

NORWEGIAN MEMORIAL; LAKE OZETTE (3B). Captain Hans Markusson was piloting the Norwegian vessel *Prince Arthur* along the coastline of the north Pacific on the dark night of January 2, 1903. A storm raging outside had everybody aboard jittery, but the Captain was certain the light he saw off the starboard side came from near Tatoosh Island/Cape Flattery so he could ease into the Strait of Juan de Fuca and out of the gale. Historians will never know for sure what Captain Markusson saw that night. Perhaps it was the light shining in settler Ivan Birkestol's cabin along the shoreline. They do know, however, the *Prince Arthur* was considerably south of Cape Flattery. So when the beleaguered Captain Markusson steered his ship to the right, believing he was turning into the Strait, he ran the vessel onto the rock-strewn coastline at this spot.

Smashed upon the breakers, the *Prince Arthur* snapped in the middle like a toothpick and floundered in two pieces in the heavy seas. The captain and his 19 crewmen - most of whom were young apprentice seamen - were washed off the boat one by one; a total of 18 men died and were later buried here. Two sailors, Chris Schjodt Hansen and Knud Larsen survived to relate the horrible story.

Today a concrete monument, installed around 1904 by Seattle Norwegians, marks the site of this sea tragedy. 120, 152

NYLUND RUINS; LAKE OZETTE (3E). Anders Nylund, a native Finn, and his wife Johanna Erickson Nylund brought their family to the Ozette area in the spring of 1895. The Nylunds homesteaded from 1905-1932 on two 40-acre tracts near the north end of Lake Ozette and there built a six-bedroom house in which to raise their children. Apple, pear, and plum trees thrived all over the Nylunds' spread, while sheep and cattle grazed contentedly nearby.

Ander Nylund, an avid, though amateur poet, maintained the large, busy and prosperous homestead at this site for 15 years until his death in 1920. The family then began to slowly drift away, and Nylund's bustling homestead ultimately

Above, Left: NYLUND HOUSE WITH GHOST. Some claim a flute-playing ghost resides within the ruins of the Anders Nylund home near Ozette Lake and that he can be seen on the balcony in this early photograph.

(Clallam County Historical Society Collection)

Right: OLYMPIC HOT SPRINGS. In 1907 Tom Farrell, Charley Anderson and Billy Everett "rediscovered" the springs at this site on Boulder Creek and named them. This photograph was taken in 1914. (Olympic National Park Collection)

OLYMPUS GUARD STATION. Manned for many years beginning around 1920 by Charlie Lewis, pictured here on the left with District Ranger Sanford Floe. The site was later named Lewis Meadow in Charley's honor. Photograph circa 1930. (Marilyn Lewis Collection)

reverted to federal ownership in 1938 when Olympic National Park was established. Ander Nylund's grave was marked by a simple, white wooden cross inscribed "A. Nylund - Born January, 1851. Died July 15, 1920."

Before the Nylund family members began to move from hearth and home, they experienced a tragedy when in 1928, 30-year-old Alfred disappeared mysteriously. Only a canoe on the shore of Lake Ozette was found, and the young man was presumed drowned. Eight years later in 1936, Alfred's body was discovered in the nearby woods propped against a tree, and though the cause of his death was never determined, most observers believe he suffered a heart attack.

There is now very little remaining of Ander Nylund's once-impressive 80-acre homestead. However, with some effort, parts of the rotting foundation and Ander's grave marker can be found just a few minutes walk from the Ozette Ranger Station.

Ghost stories about the old Nylund homestead never fade away. Most tell of an apparition often seen hovering over the ruins or of a flute-playing spirit heard after dark, its weird strains emanating from the direction of Ander Nylund's gravesite. 3, 58.5, 107

OBSERVATION POINT; MT. OLYMPUS (4G). The source of this name is unknown. Observation Point is a bend in the road enroute to Boulder Creek Campground offering a splendid view of Lake Mills and the Elwha Valley. (See BOULDER CREEK, LAKE MILLS, ELWHA BASIN.) 152

OBSTRUCTION LAKE, **PEAK** (6,450'), **POINT**; MT. ANGELES (4E). The lake also has been called Jackass Lake, but the National Park Service employees usually refer to it as Obstruction Lake, for its nearness to Obstruction Point.

Amos B. Cameron may have been the one who named the point when, in 1910, he found it to be an obstruction to his goal of building a trail along the ridge. Cameron was a well-known settler, trapper, and hunter in the area.

It is more popularly believed that a road-building project in the 1940s expecting to run a full-circle loop from the Elwha River to Hurricane Ridge and Deer Park, then on to Port Angeles was stopped here. Loose shale and inherent instability of the slopes in the vicinity were listed as the primary reasons. The obstacle was commemorated here at Obstruction Point. 12, 31, 59, 94, 120, 169

OIL CITY; FORKS (3A). Oil City, just north of the mouth of the Hoh River, was so named in 1931 by Merle Schmid, an employee of the Leslie Petroleum Company. At the time the company was attempting to develop the Jefferson Oil Seep.

Near the summit of Hoh Head, (see FORKS (2B) for HOH HEAD location) workers had stumbled onto a distinct oil seepage which created a fever of interest throughout the region. (The discovery would lead to the drilling of a major, albeit dry, well at the site one year later.) In that exciting summer of 1931, prospects for discovery of a top-grade oil well in this vicinity seemed most favorable, Schmid's suggestion that the site be officially dubbed Oil City was promptly adopted by the company. The surrounding area was platted into lots, many of which were sold anticipating a major oil find, which never occurred. Eleven wells were drilled between 1931 and 1937 at the Jefferson Oil Seep, located two miles northwest of "Oil City." In spite of excellent indications of oil, such as strong petroleum odor and iridescence in the mud pit, there was insufficient commercial oil for development.

Charley Anderson noted that when Olympic National Park was established and encompassed Oil City, it was still laid out and mapped with privately owned lots. Oil City- the city that really wasn't- is today abandoned and there is little evidence of the activity once found here. All that remains are overgrown roads, rotting oil well covers, timbers, and a few rusted vehicles. 6.5, 58.75, 76, 94, 110, 153.5, 172

OLYMPIC HOT SPRINGS, NATIONAL PARK; MT. OLYMPUS (3G). ALL MAPS AND AREAS IN THIS BOOK. The names of these landmarks derive from their location on the Olympic Peninsula - and their proximity to the fabled Olympic Mountains. The Peninsula and the National Park received their names from the derivative Mount Olympus: Captain George Vancouver in 1792 first applied the contracted term "Olympic" to the entire range - calling them the Olympic Mountains.

A local Native legend tells of the formation of Olympic and Sol Duc Hot Springs long ago. Two dragons lived, one on each side of the mountains. One lived in the Sol Duc Valley and one in the Elwha Valley. One day they met at the top of the ridge to do battle. This fight took place centuries ago and lasted for many years. It cleared off all of the timber on the high mountain slopes, creating huge bare areas (above tree line) which still are visible today. Both dragons lost most of their skin, which landed on trees and rocks all around and is still there in the form of reindeer moss lichen. When neither dragon could slay the other, they crawled back into their caves in despair and began to cry. Their tears are the source of the hot springs.

Andrew Jacobsen may have been (in 1892) the first white man to discover the 21 pools located here, which in 1892 were said to range in temperature from a lukewarm 116° to a rather toasty 138° Fahrenheit. When Jacobsen told residents of nearby Port Angeles what he had found, few would believe him. Angry and frustrated, he refused to tell anybody where the springs were located.

Fifteen years later, on June 25, 1907, Tom "Slim" Farrell, Charley Anderson, and the well-known Billy Everett "rediscovered" the mineral pools, and christened them Olympic Hot Springs. The men later established and maintained a resort there, gradually altering the interior lining of the springs as their popularity with the public increased. First the pools were merely "earth-lined," later lined with wood, and finally years later, with concrete.

The three-man partnership evidently was a good one, the only wrinkle being legal claims upon the land around the hot springs. In June 1908, Farrell filed a claim on the place calling it the "Saline Mining Claim." It still can be found in the Clallam County Courthouse records. For reasons that are now unclear (perhaps having to do with citizenship: Anderson was Swedish, Everett part-Native American), the other two partners were unable to file a similar claim. A few short years later (1913), Farrell sold his interest in the place to Billy Everett. Shortly thereafter, Carl Schoeffel bought into the partnership, the men secured a 25-year lease from the U.S. Forest Service and the Olympic Hot Springs enterprise was off and running.

Everett and his colleagues built a lodge in 1917 and replaced it entirely in 1920. A decade later in 1930, a road was constructed to the Springs. Further expansion of the lodge was carried out in 1932, but by this time, operational problems had already begun to set in. Then, on January 27, 1940, disaster struck. The entire complex burned to the ground and was rebuilt.

By 1966 Olympic Hot Springs as a commercial entity was closed permanently and ownership of the land was turned over to Olympic National Park. Deterioration over the years caused Park officials to begin thinking about total abandonment of the Springs. When a heavy snowstorm collapsed most of the remaining buildings on December 31, 1966, such official action was taken.

Since 1967, the area has been returned to its natural setting by the National Park Service. 58.5, 120, 174, 179

OLYMPIC COAST NATIONAL MARINE SANCTUARY. The Sanctuary, established in 1994, extends from the northest end of Neah Bay over 50 miles out into the Pacific Ocean and south to the Moclips/Pacific Beach area, covering 3,310 square miles. 100.5

OLYMPUS GUARD, RANGER STATION; MT. TOM (7D). Olympus Guard Station in the Hoh Valley was first located at what is now known as Lewis Meadow. Charley Lewis served as Forest Guard at this location from 1919 to 1926. In 1926 the station was moved to its present site down river from Hoh/Lake Creek where Charley continued his service. The names Olympus Guard Station and Olympus Ranger Station are used interchangeably. 43, 59, 64, 117, 117.5, 153.25

ONE TOO MANY CREEK; THE BROTHERS (2E). This creek is thought to have been named by early packers. There are 11 tributaries of the Duckabush River along this stretch of four miles; every one of them must be crossed by pack trains. It appears the last one may have been "one too many." 91

O'NEIL CREEK, PASS, PEAK (5,758'), **UPPER CREEK**; MT. STEEL (4D). The 1890 O'Neil Expedition (see INTRODUCTION) crossed over O'Neil Pass at the northeast base of O'Neil Peak enroute from the North Fork Skokomish River Valley to Quinault River Valley. Following this Olympic traverse, the features were named in honor of expedition leader Joseph Patrick O'Neil, Second Lieutenant Fourteenth Infantry, Commanding Olympic Mountains Exploring Expedition. O'Neil had named the features, but the exact dates of the christenings are not known.

Following his crossing, O'Neil said of the rugged Olympic wilds, "This country is absolutely unfit for any use except, perhaps, a national park..."

There is a depression north of the point where the trail crosses O'Neil that is actually lower and more of a natural "seam" than is O'Neil Pass. Port Angeles, Washington, resident Mike Doherty, a former Quinault Ranger, observed ptarmigan at this spot during both 1970 and 1971. Ptarmigan are virtually unheard of in the Olympics. Subsequently, some local hikers now refer to this more natural pass as "Ptarmigan Pass." 22, 169, 207, 208

ORANGE CREEK; LAKE CRESCENT (2B). According to a 1966 letter he wrote to Olympic National Park officials, Rudo Fromme named this stream sometime between 1913 and 1926. The former Olympic National Forest supervisor gave as his reason the following anecdote:

There is one small creek, which flows into the Soleduck river (sic) close to a mile below the junction of the N. Fork, for which I once wrote in the name "Orange." This seems to have gotten lost in the printing process, probably due to lack of space or explanation. This unusual name for a creek in this location was to perpetuate an unusual experience so hugely enjoyed by Ranger Morgenroth and myself on one specific occasion. We had been hiking all day during a hot spell of weather from the Olympic Hot Springs along the general route of a trail now shown on your Park map to be greeted, as we dropped down onto the Sol Duc Hot Springs road, by a large broken crate of Florida oranges. These had evidently fallen from a Hot Springs truck, but they couldn't have landed in a more delectable spot for two thirsty, hungry foot travelers. I can still taste that wonderfully juicy fruit, upon which Chris and I practically foundered. We went on our journey down river only most reluctantly, after bulging our shirts and pants pockets out of all proportions. 11, 68

OVINGTON; LAKE CRESCENT (5C). Named for an Englishman, E.J. Ovington, and his Swedish wife who together settled in the area in 1905 and opened a resort here. Prior to the Ovingtons' arrival, this area (first settled by John Hanson in 1886) was referred to as Beardslee Bay and Beardslee Camp in honor of Rear Admiral Leslie A. Beardslee, Commander of the Pacific Fleet. Beardslee was a frequent visitor to Lake Crescent when the fleet was anchored at nearby Port Angeles to conduct summer maneuvers - an annual event that began in 1895 and continued for nearly 40 years.

The Ovington Community along the shore of Lake Crescent, highlighted by E.J. Ovington's Lodge and cabins, situated on 14 acres, became sufficiently populated that it was designated an official United States Post Office on June 18, 1913. The first postmistress there was Caroline Rixon (see MOUNT CARRIE for further information about Caroline Rixon). Declining population over the years forced the Post Office to be closed on September 30, 1942. Three years later, following the death of Mrs. Ovington, the resort was closed for good. The National Park Service then assumed ownership of the property from the Ovington estate (1948) and the area has been transformed into what is now the North Shore Picnic Area. 58.5, 111, 120, 157, 160

OYSTER LAKE; MT. OLYMPUS (2F). The source of this name is unknown. However, it is commonly acknowledged that the lake's shape resembles that of an oyster, quite likely the reason it has been so labeled. There have been claims (unsubstantiated, to the best of the author's knowledge) that fossilized, or petrified clams have been found in and around Oyster Lake. 154, 209

OZETTE (community), ARCHAEOLOGICAL SITE (see INDIAN VILLAGE ARCHAEOLOGICAL SITE), **CAMPGROUND, INDIAN RESERVATION, ISLAND, LAKE, RANGER STATION, RIVER**; LAKE OZETTE (1E, 3E). The Ozette Village was previously known as "Indian Village Archaeological Site." It was excavated by a Washington State University team led by Dr. Richard Daugherty. Remnants of Ozette longhouses and other structures dating back 2,000 years were uncovered. The Ozette Dig, as it is commonly called, has yielded thousands of well-preserved artifacts, most of which are on display at the Makah Cultural Center in Neah Bay, Washington. The dig site was closed in 1981 because of a lack of funding. Ozette was one of the most significant archaeological finds in the history of the Pacific Northwest; it is one of the five major Makah villages, and was called "Ho-Selth" by white men (the closest pronunciation early white settlers achieved to the actual Native name). The beach area was the site of several major villages over the years. The latest village was abandoned in 1900.

The Makah name for the village was "use it," pronounced "u.se.it," for which there is no known English translation. The other four ancestral Makah Villages were Sooes, Waatch, Neah, and Baadah. There were more than 300 Natives in the village in 1887 (91 in 1888 according to one source), but this dwindled to 35 in 1906 and three in 1923. There were none in the village in 1960. The 640-acre reservation surrounding the village was established by presidential proclamation, on April 12, 1893. Washington State University began excavation at the Archaeological Site (the Indian Village site) in 1966.

Depending on which version is accepted, the Makahs called the lake "Ka' Houk," meaning "large lake," or "q' a uwiq," pronounced "q'a-u-wiq," meaning "the lake" (this last from the Makah Research Center, Neah Bay, Washington).

James G. Swan, noted traveler, historian, and teacher in Neah Bay, claimed that the Makah Indian word for the 331-foot-deep, glacier-carved body of water meant "Lake of the Sun." During his three-decade stay in the area (1850s, '60s and '70s), he liked to refer to it as "Webster Lake," jointly honoring the famous American Daniel Webster and his close friend, Henry Webster of Neah Bay. It is notable that many residents of Clallam County's west end formerly referred to Lake Ozette as "Swan's Lake." 24, 90, 93, 100.5, 120, 121, 152, 155, 160, 193

PACIFIC OCEAN; DESTRUCTION ISLAND, CAPE FLATTERY, FORKS, LA PUSH, LAKE OZETTE. Credit for the discovery of this vast body of water is generally given to Vasco Balboa in the year 1513. Seven years later Ferdinand Magellan named it "mar pacifico," the Spanish equivalent of "calm ocean" or peaceful." In the four centuries since that christening, the name has been corrupted to "Pacific Ocean." 134

PACKER'S CAMP; MT. STEEL (1D). This one-time camp was located about five miles up the East (Main) Fork Quinault River. According to former horse packer June Hopkins, it was a marvelous camp for travelers until the 1970s, primarily because of the presence of a huge, old spruce tree. According to Mrs. Hopkins, branches of the spruce provided almost perfect coverage from the heaviest of rain storms as far as five feet from its base. Moreover she said, a nearby berry thicket offered privacy from the trail which was located 25 yards away. Sometime during the late 1970s, the bank of the East Fork Quinault overflowed and destroyed most of the camp area and washed away the tree. 182

PALMQUIST CREEK; OZETTE LAKE (4E). Named in honor of August Palmquist, native of Sweden, who pioneered along this stream in the early 1890s. Here he built both a cabin and a post office.

The journey from Seattle to Lake Ozette , where Palmquist Creek is located, was an arduous one in pioneer days. Travelers were required to go by ship to the village of Neah Bay often on stormy seas and then walk a distance of 23 miles to the lake. Records indicate that good neighbor August Palmquist and his sister welcomed a Mr. and Mrs. Peterson into their homes and made them welcome after the Petersons had completed such a journey in mid-September 1893.

August Palmquist moved to Enumclaw, Washington, around the turn of the century, where he died in 1908. 21, 108, 120, 156

PANIC PEAK; MT. OLYMPUS (2B). Panic Peak is located about one mile north of West Peak along the Snow Dome. The origin of this name is obvious to those who have peered down its sheer west face. 146.5, 184.5

PAR CAMP; see KIMTA CAMP.

PARADISE CREEK; KLOOCHMAN ROCK (6F).

PARADISE VALLEY; MT. CHRISTIE (1D). The source of this name is unknown. However, it was apparently applied because the adjective "paradise" portrays the almost ethereal setting of this valley which is nestled among subalpine meadows. Summer wildlife sightings are common here. 91, 152

PASS CREEK; THE BROTHERS (3G). The actual source of this stream's name is unknown, but derives from the fact that it drains Constance Pass (see CONSTANCE CREEK). 152

PAULL CREEK; MT. OLYMPUS (3A). The Paull family lived at Neilton, which is three miles south of Quinault Lake. Olympic National Forest Supervisor Rudo Fromme is said to have named the creek in 1914 for Ernest R. Paull, former Quinault District Ranger. Paull held that position in 1910 when the first trail from Quinault to Killea Ranger Station on the Queets was constructed. 59, 120, 162

PEABODY CREEK; PORT ANGELES (3C). The source of this name is unknown for there are no primary data sources which can be checked, and opinions vary greatly concerning the now-mysterious Mr. Peabody. Several Port Angeles, Washington, historians are of the opinion Peabody Creek is named for a formerly-prominent sawmill operator in that town. Other sources, though, assert that Peabody was an attorney. Still others believe he was a sea captain with relatives in a Port Angeles firm. 20, 80

PEAK 5077, 6024, 6049 (see MOUNT DELABARRE), **7022**; MT. STEEL (3B). The names of these peaks reflect the actual elevations of each. Their titles may have been applied by surveyors or mountaineers. 140, 152, 184.5

PELTON CREEK, MOUNTAIN (5,301'), **CAMP**; KLOOCHMAN ROCK (7F). It is believed the U.S. Forest Service applied the name Pelton to this stream sometime between 1913-1926. The name Pelton, which may be a corruption of the surname Felton, refers specifically to a mentally deranged Astoria, Oregon, fur trader who first manifested signs of mental illness there in the year 1811. From that incident the Chinook Jargon word "Pelton" evolved, meaning "fool," "insane," or "crazy." (See ALCKEE CREEK.)

If indeed the U.S. Forest Service christened this waterway "Pelton," it was probably because in many places throughout its flow, the water rushes and tumbles in a "crazy" fashion. 12, 120, 169

P

PERKINS REEF; LA PUSH (8B).

PETROLEUM CREEK; CAPE FLATTERY (3G). The actual source of this name is unknown. However, we do know that oil seeps are found throughout the area of the stream flow. 94

PHELAN CREEK; SALMON RIVER (6C). George J. Phelan, one of two brothers who homesteaded along this stream, circa 1890, is honored here. It is reliably reported that the two men and a companion, Dave Kerr, became expert canoeists because of a near-fatal accident that occurred on the Queets River (see KERR CREEK). 1, 63, 120

PICTURE PINNACLE (5,650'); MT. STEEL (6B). The pinnacle, located on Sawtooth Ridge, was first ascended in 1941 by brothers F. Beckey and H. Beckey, who named it. There is a 100-foot stone tower located at the top of Picture Pinnacle featuring a unique see-through "chimney" which can "frame" a climber much as one might do with a camera, thus the "picture" in the peak's title. 140, 169, 184.5

PIEDMONT; LAKE CRESCENT (7C). The first man to settle in this section of Lake Crescent was one John Smith, who arrived in 1883. Two years later, Smith blazed a trail from Port Crescent to Lake Crescent. The christening of Piedmont, nevertheless, was accomplished by William Dawson who named it in 1893 because of its location and shape at the "foot of mountain" (the meaning of the word "piedmont"). William Dawson later became the first postmaster of Piedmont, receiving his official title on July 10, 1894. The post office closed 41 years later on February 28, 1935. 120, 138, 160

PIRO'S SPIRE (6,301'); MT. STEEL (8G). Piro's Spire was named in honor of Robert F. Piro, a former fire guard at Dose Meadows station, who was killed during World War II. The name was assigned to the 6,301-foot spire by Elvin R. Johnson, who, together with D. Dooley and N. Johnson had made the first ascent of the peak in 1945.

Johnson and Piro had been friends and had completed many climbs together before the war, during the time Piro was stationed at Dose Meadows (1941).

Robert F. Piro died on Riva Ridge in Italy while fighting with Company "B" of the 85th Regiment of the Tenth Mountain Infantry Division. In dedicating his friend's name to this peak, Elvin Johnson did so in a simple dignified way, writing of Piro that "he loved the mountain.... as we all do." 140, 169

P.J. LAKE; MT. ANGELES (3F).The name P.J. Lake fell into common usage among local fishermen because it was frequented by P.J. Williams, an early-day jeweler in Port Angeles, Washington. Williams was an ardent fisherman and outdoorsman who was especially fond of fishing Morse Creek and all its tributaries. Since this small lake near Eagle Point is such a tributary and one of Williams' favorite fishing holes, fellow anglers began calling it after him and the name took hold. 12, 120

PLUTO'S GULCH; MT. OLYMPUS (5B). The Bretherton party of the 1890 O'Neil Expedition (see INTRODUCTION) arrived at this section of the upper Queets River on September 19, 1890. Because it was "the bottom of an ugly gulch through which the water plunged with a deafening roar," expedition member Harry Fisher dubbed it Pluto, the Greek term for "Hades" or "Hell." 69, 120, 208

POINT OF THE ARCHES; OZETTE LAKE and CAPE FLATTERY (2G). Noted British sea captain George Vancouver applied the name to this rugged area of arches, cliffs, and magnificent sea stacks during his voyage through the Pacific Northwest in 1792. When the author visited Point of the Arches in 1981, six arches were counted among the headland cliffs and nearby rock formations. Portions of the beach at Point of the Arches can be rounded only at low tide; much of it can never be rounded because of precipitous cliffs which drop directly into the ocean. Hikers are thus forced to follow overland trails. This is an area of powerful waves which, during winter storms, are known to smash the cliffs with a roar, propelling fountains of sea water 20 feet high up their sides. (See DESTRUCTION ISLAND for Native legend relating to the area.) 39, 120, 152

POKER SPRINGS; MT. OLYMPUS (7F). Prior to 1929, U.S. Forest Service trail crews working their way through this area enjoyed visiting the springs located here and it is "rumored" they engaged in a few friendly, lunchtime poker games; thus the name.

At one time a "Poker Springs" sign erected on the flat atop Lillian Hill honored the card-playing trail crew and their foreman, Everett Frisbee. 64.5, 128

PONY BRIDGE; MT. CHRISTIE (7C). It appears that the name of this bridge stems directly from the type of structure it is. Featuring handrails and stringers, it was commonly called a Pony Bridge. Such a bridge is not to be confused with a suspension, iron, or foot log bridge. The possibility exists that the frequent use of this particular bridge by packhorses resulted in the presently accepted name. 46, 182

PORT ANGELES. Now the County Seat of Clallam County, Washington, this city of 17,500 along the shore of Juan de Fuca Strait is characterized by a prominent, three-mile-long sand spit (Ediz Hook) which juts into the harbor.

The original Makah Indian name for the area now covered by Port Angeles was "?i?i-dis," pronounced "i-ee-dis," for which there is no known English translation. In 1791, Don Francisco, sailing the *San Carlos* under a Spanish flag called it "Puerto de Nuestra Señora del los Angelos," meaning Port of Our Lady of the Angels."

Port Angeles was originally called False Dungeness, or Old Dungeness by a United States Coastal Survey Team in 1852. The name appears to have been a slightly insulting reference to the existing town of Dungeness located 15 miles eastward. Though there is disagreement as to the identity of the first non-Native settler in Port Angeles, it is known that by 1857 several white men had selected it to be their permanent home.

Port Angeles was unofficially called Cherbourg in the 1860 census, in the hope that it would eventually become a military seaport town as notable as the French port of the same name. Shortly thereafter (1862), the city was officially founded by Victor Smith and designated Port Angeles by name. President Abraham Lincoln signed an executive order that year which set aside 3,520 acres of land in the town as a military and lighthouse reservation. Finally, a scant five months later, Lincoln signed another bill into law which assigned the somewhat inflated title "Second National City" to Port Angeles, a designation no longer in use.

For further information concerning Port Angeles, see the book *Port Angeles, Washington: A History - Volume One* by Martin and Brady. 90, 120, 121, 131, 134, 158

POSEIDON PEAK; MT. OLYMPUS (4B). This peak, 1.5 miles west of Bear Pass, was given a name consistent with the "Home of the Gods" theme that carries through the peaks of the Mt. Olympus massif. Poseidon is the Greek God of the Sea, son of Cronus and Rhea. Poseidon created the horse and is the patron of horse racing. The Romans called him Neptune. 146.5

PREACHERS POINT; LAKE OZETTE (4C). The Reverend Christian Forthun conducted Lutheran church services at this spot for a few years during the mid-1890s. Reverend Forthun with his wife and two daughters homesteaded here from 1895-1897. It is reported that their Sunday morning services were attended almost exclusively by the Scandinavian homesteaders living around Ozette Lake. 21, 120

PRESCOTT CREEK; MT. ANGELES (1E). It appears this stream was named for a certain Mr. Prescott, who with his companion Mr. Shellhorn prospected here in the spring of 1900. We know that Prescott and his friend stayed with William E. and Martin Humes in April of that year, just before starting their mining efforts above the Elkhorn.

In the early days of the century, with so many geographic landmarks unnamed and perhaps not even shown on existing maps, it was relatively easy for well-known settlers such as the Humes brothers to arbitrarily tack names onto such landmarks. For this reason it is thought that Prescott Creek, Idaho Creek, and Martin's Park were all named by some member of the Humes family.

Coincidentally, the author had the privilege of reading a letter dated January 7, 1905, from Will Humes to Myron Humes which seems to link all three of the landmarks mentioned above in just one sentence: "I just received a letter from Mr. Prescott," Will wrote, "the man who had been with Martin all the time in Idaho stating that Martin died on December 24." 98, 100, 152

PRESS VALLEY; MT. ANGELES (2C). The first recorded white visitors to this middle Elwha region may have included Civil Engineer H. Hawgood, a member of the O'Neil Expedition, and other expedition members. Hawgood descended from Hurricane Ridge to the Lillian River in August 1885 and while trying to cross the Elwha, he lost all provisions. Thus ended their lone trek into the middle Elwha and they were forced to return to Hurricane Ridge.

Later, members of the 1889-90 Seattle Press Expedition (see INTRODUCTION) assigned the name "Press" to this valley (specifically, the portion of Elwha Valley between its headwaters and the Goldie River mouth) in honor of their sponsor, the *Seattle Press* newspaper. This was done on April 18, 1890. 120, 207, 207.5

PROMISE CREEK, DIVIDE; MT. CHRISTIE (4F). Olympic National Forest Supervisor Rudo Fromme named the creek because it seemed to promise a high route from Low Divide to Quinault Lake via the Skyline Divide. This seemed to be a better route than the one leading along the North Fork Quinault River, taken by the 1913 Mountaineers' expedition. Promise Creek was previously called "Sims River" in 1890 by the Seattle Press Expedition (see INTRODUCTION) for a member of their group, John William Sims. 68, 120

THE PYRAMID (7,650'); TYLER PEAK (4A). Rick LaBelle likely named the peak in the early 1970s. The peak lies on the Inner Constance ridge about halfway between Inner Constance and CF-141 Peak summit, and has a pyramidal shape. 140, 184.5

PYRAMID MOUNTAIN (3,125'); LAKE CRESCENT (6C). The previous name, "Sugarloaf Mountain" was the direct result of a conversation Ranger Chris Morgenroth had in August, 1918 while visiting a friend at the old Rosemary Inn on Lake Crescent. Musing over the birth of Chris's new son, John, the friend gazed across the lake at the yet unnamed mountain and since wartime rationing was still in effect, said to Chris, "You get an extra pound of sugar now." The mountain was officially known as "Sugarloaf" for the next ten years until the U.S. Board of Geographic Names changed the name to Pyramid Mountain, more accurately describing its shape. 29, 94, 120, 138

PYRITES CREEK; MT. STEEL (3E). The name Pyrites Creek has evolved logically since the discovery there in the late 1800s of light crystals of iron pyrite or "fools gold."

Prior to gradual acceptance of the name Pyrites Creek, the stream was called by two other titles simultaneously. Bernard Bretherton of the O'Neil Expedition christened it "Fire Creek" after an ugly encounter with yellow jackets while ascending the creek, September 14, 1890. Nelson Linsley also assigned a name to the winding little streamlet, calling it "Smokey Creek" on account of an accidental fire the expedition started at the head of the creek. Bill Goodpaster, a local resident contacted by the author, recalls scooping up "fools gold" along Pyrites Creek when he was a trail builder there during the 1920s. 74, 120, 208

QUATEATA; LA PUSH (4E). Quateata is a steep headland point featuring several sheer cliffs. Located near La Push, it isolates First Beach from Second Beach (see FIRST BEACH and SECOND BEACH). Quate (Kwate) in Queets, Hoh, Quinault, and Quileute Native legends is the Creator, supposedly in turmoil with another being who opposes him. (See QUEETS BASIN for further information concerning Kwate) 20

QUEETS BASIN, CAMPGROUND, GLACIER, MOUNT (6,480'), RIVER; MT. CHRISTIE (3G), KLOOCHMAN ROCK (2D), MT. OLYMPUS (4A), SALMON RIVER (7D). According to Queets and Quinault Indian legend, the river was originally called "K' witz qu," or "qu itz qu," pronounced "kw a tz," meaning "out of the dirt of the skin." The legend tells us that Kwate, the changer, or "s' qitu," the Great Spirit and Transformer, was walking along the beach one day and came to the Queets River. Seeing no people, he sat down to meditate. When he rubbed his legs to restore circulation from the cold crossing, small rolls of dirt formed under his hand. He threw them into the water and from them a man and a woman came forth. Kwate placed them on the river bank as ancestors of the present tribe, saying, "From this time, you shall remain on this river and your name shall be 'K' witz qu,' because from the dirt of the skin you were made."

The name Queets River first appeared on the Surveyor General's map of Washington Territory and was later applied to the other features. It was derived from the Quai' tso (Queets) tribe which was first described by James Swan in *Northwest Coast* in 1857. Notwithstanding the official name, "Quai' tso," white settlers called the Queets River "Big River" for many years, thus differentiating it from its smaller tributary, "Little River" (known today as the Clearwater River).

Above: QUEETS VALLEY AND HUMES GLACIER. Humes Glacier was first explored by William Humes, brother of well-known Elwha settler Grant Humes. (Olympic National Park Collection)

Below: QUI SI SANA. The grounds of this health spa on Lake Crescent were decorated with magnificent statuary. Photograph circa 1910. (Olympic National Park Collection)

The 1889-90 Seattle Press Expedition (see INTRODUCTION) named Mount Queets "Mt. Hearst," for William Randolph Hearst, proprietor of the *San Francisco Examiner*, but the name "Queets" is the accepted title today. The Mt. Queets/ Mt. Meany area was depicted as Mt. Mesachie on the 1896 Gilman National Geographic map. 39, 73, 93, 155, 180

QUI SI SANA; see CAMP DAVID JUNIOR.

QUILEUTE INDIAN RESERVATION QUILLAYUTE NEEDLES, RIVER; LA PUSH (4E). It is popularly believed that "Quileute" in the language of these coastal Natives, means "joining together" referring to their home at the confluence of the Sol Duc and Bogachiel Rivers and along the six mile Quileute River. It is further believed that Quillayute (pronounced Quileute by most) is merely a corrupted version of Quileute.

Sea explorer Bruno Heceta, a Spaniard, first charted Quillayute Needles on July 12, 1773. The Quileute Indian Reservation was created in 1889 by presidential proclamation to cover a total of 837 acres. This did not sit well with the local settlers who claimed prior rights back to the 1855 treaties. In the summer of 1889 the Quileute village at La Push was burned to the ground. In hastily built, temporary shelter, the Quileute People suffered extreme hardship during the record winter of 1889-90. In 1896 the Quillayute River appeared on the Gilman National Geographic map as "Quillyhute R."

Huntington Rock, located in the Quillayute Needles and Refuge, is 133 feet high and in 1906 was reported to have hosted 40,000 Leach Petrels, a type of small, open-water bird. 12, 73, 120, 155

QUINAULT GLACIER; see LINSLEY GLACIER.

QUINAULT LAKE, NORTH FORK RIVER, RANGER STATION, RIVER; MT. CHRISTIE (4B), KLOOCHMAN ROCK (6A), QUINAULT LAKE (4G), MT. STEEL (4E). "Quinault" comes from the word "Kwinaithl" or "Kwinaithi," the largest village of the Quinault tribe residing in the valley between the Raft River and Joe Creek. One source claims that the root word is " 'wi ni lth," pronounced "kwee ni lth," the meaning of which is unknown. Another source claims that the word means "lake on the river." The name "Quinault" was first charted by Captain Charles William Barclay in 1787 for the "Quin-ni-ult" tribe living at the mouth of the river.

Word of the lake first came to the outside world in July 1854, when James G. Swan, an early settler on Willapa Bay, visited the mouth of the Quinault River and heard from Natives of the existence of a "fine sheet of water called Queniult Lake."

Quinault Lake first appeared on the 1855 Pacific Railroad Survey Map of Washington Territory. Indian agents Michael T. Simmons and Benjamin F. Shaw are said to have journeyed across the Olympics from the Quinault to the Skokomish River and probably saw the lake that same year, 1855.

The first settler on the shores of Quinault Lake was Alfred Noyes who arrived in the winter of 1889. In 1890 John Crumback and William Wiser (alias William Marsh, see MOUNT STONE), two men who had been charmed by the 300-foot deep lake when they first saw it as members of the Press and O'Neil Expeditions respectively (see INTRODUCTION) - may have come back and settled there.

The Seattle Press Expedition christened many landmarks while in the Quinault area. Most of the names expired to more common usage but in the interest of accuracy the following should be noted: The Press Expedition christened what is now the Quinault Ridge "Kemp Range" honoring Alfred C.G. Kemp of Montesano. Two different streams, Promise Creek and Seattle Creek were all lumped into one title, the "Sims River" by the Press men in honor of John William Sims who was a member of their group. What is now known as the East or Main Fork Quinault River, Press Expedition members dubbed the "Crumback River" for John Henry Crumback, the expedition's cook during their traverse of the Olympics. 73, 93, 120, 155, 169, 180, 183, 207, 207.5

QUINN CREEK; LAKE OZETTE (5C). The Haugland family, Norwegians, settled along Quinn Creek, circa 1900. It is thought that they applied the name "Quinn" to the stream in honor of their hometown in Norway. Considerable research does not reveal any cities with spelling similar to this one. One source thinks the Haugland's hometown may have been Kvinsdal, Norway, but this could not be verified. 193

THE RAGAMUFFIN AND THE URCHIN (6,000'); MT. OLYMPUS (6C). On Aug. 6, 1961, Kent Heathershaw, Doug Waali, and Robert Wood climbed five peaks, three of which were previously unnamed and unclimbed. They dubbed the peaks The Urchin, The Hoodlum, and The Ragamuffin to continue the theme of Mt. Childs (children) which lies immediately to the south. The name of The Ragamuffin stuck. The mountain they called The Urchin, however, is now unnamed. The peak they christened The Hoodlum is now known as The Urchin. 69, 140, 184.5, 207.5

RANGER PASS; MT. STEEL (5F). Two seasonal rangers with the National Park Service and a part-time topographer are credited with naming Ranger Pass. Donavan Rafferty, who worked in 1973 and 1974 at Duckabush and the following four summers at Honeymoon Meadows as that area's first seasonal ranger, Craig Holmquist, a Dosewallips seasonal ranger, and Mark Jefferson, who worked on mapping the Marmot Lake area in 1973, noted that the pass created a shortcut between Honeymoon Meadows Ranger Station and Marmot Lake Ranger Station. This scramble up steep snow and scree becomes more difficult late in the year but markedly shortens the hiking distance. 13, 27, 106, 176, 182, 197

RECTAGON (5,600'); MT. STEEL (6B). The source of the name is unknown, but logical. The shape of this spire, located on Sawtooth Ridge, is noticeably rectangular. 140, 184.5

REFLECTION LAKE; MT. CHRISTIE (2D). It is not known for certain who applied the name to this body of water. However, the descriptive appellation is noteworthy because Mount Christie's reflection as it appears in this lake seems actually to be "sharper" than the direct view! 91, 152

REMANN'S CABIN; MT. ANGELES (2D). This structure is now a shelter for back-country hikers. It was formerly the site of a summer fishing cabin built in 1929 by Grant Humes (see HUMES RANCH) on behalf of Tacoma, Washington jurist, Frederick Remann. The site for the summer retreat had been selected by Truman Drum. (see DRUM'S CABIN) After it was built Judge Remann secured a 99-year lease on the land. After Remann's death, his wife turned ownership back to the U.S. Government. 51, 54, 58.5

RHODES CREEK; MT. CHRISTIE (5D).

RIALTO BEACH; LA PUSH (4E). It is thought this name was applied by a resident of the area, popularly known as "The Great Alexander" (see ALEXANDER ISLAND). The man's real name was Claude Alexander Conlin, a performer on the Vaudeville circuit. The word "Rialto" is Italian in origin and was a common name for theaters throughout the United States.

Rialto Beach was also the site of an early encounter between Russian sailors and Quileute Natives. On November 1, 1808, the Russian fur trading brig, Sv. Nikolai (Saint Nicholas) foundered on Rialto Beach. The brig's 22-member crew abandoned ship and was attacked later the same day by the Quileute tribe. Their guns drove off the Quileute, killing three, and the Russians fled south with the hope they might reach Grays Harbor and ultimately be picked up by a sister ship. The Quileutes followed but stayed at a comfortable distance, since they were armed only with spears and bows.

Records indicate that when the Russian sailors reached the Hoh River, they negotiated with some Natives they thought were local (Hoh) villagers for passage across the river. Some of the sailors were taken aboard two small canoes and rowed to mid-stream where the natives removed cedar plugs from the bottom of one of the dugouts and swam for shore. Four castaways were taken captive, (including the captain's wife, Anna Petrovna) while the remainder fled upstream on foot, where they spent the winter on the Upper Hoh. It was only later that the Russians learned what actually happened when the "local" Hoh Natives tried to drown them in the middle of the river: They weren't all Hoh Tribe. About fifty of the pursuing Quileutes had preceded the sailors down the coast and prearranged a plot with the Hoh. The story of 18 months of captivity and enslavement comes to us through the debriefing of supercargo Timofei Tarakonov by Russian Naval Commander Vasilii Golovnin, done shortly after the survivor's return May 10, 1810 to Sitka, Alaska. (Seven died in captivity including the captain and his young wife) Corroborating this story is Quileute elder Ben Hobucket's version transcribed by Indian agent Albert Reagan prior to 1910 and published in 1934. Ben's ancestral family owned one of the castaways, an Aleute woman. From a Native perspective, Hobucket tells the story of the first white people to come to Quileute country. 20.5, 63, 65, 120, 148.5

RICA CANYON; MT. OLYMPUS (6F). This canyon earns the name of the only daughter of J. Lloyd Aldwell, owner of the prospective Glines Canyon dam site for many years. J. Lloyd's brother, Thomas Aldwell, promoted and built the dam. The name was applied by Lloyd Aldwell around 1913 when he acquired the property. The canyon had previously been known as Anderson Canyon after Billy Anderson who had by 1911 developed a nearby ranch. Anderson left the area in 1927.

The 1889-90 Seattle Press Expedition (see INTRODUCTION) originally called the lower portion of this canyon "Goblin Canyon," but this was never accepted as common usage. Goblin's Gate is found at the head of Rica Canyon (see GOBLIN'S GATE). 58.5, 83.5, 114, 179, 207, 207.5

RIDGE OF THE GODS; MT. OLYMPUS (2B). This area of peaks north of the White Glacier and enclosed by Falls Creek, the Hoh River, and Glacier Creek drainages, includes peaks such as Janus, Prometheus, Phaeton, Perseus, Atlas, and Parnassus. This ridge name, its peak names and the name, "Lakes of the Gods" have met with general acceptance to date. 146.5, 184.5

RING LAKE; MT. TOM (3F). Ring Lake was named by local resident and cougar hunter Pete Brandeberry just prior to World War II. Brandeberry named the lake for his dog Ring who once treed a bobcat near enough to the lake that his owner, following closely behind, discovered the body of water. It is reliably reported that Ring was a fine cougar-hunting dog who earned his name because of the colored "rings" on the white fur just above his eyes.

> Brandeberry, his brother, Virgil, and Oscar Peterson once stocked Ring Lake with trout, packing the fish in five-gallon cans on mule back. Ring Lake is still a popular fishing spot, though difficult to reach. 28, 29, 154

ROARING WINDS CAMP; MT. ANGELES (6F). Cold winds rush and "roar" through this isolated area located at the 6,000-foot level between Maiden Peak and Elk Mountain. 94, 209

ROCKY CREEK, PEAK (6,218'); MT. ANGELES (3G). Since the earliest days of white settlement of the Olympic Peninsula, this mountain has been known as Rocky Peak. It is characterized by large outcrops of rocks and sediment on both its summit and its flanks. Although the source of this name is unknown, it is apparent that Rocky Creek was so dubbed because of its proximity to Rocky Peak. It drains that mountain to the northeast. 19, 152

ROCKY CREEK; MT. TOM (8F).

ROCKY POINT; LAKE OZETTE (4D). The source of the name is unknown, but in the summer when Lake Ozette's water level drops, numerous sizable rocks are exposed on the beach at this point. No doubt the term Rocky Point fell into common usage because of this phenomenon. 83

ROOSES PRAIRIE; OZETTE LAKE (2E). Before the coming of the white man, it was customary for Indians to burn areas such as this to produce "prairies" and thus provide food for deer.

Peter Roose (pronounced "rose") was born in Arvard Hammerlund in Volnnos, Sweden. When he immigrated to the United States in the early 1900s, this country's Immigration Department forced him to pick a new name and he chose Peter Roose. Peter settled as a bachelor on this prairie to the northwest of Ozette Lake where he lived with his brother for a year or so. Pete then built his own home and stayed on the prairie from 1905 to 1930.

Peter Roose was a cousin of famous Ozette settler Lars Ahlstrom. Even though relatives lived close, Pete was known to be somewhat aloof and would today be called a "loner." As the story goes, Pete used to live much like a hermit for long periods of time accompanied only by a radio and would then unexpectedly visit neighbor Curt Barnard and his father for three days of non-stop talking!

Even when living a lonely bachelor's existence, Pete found ways to stay busy. For company he had an Australian Shepherd named Spruce, a horse, and a chicken which (supposedly) could swivel its head 390 degrees in either direction! Pete raised sheep, later butchering them to be canned and sold along with fresh strawberries. (He claimed he always butchered the meanest sheep first since he felt bad about having to kill them!)

But the old man was tough on himself. He never visited a dentist, but when, one by one, his teeth became infected ("obsolete" he called it) he actually would take a hammer and chisel and chip the whole thing away. Sadly, it would appear that the unusual form of do-it-yourself dentistry finally caught up with the old Swede. Peter Roose died in 1943 of cancer that originated in his mouth; he was buried at Ocean View Cemetery in Port Angeles, Washington. His home on the prairie at Ozette Lake is now a national historic site. 107, 120, 165

ROUND LAKE; KLOOCHMAN ROCK (8D). The actual source of this name is unknown. However, it is obviously a reflection of the lake's round shape (which for some reason appears on many maps as a heart-shaped body of water). 152

ROUND LAKE; MT. TOM (6E). Again, the source of this name is unknown. No doubt, though, it is so designated as a result of common usage by local climbers and hikers. 152

ROUND MOUNTAIN (3,541'); PORT ANGELES (5A). The source of this name is unknown, but the mountain does have a round profile due to past continental ice-sheet scouring. 152

ROUNDED ISLAND; LA PUSH (7C). This island has a pronounced rounded contour as viewed from various angles. The author personally observed this feature while backpacking the south wilderness coastal stretch of Olympic National Park in 1981. The source of this name is unknown. 152

ROYAL CREEK, LAKE; TYLER PEAK (2C). It is thought that the source of these two landmarks' names was G.A. Whitehead who was a Quilcene District U.S. Forest Service Ranger early in this century. Whitehead, Roy Strom (also a U.S.F.S. employee), and another friend whose name is not known reportedly hiked up Milk Creek and over into this basin in approximately 1917, becoming among the first white men to see it. The men agreed that Royal Creek lay in the finest, unblemished subalpine basin they had ever seen and so it is thought they arbitrarily assigned the names Royal Basin and Royal Lake at that time. (See MOUNT MYSTERY, MOUNT NORTON, and WELLESLEY PEAK for further information concerning G.A. Whitehead.)

There is also evidence that the men applied a name to the stream found here, calling it Roy Creek for Roy Strom, a member of their party. Mapmakers, however, later misspelled it "Royal Creek."

It was thought at one time that members of the first expedition led by Lt. Joseph O'Neil in 1885 named these landmarks, but there is little evidence to support this theory. 91, 210

RUBY BEACH; DESTRUCTION ISLAND (3F). Red pebbles vaguely resembling rubies, garnet-like sand, and pebbles of a peculiar, iridescent quality found on this beach probably account for the name. As the "rubies" eroded from the bank, enterprising pioneers living nearby began practicing a unique type of fraud. They conned outsiders into investing in their "gold" and "rubies" and even went so far as to construct a fake refinery building. A photograph was even circulated, depicting smoke spewing from the building's smokestack! Some local residents actually sold gold stock and blatantly told potential investors that gold was there for the taking. Traces of the old "refinery building" still exist.

In 1932 John and Elizabeth Fletcher began developing a resort at Ruby Beach which eventually included a lodge, store building, fifteen cabins, a gas station and a light plant. This property was added to the Olympic National Park in 1953 as a part of their coastal strip acquisition. No signs of this enterprise remain at this site near the parking lot for the beach. 59, 117, 189

RUGGED RIDGE; SPRUCE MTN. (5F), MT. TOM (1F). It is thought that Stanley I. Undi, a surveyor working in this area circa 1950, applied the name to this 3,000-foot ridge because of its steep, rugged topographic character. Undi, accompanied by a man thought to be Ted Burgess, probably climbed the ridge and believed such a descriptive title was appropriate. After bushwhacking up its flank one foggy day in 1981, the author can attest to the appropriateness of the title! 194

RUM JUNCTION; MT. STEEL (4E). This landmark's name stems from what must have been a terrific party which took place in the summer of 1938. According to Port Angeles, Washington, resident Julian McCabe, two trail crews, one camped at White Creek Basin where McCabe worked and the other miles away at Hart Lake, were assigned the task of building a trail between those two points. Working toward each other, the crews met on this little timbered ridge and there followed a noteworthy celebration. For openers, cooks for the two trail crews prepared salads and main dishes to satisfy the palates of the ravenous workers. Afterwards when they were washing down dinner with wine, whiskey, beer, rum, and eggnog the party really swung into high gear. Much later that evening everyone returned to their respective camps, except for the cooks. It is said that the White Creek Basin cook staggered in far behind his companions and the Hart Lake cook didn't make it back at all, slumbering off his euphoria while the crew made their own breakfast next morning. 46, 128

RUSTLER CREEK; MT. CHRISTIE (7E). Trapper Jasper Bunch is credited with naming Rustler Creek, circa 1901. Bunch often set his trap lines along this stream and maintained a cabin on the bank about halfway up its length. It is not known for certain whether he christened the creek for his dog "Rustler" or whether he was trying to commemorate the sound or "spirit" of the area.

R

Rustler Creek had previously (May 1890) been named Alexander River by James Christie, leader of the 1889-90 Seattle Press Expedition (see INTRODUCTION). It was so named in honor of a relative of the leader, Alexander Christie. Subsequent to the Press Expedition's christening of this waterway, Rustler Creek was mistakenly referred to in notes by Harry Fisher of the 1890 O'Neil Expedition as the "west branch of the Quinault." Later in the nineteenth-century, it was misnamed on a few other maps (such as the 1896 Gilman National Geographic map) as "The Rusher" and "The Rustler." 120, 146, 207.5

SAGHALIE CREEK; MT. CHRISTIE (4G). Rudo Fromme, Olympic National Forest Supervisor, named this creek following Roy Muncaster's hike to Mt. Olympus in the summer of 1914 (see MUNCASTER MOUNTAIN for further information on Roy Muncaster). Fromme looked up Saghalie in a small Chinook Dictionary (see ALCKEE CREEK) and thought the word appropriate; its English translation is "up," "heaven," "sky," "upwards," "over," or "celestial." Other spellings are "Saghale" or Sahale." 12, 68, 120, 178, 192

SALAL RIDGE; MT. OLYMPUS (7F). Salal is an evergreen, berry-producing shrub, common to this ridge and elsewhere throughout the lower and middle elevations of the Olympics. It is not known who applied the name to this ridge or when it was done, but long-time Port Angeles, Washington, resident Lyle Beam recalled that it was in common usage during the 1920s and 1930s. 26, 51, 152

SALMON RIVER; SALMON RIVER (2B).

SAMS RAPIDS, RIDGE, RIVER; KLOOCHMAN ROCK (3D). Two different stories purport to explain the christening of these landmarks. The first suggests that they are named for Harry and Sam Sams, members of a prominent Quinault Indian family, who poled their dugout cedar canoes to this site on the Queets River each fall. Such Christian names were arbitrarily assigned to Native Americans by white men in the early days. Here they hunted and killed elk and caught salmon which they would smoke and sell to white settlers, living off the remainder for the rest of the year.

Some historians think the term for these landmarks derives from the word "sams" or "samis," an abbreviated form of "Samms-mish," a prominent Quinault tribal group which once lived on this stream. 13, 167, 178

SAND POINT; LAKE OZETTE (2D). The Makah name for this point is "?aba.pi-?," pronounced "ah-ba'h-pee-is," meaning "halfway point." The original settlers' name for it was "Sandy Point," due to the shape of the peninsula of land, pointing seaward. Later the "y" was removed. It is not known exactly when this name was applied. 121, 152

SARATOGA POINT, LAKE CRESCENT (8C).

SAWTOOTH RIDGE; MT. STEEL (6C). The ridge is jagged and irregular, somewhat like a saw. Circumstances of the specific naming of this landmark appear to be lost in history. 91, 94, 207.5

SCHOEFFEL CREEK; MT. OLYMPUS (3F). Named for Harry Schoeffel, long-time Clallam County resident whose relatives and ancestors had been Quinault area settlers. Schoeffel, still living in the community of Joyce, Washington, when this book first went to press, was a second cousin to Billy Everett (see EVERETT PEAK). It is not known when the name was applied to this stream. 59, 174

SCOTT CREEK; LA PUSH (7D). Named for settler R. Scott who lived in this area, circa 1893. Just offshore from the site of Scott's homestead is the spectacular, rocky pinnacle known as the Graveyard of the Gods. 120, 152

SCOUT LAKE; THE BROTHERS (1D). What is now labeled Hagen Lake on maps, was shown on the 1941 U.S. Forest Service map as "Scout Lake." The Scout Lake name was moved to this lake on the east side of Mt. Stone because of a mapmaker's error.

Scouts were active in the area from 1914 to the late 1940s and named the lake. A main camp for Tumwater Council was located on Lower Lena Lake. 140

SEA LION ROCK; LA PUSH (2G). Labeled "Jagged Island" in Harry A. Major's book *Washington*, the more commonly-used term is Sea Lion Rock. It is one of only two islands off the shoreline of the State of Washington which serve as sea lion rookeries. It is not known who applied the name to this area. 120, 152

SEAFIELD LAKE; LAKE OZETTE (3F). The source of this name is unknown for certain. However, there are two theories as to how it was christened.

The first suggests that it was named for the wet, marshy prairie located one-half mile from the lake itself. Another, albeit less-supported account, states that it is named in honor of an early settler named Seafield. 91, 196

SEATTLE CREEK, MOUNT (6,246'); MT. CHRISTIE (6G). This mountain was christened on April 29, 1890, by Barnes and Christie, co-leaders of the 1889-90 Seattle Press Expedition (see INTRODUCTION) while hiking near Deception Divide (see DECEPTION DIVIDE). That day they decided to name the peak "in honor of the city of Seattle," (the expedition's "sponsoring" city). From this mountainside, Barnes made observations enabling him to complete his map of the Olympics.

The three streams now shown on maps separately as Seattle Creek, Promise Creek, and the North Fork Quinault River were all lumped together by expedition members and dubbed "Sims River" in honor of a member of their group, John William Sims (see PROMISE CREEK).

The city of Seattle (originally called Duwamps) owes its name to the venerable Indian, Sealth. Sealth was Chief of all the Suquamish Tribe, signer of treaties, orator, statesman, and was a true friend to early white Puget Sound residents. It was an early settler Doctor David Swinson "Doc" Maynard, one of the city's founders, who is credited with naming Seattle in honor of the wise, eloquent old Chief.

First-hand reports suggest that Chief Sealth was a formidable person, courageous, bright, and with a deep love of the land. 6, 7, 12, 73, 169, 207, 207.5

SECOND BEACH; LA PUSH (5D). The source of this name is unknown. This is the second beach south of La Push, Washington, each one separated by impassable headlands. 59

SECOND TOP (6,000'); PORT ANGELES (2A). This summit is the second "top" that climbers encounter when trying to ascend Mount Angeles (see MOUNT ANGELES) from the north. Apparently it was christened by climbers in the early days of the twentieth-century along with its summit pinnacle dubbed "Webster's Cliff" in honor of prominent Port Angeles, Washington, publisher E.B. Webster. The story is told of a party of weary climbers clambering up the Angeles mountainside, circa 1920, who were startled to see a proud, red banner (planted by unknown parties) on Webster's Cliff boldly proclaiming "Votes For Women!" 46, 94, 200

SEGE CREEK; MT. OLYMPUS (5G). Named for an early settler named Otto Sege "Serge" who homesteaded along this stream, circa 1890. He "proved up" on his homestead (cleared and established a legal home upon), which was adjacent to the six-mile post on the Elwha River. Sege's place was directly above what was then the Wolff Ranch (one source says it was below Wolff (Wolf) Ranch (cabin)). Because of the completion of Glines Canyon Dam in 1927, part of the homestead now lies beneath the waters of Lake Mills. Port Angeles, Washington, resident Harold Sisson remembers traveling to the Sege Creek area on hunting trips with his father, C.D. Sisson, and recalls the homestead being in a good state of preservation as late as 1927. It has been reported that more recently that a remnant of Sege's old cabin was observed in the forest above the road near Sege Creek. This sighting could not be verified. 12, 20.75, 58.5, 64.5, 98, 120, 156, 173, 179, 195

SEMPLE PLATEAU; MT. ANGELES (2C). The 1889-90 Seattle Press Expedition (see INTRODUCTION) crossed this plateau April 21, 1890. The two leaders of the expedition, Barnes and Christie, discovered an area of blazed and injured trees which may have been bear or elk markings, but which they attributed to earlier occupancy by Indians. Musing over the appropriate term for the place, the men were reminded of why they were there. Governor Eugene Semple, former Washington Territorial Governor, had referred to the inner Olympics in a June 30, 1888 report to the Secretary of the Interior of the United States. In that report he referred to peripheral exploration of the mountain range, while lamenting

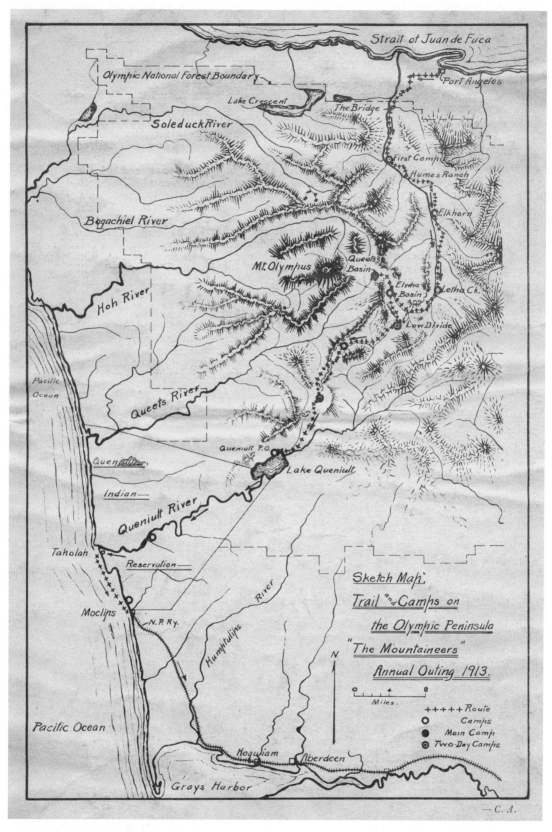

1913 SEATTLE MOUNTAINEERS MAP. Seen here is the route across the Olympics taken by the Seattle Mountaineers in their **Annual Outing (1913).** (Clallam County Historical Society Collection)

MT SEATTLE. Seattle Mountaineers are in this photograph negotiating the upper slopes of Mt Seattle, during their 1913 Annual Outing. Note the lack of ropes. Seattle Mountaineer leadership considered ropes hazardous when used by inexperienced climbers. (Clallam County Historical Society Collection)

the fact that red and white men had not yet probed the interior of this mighty wilderness. He observed:

...a land of mystery, awe-inspiring in its mighty constituents and wonder-making in its unknown expanse of canyon and ridge...Red men and white men have gone all around this section as bush men go all around a jungle in which a man-eating tiger is concealed, but the interior is incognita. In tradition alone had man penetrated its fastness and trod the aisles of its continuous woods.

The Press men applied Semple's name to the spot the day they discovered it. (See also MOUNT FERRY.) 90, 120, 207, 207.5

SENTINEL PEAK (6,592'), **SENTINEL'S SISTER** (6,301'); MT. ANGELES (5B). Named during a Mountaineer outing by Fairman Lee, Norman Huber, and Ralph Leber after they passed through the area on Aug. 1, 1920. The twin peaks stand as "sentinels" over Hayden Pass and the upper Dosewallips Valley.

"Sentinel's Sister" is a term indicative of that summit's slightly smaller size, as in the physical stature of a woman to a man. 152, 169, 207.5

SERVICE FALLS; MT. OLYMPUS (3A). Although there have been reports that famed poet Robert Service (who visited the Staircase area) may be honored here, it is more likely the term "service" honors the U.S. Forest Service which controlled this land from 1905-1938.

George Shaube homesteaded on Smith Place (see SMITH PLACE) on the Queets River 1922-1929. He built several trails up the Queets near this falls which seem to pour from a milk pitcher down the steep canyon hillside. In letters he wrote to relatives and friends, Shaube referred to the U.S. Forest Service as the "Service." Many other employees of the U.S. Forest Service likewise used this terminology. 64.5, 152, 178, 197, 207.5

SEVEN LAKES BASIN, CREEK; MT. TOM (7F), MT. OLYMPUS (1E). The basin is said to have been named by Chris Morgenroth who first explored the region. Morgenroth first counted seven lakes but there are actually many more. 94, 152, 207.5

SEVENMILE CAMP; MT. OLYMPUS (2F). The source of this name is unknown, but it was no doubt applied by early trail crews who noted that the shelter is located approximately seven miles up the Soleduck River trail from Sol Duc Hot Springs. 152

SEVEN STREAM; MT. STEEL (3C). Though not actually named by members of the 1890 O'Neil Expedition, this was the site of their Camp Number Seven. For that reason, local settlers began calling it Camp Number Seven Stream and for purposes of simplification, finally shortened it to Seven Stream. 208

SHAFERS POINT; LAKE OZETTE (4D). Named for settler Stephen Schaeffer who lived here, circa 1895. The spelling of the name as known today (Shafer) is a corruption of the settler's real surname.

Schaeffer, nearly blind due to an accident when gunpowder blew up in his face, raised goats here (until they died from eating a poisonous plant, foxglove) and geese (which were accidentally shot by some of his fellow settlers). From all accounts Stephen Schaeffer was a popular neighbor, often playing his violin in accompaniment to Lars Ahlstrom's accordion and Als Anderson's harmonica. It is said the men provided many lively Scandinavian tunes during the Anuelsons' New Years parties and dances. 4, 107, 120

SHELTER ROCK; TYLER PEAK (2C). Also referred to as "Big Rock," this huge overhanging stone is said to be capable of providing a natural shelter for 50 or more people. It is not known who actually assigned the name. 116, 152

SHI SHI BEACH; CAPE FLATTERY (3A). Named by the Makah Indians, their term for this beach is "sa sayi s," pronounced "sh'ah-sha-yees," meaning "smelt beach" or "surf beach." Shi Shi is a picturesque, broad beach, especially at low tide. 121, 152

SILT CREEK; MT. STEEL (5G). Though we do not now know who applied the term "Silt" to this stream or when, it was quite obviously named because of glacial "milk" washing into it from the grinding of Eel Glacier located at its headwaters. The "silty" appearance is a year-round phenomenon, especially pronounced during the warm summer months. 27, 152

SIWASH CREEK; LAKE OZETTE (5C). Siwash is a Chinook jargon term (see ALCKEE CREEK) meaning "savage." It is a corruption of the French root word "sauvage" and carries with it the connotation of a powerful being.

Native legends state that a tribal medicine man once became lost, turned into a bad Siwash, and killed many people in the Wynochee River area, in the southwestern Olympics. 11, 208

SIX RIDGE, STREAM; MT. STEEL (3B). Located at the confluence of Six Stream River and the North Fork Skokomish River, this was the site of the 1890 O'Neil Expedition's (see INTRODUCTION) camp number six. Technically, it was the sixth major camp established by O'Neil after his party left the Lilliwaup River on the Hood Canal. Though the creek itself was not actually named by O'Neil, local settlers began calling it Camp Number Six Stream, a term later shortened to the simpler Six Stream.

Lt. O'Neil and his men did christen the mountain we now know as Six Ridge. They called it "Deer Mountain," probably because of the deer sightings in that area. The name Deer Mountain did not take hold, however, and the entire area is today known as Six Ridge. A pass at its western end is called "Six Ridge Pass." 152, 208

SIXTEENMILE; MT. CHRISTIE (5F). Because of alterations made to the North Fork Quinault trail—the road was extended from the Main Fork Quinault River to the North Fork—today's hikers need only travel thirteen miles from North Fork trailhead to reach this spot. Before the road was modified, it was a full sixteen-mile journey to the shelter that once existed here. 94, 152

SKI LAIR; MT. OLYMPUS (7G). Built and named by Herb and Lois Crisler in 1944, Ski Lair was a roomy, comfortable dugout on a hillside that served as a convenient shelter for the Crislers and their weekend skiing visitors from Seattle. After a day of skiing up the mountain from the halfway house above Whiskey Bend, the group would spend the night at Ski Lair sitting on orange crate-seats and sleeping on bunks built by the famous photographer. Half-hidden beneath the snow-laden boughs of huge fir trees, Ski Lair was, from all accounts a cozy shelter for the Crisler party. It reportedly included sleeping bags, and even a sheet-tin stove with a stovepipe! 95

SKOKOMISH RIVER (NORTH FORK), MOUNT (6,434'); MT. STEEL (5C). Skokomish is a corruption of a Twana word or words, "s'kaw" or "kaw," meaning "fresh water" and "mish," meaning "people." Others have defined the word to mean "S-kaw-kaw-bish," or "river people." The Quinault name for the Twana tribe is "quo-quo-lb-dbish," pronounced "Kwo kwol'mish," meaning "the people living near the lake with a monster in it." The "mish" in this case is Salish, referring to "the people of that place." Of these two basic definitions, "fresh water people" is most accepted. (See DOSEWALLIPS for a Native legend which relates to this area.)

Augustus Case of the 1841 Wilkes Expedition discovered the mouth of the Skokomish River in June of that year, describing it as "a large inlet, called Black Creek," thus naming it for a trader named Black at one of the northern posts. The name of this, the largest river in Mason County, was later changed back to the original Native designation.

The original Mt. Skokomish is now called Mt. Henderson and vice versa. 12, 39, 50, 53, 70, 74, 180, 184.5

SKYLINE TRAIL, RIDGE; MT. CHRISTIE (3F). This term is descriptive of the topography of the trail, which follows the "skyline" of ridges southwest of Mount Seattle. The trail was begun in 1913 and extended in 1920 by the U.S. Forest Service. (The chalet was then located at Low Divide. See LOW DIVIDE, ENCHANTED VALLEY, HALFWAY HOUSE.) 95, 152, 208.5

SLAB TOWER (5,500'); MT. STEEL (6B). Located on Sawtooth Ridge, the tower has a flattened, steep profile. 140, 184.5

SLATE CREEK; MT. STEEL (6B). At several points in the flow of this stream, the creek bank is badly eroded, exposing large walls of slate. Some slate exposure is found near its headwaters. 53

SLATE CREEK; MT. TOM (5A).

SLEDGEHAMMER POINT; LAKE CRESCENT (8C). The road around the south shore of Lake Crescent (now U.S. Route 101) was built in 1920 and reconstructed in 1949. The latter job was completed with the assistance of inmates from Walla Walla Prison.

This part of the roadway was named Sledgehammer Point because of an incident that reportedly occurred here. The "chain gang" was busy hammering the roadbed out of the vertical hillside at this spot when one worker swung mightily at a rock with his sledgehammer but the stone didn't break. The sledgehammer careened out of the man's hands and flew back at him. When he ducked it continued on into the depths of Lake Crescent. Thus, the name Sledgehammer Point was born. 75, 109, 120, 122, 138

S

SLEIPNER (5,550'); KLOOCHMAN ROCK (8G). Jim White, Mike Lonac, and Bill Larson likely named the pinnacle during their first ascent in 1978 in keeping with the "Home of the Gods" theme. In Norse mythology, Sleipner or "Slippery," is a gray, eight-legged horse belonging to the god Odin. Odin, the oldest god, often referred to as Allfather, wore a gold helmet and clutched a magical spear as he rode the mighty stallion over bloody battlefields. It was Odin who selected slain warriors whom he felt had demonstrated sufficient bravery to be brought to the Valhallas (see VALHALLAS). 69, 78, 120, 140, 169, 184.5

SLIDE CREEK; MT. OLYMPUS (2E). The source of this name is unknown. The creek flows through a canyon which is host to recurrent mudslides. 154

SLIDE CREEK; QUINAULT LAKE (4G).

SLIDE CREEK; TYLER PEAK (2A).

SLIDE PEAK (4,310'); MT. TOM (4F).

SMITH CREEK; LAKE CRESCENT (6B).

SMITH LAKE; MT. STEEL (6C).

SMITH PLACE; KLOOCHMAN ROCK (3E). George Shaube (see SERVICE FALLS) filed a claim on this site in 1922, "proved up" on it in 1923 (established a clear and legal home thereon) only to move out in 1929. Scribing on his cedar plank door read "Geo Shaube Homestead 1923." Shaube, whose career included trail building for the U.S. Forest Service along the Queets River, Tshletshy Creek, and Sams River, died on December 4, 1966, without having his name affixed to his original homestead.

George sold the cabin and property to Oscar Smith in 1929, and moved to Killea Guard Station near Kelly Dude Ranch in the "upper Queets Country," which allowed their son Lorne to attend school. Oscar maintained "Smith Place" for several years during which time other homesteaders in the vicinity moved out rather than accept direct government control in the form of Olympic National Park. Smith finally relented, and sold the property now bearing his name to the U.S. Government in January, 1941.

The Shaube-Smith cabin was located in a meadow by the Queets River at a point where once there was a cable crossing to assist travelers in fording the turbulent waters. Though the cable has been washed out (circa 1964), some rehabilitation of the cabin was carried out by the Student Conservation Association in recent years. The author can attest that the Smith Place was a welcome sight to hikers completing a bushwhack down the Tshletshy Creek route or who have forded the Queets River. The historical portion of the Shaube-Smith Place caved in during the winter of 2005-2006. 59, 64.5, 119.5, 167, 198, 203, 207.5

SNAGTOOTH (6,283'); see MOUNT PULITZER

SNIDER CREEK; MT. TOM (2C). It appears likely that Snider Creek was named for Charlie Snider, a Sol Duc River homesteader who worked for the U.S. Forest Service. Upon his death, it is thought that co-workers applied this name because of Snider's popularity and the respect they had for him. Snider Creek is located on the Hoh River side of the old Snider-Jackson trail.

It should be noted, however, that another source claims that Snider Creek was named in honor of a carpenter from Clallam Bay who traveled and worked in this region. This story could not be verified. 113, 154, 157

SNOW DOME-MOUNT OLYMPUS. Left to right; Joseph Hazard, Winona Bailey and unknown. Seattle Mountaineer Joseph Hazard (Camp Hazard-Mt. Rainier) was a noted early Mt. Rainier guide, famous for his climbing exploits not sanctioned by the Club. On this 1927 outlaw climb Hazard was accompanied by Winona Bailey who climbed with the Seattle Mountaineers on their historic 1907 Olympus first accent but took a serious fall and failed to summit. However the intrepid woman came back successfully to climb Mt. Olympus with the Club in 1913, 1920, and 1926. (Peterson Collection)

SNOW DOME; MT. OLYMPUS (2C). The source of this name is unknown but obviously derives from the deep snow and ice which blanket this relatively flat table or "dome." Snow Dome forms part of the head of the Blue Glacier (see BLUE GLACIER) and is the location of a glacier research hut at its northwest end near Panic Peak. 94, 152

SNOWFINGER, ELWHA; MT. OLYMPUS (6A). This ravine houses a long, relatively narrow and persistent patch of snow and ice fed by avalanches from the slopes above it. Its fingerlike tongue of snow accounts for the name which may date to early Seattle Mountaineer days. The finger has receded dramatically in recent years.

In 1896, the Gilman National Geographic map called the ravine "Tunnel Creek" because of its "beautifully arched tunnel, 20 feet high and 40 feet wide in summer, through which it flows for two and 1/2 miles under an accumulation of ice that fills the gorge to a depth of 100 to 200 feet." Since 1896, the size of the Snowfinger has decreased. 73, 152, 184.5

SODA SPRINGS; THE BROTHERS (2G). Mineral water seeps to the surface 1/2-mile below the Main Fork/West Fork Dosewallips River confluence, attracting animals - and accounting for this name. 57.5

SOL DUC CAMPGROUND, FALLS, CAMP, LAKE, NORTH FORK RIVER, NORTH FORK CAMP, RANGER STATION, RIVER, SOL DUC HOT SPRINGS; MT. TOM (5G). According to Quileute linguist Jay V. Powell, Sol Duc is the corruption of a Quileute word whose meaning has been lost in antiquity. He describes any imputed meanings as "erroneous folk etymologies."

Nevertheless, it is known that sometime during the decade of the 1880s, a Quillayute Valley settler named Theodore Moritz "discovered" the mineral water seepage after being taken there by a grateful Native to whom he had administered medical assistance. Moritz later returned to the site, built a cabin and filed a claim on the land.

Some years later, following the death of Moritz, Sol Duc Hot Springs became the site of one of the most lavish pleasure and health resorts in the Pacific Northwest, perhaps in the country.

In 1910, entrepreneur Michael Earles formed the Sol Duc Hot Springs Company with four other men, quickly constructed a $75,000 road from Fairholme on the west end of Lake Crescent (see Fairholme campground) to the Hot Springs, then proceeded to spend approximately a half-million dollars on this new, opulent health spa.

Featuring a four-story, 165-room hotel in the center of the complex, Earles' resort held its grand opening on May 15, 1912. Thousands of guests from all over the United States and Europe (10,000 in one year alone) flocked to Sol Duc for the next four years to relax in the sanatorium and bathhouses and to soak in the 130°-140° waters. All were convinced of the healing powers of the mineral springs located there. Since the water contained hydrogen sulfide, sodium, potassium, magnesium, silica, iron, and other minerals, it also was common practice to drink from the springs. When consumed internally, it was widely believed that the waters were good treatment for everything from rheumatism to anemia and from ulcers to blood disorders.

Guests disembarking from steamboats in nearby Port Angeles were transported via company-owned Stanley Steamers to the luxuriously decorated and furnished resort. There they stayed in steam-heated rooms with hot and cold running water, electric lights, and telephones. Outside, the grounds were beautifully landscaped, featuring flower gardens, fountains, tennis courts and golf links. Surrounding buildings and shelters to which Earles conveniently piped hot mineral water for his guests to drink featured billiard rooms, bowling alleys, and a theater. In short, it was a splendid place to rest and relax.

Then, on May 26, 1916, just four years after the grand opening, sparks from a defective flue set fire to the shingle roof of the main building. Since the summer season had not yet opened, the water was still turned off, and staff members were unable to douse the flames. Strong winds quickly scattered sparks throughout the compound. All the buildings caught fire and within hours the greatest resort in the Pacific Northwest was in ashes. Employees recalled that as the resort burned, the electric organ, its wires short-circuited, continued playing Beethoven's "Funeral march" until it was totally destroyed in the flames.

Today the resort area is operated as a small "destination" resort by private concessionaires under contract with the National Park Service. Up river a nearby trailhead offers hikers access to the Olympic backcountry. On the North Fork a shelter marks the official trail-end. At one time this trail continued on to Happy Lake Ridge. 50, 60, 73, 94, 120, 155, 156

SOURDOUGH MOUNTAIN (4,600'); LAKE CRESCENT (5B). Pioneers who came here from Alaska were called sourdoughs, a term descriptive of a way of life in the old days. That, or possibly some old-timer who had made some sourdough pancakes or bread here, probably accounts for the name. 75, 175

SOUTH CREEK; LAKE OZETTE (4B). This creek flows into the south end of Ozette Lake, no doubt accounting for its name. 152

SOUTH FORK BOULDER CREEK; see BOULDER CREEK.

SOUTH ROCK; DESTRUCTION ISLAND (2G). This rock is the southernmost of three prominent sea stacks offshore from the mouth of the Hoh River (see MIDDLE ROCK and NORTH ROCK). 152

SPAWNER CREEK; SPRUCE MTN. (6E). The term "Spawner" has fallen into common usage, but it is not known who first applied the term to this stream. In the spring hikers standing on the trail alongside this stream can often view a dozen or more steelhead trout as they are spawning. It is the first major creek crossing after Flapjack Shelter and Sunday Creek on the Bogachiel Trail. 182

SPIKE ROCK; CAPE FLATTERY (2A). The Makah Indian name for the rock found here is "sackqu," pronounced "shack-qee," meaning "sharp rock," a most descriptive term for this prominent landmark. More than a mile from the nearest shoreline, it looks like a spike when viewed from the northeast. However, viewed from the east to southeast, the rock appears to be more two-pronged. 121, 152

SPRUCE BOTTOM CAMP; KLOOCHMAN ROCK (3E).The "Bottom" is named for a large stand of tall Sitka spruce trees located here. 59, 207.5, 209

SPRUCE CREEK, MOUNTAIN (3,018'); SPRUCE MTN. (6D). The source of this name is unknown, but it is obviously appropriate since Sitka spruce trees abound along the creek area and on adjoining lower mountainsides. Another Spruce Creek flows into the Hoh outside the Park south of here. 29, 60, 64.5,

SQUAW CREEK; MT. CHRISTIE (4D).

STAIRCASE RAPIDS, RANGER STATION (Lincoln Guard Station); MT. STEEL (6A). It is thought that the "staircase" near the present campground on the south side of the North Fork Skokomish River was traversed and bridged by members of the 1890 Lt. Joseph O'Neil Expedition (see INTRODUCTION) to allow their mules to continue up the valley. A cable crossing once existed here and was often used by people to assist them and their horses in traversing this difficult section of the river. Though the cable crossing is gone, remnants of the cables are still visible today.

Directly across from the campground located here is an obstruction formerly known as Fisher's Bluff. It created a particularly difficult passage along the river, one which an 1890s visitor bitterly dubbed "The Devil's Staircase" when he tried to get through. "The Devil's" later disappeared from the name. 19, 74, 120, 156, 159, 207.5, 208

STALDING CREEK; MT. CHRISTIE (3E).

STARBUCH MINE; OZETTE LAKE (3A). J.M. Starbuch owned and probably worked the Starbuch (alias Cedar Creek) placer here sometime between 1910-1920. The mine was abandoned by 1940. 58.5

STARVATION FLATS; PORT ANGELES (3A). Located on a north-facing slope which maintains a snow covering long into the summer months, Starvation Flats is the name applied to the Ennis Creek Basin by the Port Angeles-based Klahhane Club, circa 1940. This area is sometimes called "Poverty Flats." The author can attest to the barren nature of this basin and concurs with its bleak title. 46, 152

STATION CREEK; THE BROTHERS (3G). This stream is so named (it is not known when) because it enters the Dosewallips River at the point where the Dosewallips Ranger Station is now located. 152

STEAMBOAT CREEK; DESTRUCTION ISLAND (4F). In 1903 the steamboat *Far West* wrecked just off Destruction Island. Rolling tides and high winds ultimately caused it to drift, until a year later when it lodged on the ocean shore near the mouth of this stream. It was visible until 1926 when the remnants of it were totally washed away. 63, 120

STEEPLE ROCK (5,567'); MT. ANGELES (2G). The source of this name is unknown. Its christening describes the church steeple-shaped pinnacle of basalt exposed here. 152

STEPHEN PEAK (6,430'); MT. OLYMPUS (5D).

STONY CREEK, POINT, CAMP; MT. ANGELES (2D). This area is coated with many small stones from old river wash action. 75

STORM KING (4,534'); see MOUNT STORM KING

STRAWBERRY BAY, POINT; LA PUSH (6D). The source of this name is unknown, but no doubt it was applied by settlers because of the abundance of wild strawberries found on this coastal bluff area. 154

STREATOR FIELD; SALMON RIVER (4C). Today's casual visitor to Streator Field would be hard-pressed to imagine the noisy hustle-bustle of activity which must have characterized this spread when it was first populated by the nine-member Streator family. Frederick Streator settled here (on property originally opened up by an ancient forest fire) in 1891 and later his son George, ran the homestead until 1920.

Another son, Charley Streator, and his friend, Bill Hunter, (see ANDREWS FIELD) stayed busy playing their violins throughout the Queets Valley. For many years during this time, Streator Field was alive with thirty-five Jersey and Holstein cattle, 15-20 chickens, some pigs, and two oxen. Numerous buildings were scattered throughout the property, including three houses, a barn, a woodshed, and a chicken coop. A large three-acre orchard hosted apple, Bing cherry, green gage plum, Italian plum, and prune trees. Gooseberries, raspberries, and various other ornamentals graced the magnificent thirty-acre property.

The Streators sold out to the Higley family in 1920 and the Higleys stayed at Streator Field for five years. Today the property is merely an open field. 203

STUKEY CREEK; JOYCE (5A). This creek is named in honor of Jim Stukey (sometimes spelled Stubey) who maintained a homestead at a spot above the Glines Canyon Power Dam. Stukey, a prospector and frustrated miner, (he sank a shaft or two in this region, but only worked up a sweat) established his homestead, circa 1892, when the area was officially surveyed. Stukey Creek is the first main stream one encounters when traveling above the Glines Canyon Dam on the west side. 179

SUCCESS CREEK, LAKE; MT. STEEL (2C).

SUGARLOAF MOUNTAIN (3.565'); MT. TOM (1E).

SUNDAY CREEK; SPRUCE MTN. 6E). It is thought this stream was named by an early trail crew whose members established their main or base camp here on a Sunday. This version of Sunday Creek's christening, however, could not be positively verified. 63

SUNDIAL (7,150'); TYLER PEAK (2C). When standing in Royal Basin 1/2 mile west of Royal Lake, one can watch the morning sunlight gliding down this peak's east face and be able to approximate the time of day from the position of the sun's rays. Keith Spencer provided the name on his first trip into Royal Basin around 1954. 140, 184.5

SUNDOWN LAKE, PASS; MT. CHRISTIE (8B). The orientation of the Sundown Lake Basin is nearly due east-west. Steep walls hem in the south, east, and north sides. Only the west end of the basin is open, and this is where Graves Creek drains the lake. The evening sunset can slip through this opening to produce direct sunset views from Sundown Lake in summer. With a snow bank on the east cirque wall behind the lake, the sunset casts a beautiful alpenglow and creates a truly marvelous scene at dusk. The lake is located 1,400' above Graves Creek, a lofty perch necessary for this spectacular view. Sundown Pass is also a potentially good viewpoint for lovers of sunsets. 41, 53, 152

SUNNYBROOK (CREEK), MEADOWS; TYLER PEAK (3A). Boy Scouts at Camp Parsons are said to have named the meadows in 1926. 207.5

SUNRISE POINT (5,450'), **RIDGE**; MT. ANGELES (1G). Harold N. Lee, Professor of Philosophy at Tulane University, New Orleans, Louisiana, called what is now designated Alpine Hill "Sunrise Hill" because once, while he was standing atop that gentle rise, he witnessed a gorgeous sunrise over Cox Valley. Lee's term "Sunrise Hill" was later shifted by mapmakers to a point 0.1 miles north.

The sun does rise and shine directly on this point as well as the ridge which extends northeast from Sunrise Point to Mount Angeles. The stretch of Hurricane Ridge Road just below Sunrise Point is now referred to as "Sunrise." 12, 94, 114

SWAN BAY; LAKE OZETTE (5D).Some historians believe that swans nesting here in the late nineteenth-century resulted in the great bird's name being applied to this bay. That account, however, cannot be verified nor can it be disproved. It is more likely that Swan Bay is named in honor of Judge James G. Swan, famous early explorer and educator who first mapped Ozette Lake in August 1861, and first publicized its existence. For a time Lake Ozette was known to local residents as Swan's Lake (see OZETTE LAKE) lending credence to the theory that Swan Bay was christened in his honor. 83, 90

TACOMA CREEK (EAST FORK); SALMON RIVER (4C). Named in honor of forty settlers from Tacoma who homesteaded near this stream at the mouth of the Queets River in May 1891. Led there by John Banta and S. Price Sharpe, these and other settlers established a thriving colony known as Evergreen, which lasted as a colony until approximately 1940. (See EVERGREEN and HIBBARD CREEK) 1, 167

TAFT CREEK; MT. TOM 2D). U.S. Forest Service crew foreman Charley Anderson was responsible for naming many creeks flowing throughout the Olympic Mountains; some were christened in a lighthearted fashion. Such was the case here at Taft Creek. Anderson and fellow Ranger Chris Morgenroth, as the story goes, noted that this stream had no "head" and that it wandered aimlessly through flat wetlands as though it didn't know where it was going. The two men agreed that this seemed to be an accurate description of then-President William Howard Taft, and so they gleefully applied his name to the irregular little streamlet. 63

TAYLOR POINT; LA PUSH (6D). Taylor point is a dangerous headland which cannot be safely rounded. The name commemorates William F. Taylor of Mora, who purchased the James Dodge homestead here about 1909. His wife, Mrs. W.F. (Fannie) Taylor, recorded a stunning visual history of West Clallam County. In addition to many of her photos, parts of Fannie's diary from this period have survived and been published in Jacilee Wray's, *Postmistress—Mora, Wash. 1914-1915: Journal Entries and Photographs of Fannie Taylor.* 120, 167

TEAHWHIT HEAD; LA PUSH (5D). The Quileute name for this peninsula is "tseal tal oqu," pronounced "t seal' tla 'ok," meaning "a creek going over a high bluff" or "a waterfall." The present name is said to come from "teahwhit" or tealwhit" in the Chinook Jargon (see ALCKEE CREEK) and to mean "leg" or "foot," a descriptive term applied by coast surveyor John F. Pratt in May 1887. According to Quileute tradition the headlands were created by a "Changer," (powerful sprit being), who to escape a pack of wolves, used his comb to form headlands and whale oil to form rivers.

Theodore Rixon, pioneer surveyor of the Olympic Mountains (see DODWELL-RIXON PASS) settled on Teahwhit Head with his wife, Carrie, (see MOUNT CARRIE) in 1916. When they left, circa 1920, the area reverted to nature, became completely overgrown and was later almost destroyed in the famous storm known as the "1921 blow down." The forest area around Teahwhit Head was so devastated by that storm that when Theodore Rixon's son-in-law and cousin, Bob, decided to hike there a few years later, he clambered the entire distance from the nearest roadway to his father-in-law's homestead, a full mile, on fallen logs! 111, 120, 153.75, 157

TENMILE CAMP; THE BROTHERS (3E). The camp is around ten miles from the Duckabush trailhead. 152, 207.5

THIRD BEACH; LA PUSH (6D).This is the third beach south of the Native Village of La Push, Washington, each separated from the next by impassable headlands.

In 1902, an attempt was made to drill for oil at this site. What became known as The La Push Oil Well was dug at the west end of the beach. It had to be abandoned at only the 55-foot level when the sides of the shaft caved in. Remnants of the rusted boiler from that venture can still be found today. (See TAYLOR POINT for related story.) 59, 120, 152

Above: TEAHWHIT HEAD. Aerial view looking Southeast taken above Second Beach area. Note the resemblance to a human foot. (Olympic National Park Collection)

Left: THEODORE AND CARRIE RIXON. Theodore and Carrie are honored by the names Dodwell-Rixon Pass and Mt. Carrie. This photograph is circa 1900. (Polhamus Collection)

THIRD PEAK; MT. ANGELES (2G). This peak is situated on the Hurricane Ridge Road, 14 miles south of the city of Port Angeles, Washington, and 1/4 mile below the Switchback Trailhead to Klahhane Ridge. Just beyond Third Peak parking area (the last spot at which the Ridge Road can be closed during blizzards), one can glimpse the third and highest peak of Mount Angeles. Adjacent to Switchback Trailhead is the Ghost Forest where a fire occurred in the 1940s or '50s. (See map under DOUBLE PARKING). 94, 152, 207.5

THOMPSON POINT; LAKE CRESCENT (4C). This location was named in honor of David Thompson who settled here in 1915. Thompson is credited with donating land to Clallam County which now has been developed into a favorite recreation spot, Camp David Junior. (See CAMP DAVID, JR.) 120, 195

THOR (5,950'); MT. OLYMPUS (1A). This peak was first climbed in 1971 by R. Beckett, D. Haley, G. Kelsey, M. Lennox, D. Michael, D. Stevens, and R. Yekel. On this same trip these men also made the first ascent of Loki Spire (see LOKI SPIRE).

Harold Pinsch and Glenn Kelsey of Bremerton named the Valhallas (see VALHALLAS) in 1970 drawing upon Norse legends to complement the Greek and Roman mythology so prevalent in the immediate Mount Olympus area. In Norse myth, Thor is the son of chief god Woden (see WODEN) and is himself the god of war, thunder and strength. He rules the Paddocks of Power, driving a chariot drawn by two goats named Toothgnasher and Toothgrinder. Thor (from whose name the word Thursday is derived) is the adversary of giants and trolls and creates lightning merely by throwing his hammer. Though a god and presumably immortal, he was said to have been killed by the World Serpent. 69, 78, 140, 169, 184.5, 207.5

THOUSAND ACRE MEADOW; MT. ANGELES (6B). Frank Shaw, after returning from a camping trip in the area in 1932, was told by Lloyd B. Hunt that the area was called "Thousand Acre Meadow" (or Meadows). It is thought that Hunt may have named it. Thousand Acre Meadows is certainly one of the largest of its kind in Olympic National Park. It should be noted, though, that its size measures less than 500 acres. 69, 152, 207.5

THREE FORKS; TYLER PEAK (1E). One of the more descriptive names applied to a geographic feature in Olympic National Park (although there are actually only two forks). Three Forks is the point where the Grand, Cameron, and Graywolf Rivers merge to become the even larger Graywolf River. Famous early settler and trapper Amos B. Cameron maintained a hunting cabin here. Today, however, no remnants of the cabin can be found. 34, 152, 207.5

THREE HORSE LAKE; MT. OLYMPUS (1G). It is known that names of some landmarks found throughout the Olympic National Park were applied casually and without a great deal of forethought. From information found relative to the christening of Three Horse Lake, it would appear that just such a spontaneous process occurred here.

As the story goes, Billy Everett and some of his friends (whose names could not be verified, but among whom were probably Johnny George and Ed Lippert) led three horses to this lake on elk trails, open areas and some tricky route changes. Perhaps the journey was dangerous, adventurous, or in some other way momentous. Whatever the reason, after their arrival, the men were inclined to affix the label "Three Horses" to the lake. The name took hold, became a commonly accepted term, and remains permanent today. 173, 179

THREE LAKES; MT. CHRISTIE (2D). The source of this name is unknown. Apparently, it was christened because of the three bodies of water clustered here. 94, 152

THREE PRUNE CAMP, CREEK; MT. CHRISTIE (3E). With his typical sense of humor, early Olympic National Forest Supervisor Rudo Fromme dubbed this spot Three Prune Camp, circa 1913. As Fromme explained the name:

Here is where about 60 women, the female contingent of the 1913 Mountaineers Outing, had to go without the usual evening meal, because they had walked on ahead of the pack ho(r)ses, which were carrying the food supplies. The plan, of course, was to follow right along with the food as well as all the bedding, but the unfini(s)hed condition of Kimta Creek, in the matter of tread and pack clearance, required unpacking every horse, about 35 in number, leading each down the steep slope to the water crossing and up the other side. Food and other baggage likewise had to be carried by hand for repacking the horses after the crossing. The cook crew with cooking equipment and several horses carrying bedding were at the head of the line and in good enough shape to make it through to the previously planned night camp. The heavier loaded food carrying cayuses were, however, too played out to get much beyond the Kimta

Creek ordeal. Three of we men went on afoot to supply the sad news, and were naturally greeted with grins and lamentations, particularly after we had pulled a cruel prank at pretending to be approaching with a bunch of horses in the 8 o'clock darkness. However, by pooling the dried prunes I was carrying in my packsack with a larger supply in the cook's lunch assignment, we counted out practically 200, which permitted the doling out of three prunes per person, stewed thoroughly to look as large as possible.

The total number of persons in the party described by Fromme was 115. They were crossing the Olympics enroute to the Pacific Ocean, having recently headed south from the Low Divide area. 67, 68, 94, 120, 202

THE THUMB (6,600'); TYLER PEAK (4A). This peak is named for its appearance which actually resembles a rock "thumb." It is not known who applied the name or when this occurred. 140

THUMB ROCK (5,485'); PORT ANGELES (2A). Sometimes referred to as "Egg Rock," this tower was so designated by unknown early mountaineers because it projects skyward like a "giant sore thumb." Thumb Rock is a massive block of erosion-resistant basalt surrounded at one time with shale and sandstone, most of which is now worn away. 46, 140, 152, 200

THUNDER CANYON; MT. ANGELES (2D). The 1889-90 Seattle Press Expedition (see INTRODUCTION) camped here early in April 1890 and named this canyon on April 14th for the "heavy booming sound, as of water pounding into a cave or hollow." The resonance they described is created by the slate cliffs on each side of the Elwha River which swirls through this gorge. 120, 207.5, 208, 209

THUNDER FIELD, ROAD; LA PUSH (4E). Although the person responsible for this name is unknown it certainly follows logically from the field's proximity to the surf of First and Rialto Beaches. According to locals the road's christening was inspired by the movie of the same name. The 163-acre parcel that includes Thunder Field was purchased by Harvey H. Smith from the Federal Government on Feb. 7, 1889, under the 1820 Cash Sale Law. Subsequently the property was acquired by Harvey B. Smith, son of Quillayute pioneer, A. J. "Salvation" Smith.

Of historical significance is the fact that Harvey's brother, Alanson Wesley, while serving as Indian Agent and teacher at La Push, gave the Quileutes their European names. Also notable is the fact that Harvey's sister Harriet and her husband, Dan Pullen, owned a sizable spread in La Push that through the courts was reclaimed by the Quileute People. In 1897 Harriet pulled up stakes in La Push and joined the Alaska Gold Rush. This resilient woman lived out her life in Skagway becoming an icon in Alaska history.

The land was added to the Park as part of its 1953 coastal strip acquisition. Until the mid-sixties the farm was under Park lease to Betty and Art Munson, Harvey B. Smith's daughter and son-in-law. 153.25, 178.25

TIPPERARY CAMP; MT. ANGELES (2C).

TIVOLI ISLAND; LAKE OZETTE (4C). This island, located in the southern portion of Ozette Lake, was named in 1892 by Scandinavian immigrants in honor of an amusement park and gardens in Copenhagen, Denmark. One of these settlers, E.F. "Tivoli" Neilson, spent his 160-acre homesteading rights on the 22-acre island intending to make it a great showplace like the garden portion of Denmark's Tivoli. Here he planted Norway maples, chestnut, beech, and cork trees and other, more exotic items. Neilson, who had worked in a nursery, even tried to bring in frogs to complete the gardens but the attempt failed. After his first cabin burned, he deeded the island to a nephew in Seattle.

Tivoli Island is now owned by Olympic National Park. Norway maples, American chestnut (rare, healthy specimens), and beech trees still stand in the originally-planted rows, although other signs of human habitation have largely disappeared. 21, 120, 147, 167

TOLEAK POINT; LA PUSH (7C). Coast surveyor John F. Pratt named this point on May 28, 1887. Toleak is a contraction of a Quileute word "t lo' que a'h'l quil qu," pronounced "tlo'kwe'ah lqui ok," meaning "hole in the wall rock." It is also claimed as a Klallam word, pronounced "toluks," meaning "mussel," which would be most descriptive. Many shellfish can be found on rocks around the point.

On August 11, 1774, just off Toleak Point, Spanish naval explorer, Juan Perez "discovered" the Olympic Peninsula. He was the first European to view any part of the Washington State area. 120, 180

TOMBSTONE PASS; see HEATHER PASS

THE TRYLON (5,700'); MT. STEEL (6B). Fred and Helmy Beckey of Seattle christened this three-sided pinnacle (the world "trylon" refers to the peak's three flanks) located on Sawtooth Ridge as they were making the first known ascent of it in 1951. 140, 146.5, 169, 184.5

TSHLETSHY CREEK, RIDGE; KLOOCHMAN ROCK (6E). One theory concerning the origin of this name asserts that it comes from the Chehalis Native word "tAs lot chi," pronounced "tus-lot-shee," meaning "pull up roots and all." The phrase is found in one of the Native legends describing a Chinook wind that was so strong that it "pulled up roots and all." Any hiker struggling along the old creek trail would understand this name!

George Shaube (early settler; see SMITH PLACE), however, says an Indian friend told him that "Tshletshy" means "halfway," possibly referring to the creek flowing into the Queets River about halfway to its headwaters. In either case, the word has Indian origins. Shaube, descendant of a family who settled on the Queets, took up a homestead in 1922 about a mile below the mouth of Tshletshy Creek at the site of Smith Place (see SMITH PLACE).

It is thought that Rudo Fromme, a U.S. Forest Supervisor 1913-1926, was the first to officially apply the name to this specific area. 64.5, 68, 167

TSKWAHYAH ISLAND; see CANNONBALL ISLAND

TUMBLING CREEK; THE BROTHERS (4G). This creek indeed "tumbles" - down 3,000 feet in 0.9 miles! The section of the stream the author walked across while hiking the practically nonexistent Muscott Creek lower trail was precipitous indeed. 152

TUMWATA CREEK; SPRUCE MTN. 96D). "Tumwata" is Chinook Jargon (see ALCKEE CREEK) for "rapids," "cascades," or "waterfall" - all descriptive of the nature of this creek as it drains Geodetic Hill. It is also claimed that Natives used this word to connote a sound like "tum-tum," the sound of the human heart. Most Chinook creek names were applied by U.S. Forest Service rangers prior to establishment of Olympic National Park. 28, 101, 120

TWELVE MILE CAMP; MT. CHRISTIE (5F). This area is located twelve miles up the North Fork Quinault trail. 94, 152

TWENTYONE-MILE CAMP; MT. TOM (3F). Possibly named by early trail maintenance crews, Twentyone-Mile Camp is located about 20.6 miles from the Bogachiel River trailhead. Certainly that is close enough to the number "21" to account for the name. 152, 207.5

TWIN CREEK; SPRUCE MTN. (8C), MT. TOM (1C). This stream flows into the Hoh River approximately 150 meters west of the point where East Twin Creek enters the Hoh. Some maps show Twin Creek merging with East Twin Creek prior to the Hoh. (See EAST TWIN CREEK and WEST TWIN CREEK.) 63, 152

TWO BEAR CAMP; MT. STEEL (6D). George Conaway was foreman of a crew constructing the North Fork Skokomish trail in 1924. Every morning, while camping at this site and working in the area, crewmen observed two bears. Conaway thus proposed the name. 207.5

TWO MAN ROCK; LAKE OZETTE (2A).

UMATILLA REEF; LAKE OZETTE (1F). Spring and fall migrations of northern fur seals pass just west of Umatilla Reef enroute to and from the great rookeries on Alaska's Pribilof Islands. The Makah Natives called the reef "*' abac' ?at'," pronounced "*'a-ba't's-at'," which means "blubber rocks," probably in reference to the fact that this once was a popular spot for whale and seal hunters.

The present name came about when the steamship *Umatilla* was driven onto the reef in a blinding gale and snow storm on February 8, 1884. The crew survived and left the area, but several of them returned later and, by maneuvering the sails (at that time, some steamships were still being fitted with sails, "just in case!"), were able to disengage the steamer from the reef. It was then towed to Victoria for repairs.

In 1898, a lightship (a ship with a powerful light moored at a place dangerous to navigation) was positioned about three miles southwest of this reef; it was removed in 1971. 120, 121, 134

UMBRELLA BAY, CREEK, POINT; LAKE OZETTE (4D).

UNDERGROUND PASSAGE; see BIG CREEK

UNICORN HORN (5,050'), **PEAK** (5,100'); JOYCE (7A). Clallam Native legend relates that during a great flood, water rose to near the mountain tops so high that canoes were tied to the top of the mountain. The mountain top then broke off, leaving these two peaks visible at the end of a saddle-like ridge. It is said that all of the canoes floated away to where Seattle now is located and the people in them became the ancestors of the Natives living in Puget Sound today.

Unicorn Peak and Unicorn Horn once were called "The Pinchers" by the Port Angeles-based Klahhane Club because when viewed from Hurricane Ridge they looked like pinchers of a crab.

The present names probably refer to the fact that, from just the right angle, Unicorn Peak by itself looks somewhat like the horn of this mythical beast. Viewed from the north, Unicorn Peak and Horn become as one and look very much like a unicorn. From other perspectives, they are quite distinct and pincher-like or horn-like, as is common for horned animals. 20, 39, 114, 136, 152, 195

UNIVERSITY GLACIER: see JEFFERS GLACIER

UPPER TWIN CREEK; TYLER PEAK (2A). The source of the name is unknown, but the name obviously derives from the fact that Upper Twin Creek is located just uphill from Lower Twin Creek and enters the Dosewallips River less than 1/4 mile above the spot where Lower Twin Creek enters it. 152

101, U.S. HIGHWAY; MAPS ENCIRCLING THE OLYMPIC PENINSULA. A major interstate artery, the portion of U.S. Highway 101 that serves the Olympic Peninsula encircles all but the southernmost section of the mountain range. The highway is odd-numbered (101) because of its north-south orientation (even-numbered roadways generally have an east-west orientation). The Highway was completed in 1931 near Kalaloch and until the late 1940s was known as the "Olympic Loop."

The numbers of interstate highways tend to become smaller as one travels south and east. For example, the next U.S. Highway with a north-south trend east of 101 is Route 99, followed by 97. U.S. Highway 95 is even farther east on the Washington-Idaho border. 47, 64.5

VALHALLAS (6,038'); MT. CHRISTIE (1G), KLOOCHMAN ROCK (8G). These infrequently climbed significant peaks were originally christened Pleiades Peaks by Robert L. Wood, referring to the seven daughters of Atlas in Greek mythology. That name, however, never fell into common usage.

The Valhallas were first visited in 1966 by Ivan Lundgren, Ernest Labistida, J. Wall, and W. Howarth. They were climbed again in 1970 by Glenn Kelsey and Harold Pinsch of Bremerton, who are credited with the final christening.

In Norse mythology, the Valhallas is the great hall into which the souls of heroes fallen bravely in battle were borne by the Valkyries (see VALKYRIE LAKE) to be received and feasted by the chief god, Odin (see WODEN).

The term Valhalla comes from "Valholl," the "hall of the slain." Its approaches are guarded by a fierce, roaring river and barred gate, Valgrind. The hall itself has 540 doors, each large enough to permit the simultaneous exit of 800 champions abreast. Its rafters are spears, the roof tiles shields, and the benches are strewn with war coats. Here the beautiful Valkyrie maidens serve drinks to brave fallen warriors. Sick and injured Norsemen would beg to be stabbed in the hope of being allowed into the Valhallas.

This christening follows the mythological "pattern" established by use of Roman, Norse, and Greek mythological names on the Mt. Olympus massif. 69, 78, 120, 140, 169, 184.5

VALKYRIE CREEK, LAKE; MT. TOM (8A), MT. STEEL (6F). It is located just northwest of Frigga on the general mountaineer approach route to the Valhallas; (see FRIGGA) Harold Pinsch and Glenn Kelsey named this creek for its proximity to the Valhallas during the period of first ascents of the neighboring peaks.

Valkyries are wondrous creatures found in Norse mythology. They are said to be beautiful maidens who ride through the air astride magnificent steeds, resplendent in shining armor and adorned with helmets. The gleam of their armor is the source of the Aurora Borealis. Valkyries carry both spears and shields on their airborne journeys. It is they who bear brave, fallen warriors to the great Valhallas. It is they who serve food and drink while the soldiers are feted by the great god Odin (see VALHALLAS and WODEN).

When Dick Pargeter went to Valkyrie Lake in 1955, he reported that the "lake" more resembled a "puddle" lying sluggishly at the base of Anderson Glacier. When he returned in 1976, though, it had become a large body of water. Pargeter dubbed it Valkyrie because of the trend toward mythological names already established in the christening of Olympic peaks. Furthermore, he thought the name was appropriate to the appearance of the lake, set as it is in a large wasteland, mists floating over it conveying an eerie "mythological" personality. 69, 78, 140, 151, 152, 184.5

VIDAR NORTH (5,650'), **SOUTH** (5,600'); KLOOCHMAN ROCK (8G). Jim White, Mike Lonac, and Bill Larson likely named the peaks during their first ascent in 1978. Vidar in Norse mythology is one of the sons of Odin. It is he who avenges Odin's death at the Ragnorok, when he tears apart the jaws of the wolf which swallowed his father. (See WODEN and VALHALLAS.) 69, 78, 120, 140, 169, 184.5

VIKING LAKE; MT. ANGELES (7C). This small body of water was first mapped by surveyors Dodwell and Rixon in 1899. In August, 1973 a sign was erected there by parties unknown who somewhat arbitrarily assigned the name Viking to the lake and so it remains today. 120

VILI (5,500'); MT. OLYMPUS (1A). Vili is the second son of Norse gods Bor and Bestla. His rank in Norse mythology's celestial hierarchy is notable: Chief god Odin and Ve' were his older and younger brothers, respectively. These three brothers are said to have made the earth from the first god's (Ymir's) corpse. The teeth and bones of Ymir became the rocks, his flesh the earth. Odin, Vili and Ve' also created mankind, Odin, bestowing soul and life, Vili giving people the gift of understanding and the ability to feel, and Ve' providing human beings with the power of speech, hearing, and sight. (See also VALHALLAS.) 69, 78, 120, 140, 169

WARKUM CREEK; SPRUCE MTN. (5E). Warkum Creek was probably named by trail construction or trail maintenance crews just prior to the advent of World War II, or at least prior to America's involvement in that conflict. It is said by some that the term "warkum" was affixed to the landmarks primarily because *war* was *coming* , but this fact and the exact name of the person who first applied the word could not be determined with certainty. We do know that Warkum Creek was given its name because of its proximity to Warkum Point, a Bogachiel River location that no longer carries that name. 154

WARRIOR ARM (7,300'); TYLER PEAK (5B). Following the theme set by Fred Beckey, Keith Spencer named Warrior Arm (6,900'), the Brave (6,900'), Squaw (6,300'), and Papoose (6,100') after consultation with the others in the first ascent party of the Squaw in 1967. This is a major ridge with fine, difficult climbing that drops easterly out of the Park. 146.5, 184.5

WARRIOR PEAK (7,300'); TYLER PEAK (5B). Fred Beckey named this summit following his 1946 solo first ascent of the mountain. His reasons for calling it Warrior Peak are not certain. 27, 169, 184.5

WASHINGTON ISLANDS NATIONAL WILDLIFE REFUGE; see FLATTERY ROCKS.

WASHINGTON (STATE); ALL MAPS IN THIS BOOK. (The word "WASHINGTON" does not appear on maps.) Olympic National Park is part of the state.

From 1525-1539, the Spanish called the entire coast of North America "California." The English called the coast "Nova Albion" in 1578.

Oregon Territory, which included all of the present states of Washington and Oregon, came into being in 1843. Ten years later in 1853, President Millard Fillmore signed a bill creating Washington Territory. The name honors former President George Washington, "Father of our country." Columbia Territory was suggested originally as the name of the new territory, but this was changed to Washington at the suggestion of U.S. Representative Richard H. Stanton of Kentucky.

Washington became the 42nd State of the Union on November 11, 1889, during the term of President William Henry Harrison. 131

WATERHOLE, SKI HUT; MT. ANGELES (3F). Waterhole, about four miles out the Obstruction Point Road from the Hurricane Ridge parking lot, is the only spring water near the ridge summit in this entire area. Conveniently enough it is almost exactly halfway to Obstruction Point. It was a picnic area in 1965 but soon closed. Until recently a ski hut was maintained at this site. 94, 152

WEDDING ROCKS; LAKE OZETTE (1E). This stone formation is located offshore from an Native rock carving area (petroglyphs). When an Ozette or Quileute marriage proposal was rejected, it is said that the humiliated man would carve a design on a beach boulder to describe his sorrow and shame. Found here now are carvings of killer whale, masks, ships, birds, and elliptical designs intended to represent human genitalia. The rocks offshore from these petroglyphs (actually four rocks "wedded" close together) were referred to as "Whispering Rocks" by pioneers, for reasons unknown. 4, 120, 152

WELLESLEY PEAK (6,758'); MT. ANGELES (7B). Quilcene District Ranger G.A. Whitehead named this peak in 1925. A friend of his, William J. Worthington of Quilcene, had a daughter, Grace, (later Mrs. L.A.W. Swabey) who had been accepted as a student at Wellesley College. Her acceptance by the prestigious school was the biggest news occurring in Quilcene in quite awhile and the mountain was so named to commemorate the event. (See MOUNT MYSTERY, MOUNT NORTON, and ROYAL CREEK for further information concerning G.A. Whitehead.) 120, 169

WELLS CREEK, VALLEY; MT. ANGELES (2G). Named for an early homesteader named Wells, who lived just below the Cox homestead in Cox Valley (see COX VALLEY). Wells' cabin was constructed alongside this creek. 136

WEST PEAK (MT. ANDERSON MASSIF) (7,365'); MT. STEEL (5G). Contrary to logical assumption, this peak may not be named such because it is west of and closely related to Mount Anderson (see ANDERSON CREEK). Rather, legend tells us that it is named after Harry West who accompanied part of the 1890 O'Neil Expedition (see INTRODUCTION) into that area. The West Fork (of the Dosewallips) was supposedly named after him in the year 1890. 152, 169, 184.5, 207.5

WEST PEAK (MT. OLYMPUS) (7,965'); MT. OLYMPUS (2B). The highest of three summits on Mt. Olympus, this peak's name is derived from the fact that it also is the westernmost spire on the mountain. (See EAST PEAK, MIDDLE PEAK, MT. OLYMPUS.) 152

WEST TWIN CREEK; SPRUCE MTN. (8C). Located approximately 150 meters from East Twin Creek, there is some confusion as to the ultimate destination of this stream. Some maps indicate that it flows into Twin Creek (see TWIN CREEK) and then flows on into the Hoh River. Other maps, though, depict it as also flowing into East Twin Creek before meeting the Hoh (see EAST TWIN CREEK). 152

WHISKEY BEND; MT. OLYMPUS (6G). During the heyday of the Civilian Conservation Corps (circa 1930s), one Jack Cosser was on a U.S. Forest Service crew constructing roadway from the Elwha Ranger Station to the area we now know as Whiskey Bend. Steep slopes created difficulty for the workers for the first few miles. Nearing the spot where the road was designed to take a sharp bend, legend has it that their foreman, working out of the Waumilla CCC Camp, told the workers he'd buy all of them whiskey if they extended the roadway to that exact point by the weekend. No record exists as to whether the goal was met or the whiskey consumed.

   Although that legend has a nice ring to it and the author would like to believe it, records of former District Ranger Sanford M. Floe tend to refute it. Floe reports that the name Whiskey Bend existed before 1927. Other old-timers contacted during the research for this book say the christening predated the turn of the century. Quite obviously, the real reason for the name is lost in antiquity.

   There is a ridge near Whiskey Bend running down to Winslow Spring. That Ridge was referred to by local settlers as Salal Ridge (see SALAL RIDGE and WINSLOW SPRING). 26, 51, 85, 94, 114, 195

WHITE CREEK; PORT ANGELES (3C). Named in honor of the earliest settler here, Captain John White who homesteaded in 1859. Captain White did some placer mining along the creek, but records indicate he found only "quantities sufficient to pay for the working." 120, 208

WHITE GLACIER; MT. OLYMPUS (1B). Source of the name is unknown, but obviously dubbed White Glacier because it is predominantly white. It is noteworthy that White Glacier is in close proximity to Black Glacier (see BLACK GLACIER), the top of which is covered with black rocks and dirt and both are near the Blue Glacier, dominated by the prevalent blue tint of the crevasses. (See BLUE GLACIER.) 152

WHITE MOUNTAIN (6,400'); MT. STEEL (6F).

WHITE ROCK; LAKE OZETTE (1E). Located directly offshore from the White Rock Archaeological Site, which was the location of a former Native village excavated by S.J. Dunn of Washington State University in 1912. The excavation was so named because of its proximity to White Rock.

This landmark's name derives from the voluminous heaping of white bird "guano" (droppings) on the large stone, a direct result of the thousands of sea birds which frequent it throughout the year. 103, 120

WILDCAT MOUNTAIN; PORT ANGELES (2B).

WILD ONIONS THERE; LAKE OZETTE (2F). The Makah word for this place is "Kwa disdit," pronounced "kwa'h-dis-dit," meaning "wild onions there." At one time Indians harvested onions at this site near Lake Ozette. 121

WILD ROSE CREEK; MT. CHRISTIE (4D). The author was unable to determine with certainty how this stream was christened. One source contacted, though, indicated that an early Quinault River area settler named Rose (surname unknown) unwittingly was responsible for it. For a number of years Rose's neighbors frequently preceded her name with the adjective "wild," bestowing upon her a nickname which prompted much good-natured ribbing. According to this source, it also led to the phrase "Wild Rose" being applied permanently to this stream. 94

WILD ROSE CREEK; MT. ANGELES (2E).The abundance of wild rose plants that here perfume the summer air, account for this name. It may have been christened by 1920s/1930s U.S. Forest Service trail crew worker Everett Frisbee, now deceased. 51, 128, 141

WILLOUGHBY LAKE; CAPE FLATTERY (3G). Named in honor of O.L. Willoughby, the first postman to carry mail from Neah Bay, Washington to the Ozette Lake area. Willoughby lived in this area, circa 1902. The lake named for him nestles in a dense coastal forest of spruce and cedar, just 1 1/2 miles up an overgrown trail from Shi Shi Beach. 120, 145, 152

WINDFALL CREEK, PEAK (5,978); MT. ANGELES (3D). The stream found here was originally called "Jane Creek" by members of the 1889-90 Seattle Press Expedition (see INTRODUCTION). The person for whom it was named was not identified, but notes of the group tell us that they crossed the creek on April 4, 1890, while three feet of snow lay on the ground.

The term "Windfall" was not originally affixed to this particular mountain. The peak so named was a summit north of the one found here. Mapmakers, though, inadvertently altered the labeling process and that mountain, originally called "Windfall," began showing up on maps renamed McCartney (see McCARTNEY PEAK). This 5,978' high peak then received the appellation "Windfall."

The actual term "windfall" as applied to landmarks found here originated around the turn of the century. A tremendous windstorm, called a "blowdown," swept through the area circa 1900 knocking trees down all over the place and especially across the Elwha Trail. As a result of that storm, the creek soon was being referred to by trail crews and others as Windfall Creek and that word was later applied to the mountains as described above. 114, 179, 207

WINDY ARM; MT. OLYMPUS (5G). Because of the topography of this area, it appears to visitors that the wind always seems to blow harder here than anyplace else on Whiskey Bend Road. The source of the name is unknown. 91, 152

WINDY HOLLOW; (see CRISLER'S HOTCAKE CAMP).

WINK CREEK; LAKE OZETTE (2D). Named for Arnold Wink, an early miner who lived here circa 1940. 58.5, 120, 204

WINSLOW SPRING; MT. OLYMPUS (6G). Named in honor of William Winslow, who maintained a homestead here, circa 1895. Winslow's spread consisted of four 40-acre claims on the hillside above the banks of the Elwha River at the end of Salal Ridge. (See SALAL RIDGE.) 12, 114, 156, 179

W

WODEN (6,038'); MT. CHRISTIE (1G). This peak might have been named "Mount O'Neil" by the 1890 Seattle Press Expedition (see INTRODUCTION) in honor of Lt. Joseph O'Neil, leader of an earlier (1885) trek through the Olympics. The present name, Woden, was applied by Glenn Kelsey and Harold Pinsch, circa 1971. Certainly, naming the peak for the great Norse god followed the trend set throughout this area of naming peaks for mythological deities.

The first ascent of Woden was made in 1966 by Ernest Labistida and I. Lindgren. It is the highest peak in the Valhallas.Woden, in Norse mythology, is the English name of Odin, the chief Norse god. He was a wise old warrior with one eye, a flowing beard, a spear, and a eight-legged horse, Sleipner. The word "Wednesday" is derived from his name. Odin, nicknamed Yffr (Terrible), alternated riding his famous warrior horse Sleipner with traveling in disguise as an old man with a staff, gray-bearded and wearing a wide-brimmed hat. Very little escaped his knowledge. (See VALHALLAS, VILI, GERI-FREKI, and MIMIR for further information on the naming of peaks in this area.) 69, 78, 120, 140, 169, 184.5

WOLF BAR CAMP; MT. CHRISTIE (5D). The source of the name is unknown. However, local settlers believe that a wolf was killed at this site, accounting for its name. 152, 171

WOLF CREEK; MT. OLYMPUS (6G). The name Wolf Creek may have been applied by one of the two formal expeditions which traveled through this area between 1885 and 1890.

It is popularly believed that the Seattle Press Expedition - which camped nearby February 15 through March 14, 1890 - is responsible for the naming.

Notes of expedition members state that one of their group did kill a wolf here (accounting for the name "Wolf Creek") and a bobcat (accounting for the name "Wildcat Creek;" see CAT CREEK) on February 27 or 28, 1890.

However, as in numerous entries throughout this text, the possibility exists that a third version of Wolf Creek's christening is the correct one. The stream might well have been named in honor of Gustus Wolff, who was an early homesteader here, with a home and spread located on four 40-acre parcels where Wolf Creek now flows. Many years after the old settler left the homestead, a man-made dam on the Elwha River created today's Lake Mills, inundating the site. 57, 98, 114, 120, 173, 179, 207, 207.5

WYNOCHEE PASS, RIVER; MT. CHRISTIE (7A). "Wynochee" is a corruption of an original Indian word meaning "shifting," which probably refers to the shifting course of the river at lower elevations, or its winding to and fro behavior. The upper Wynochee was first explored in 1875 by a party which found it to be a "succession of rapids, and having a canyon three miles in length, with walls of rock from 200 to 300 feet high." 120, 208

Y LAKE; MT. TOM (7E).

YELLOW BANKS; LAKE OZETTE (2B). K. Olof Erickson and Walter L. Ferguson, Quillayute Valley homesteaders, established a gold placer mine here in 1893. The equipment with which the men hoped to extract gold from the earth was set up on the banks of an unnamed stream (NOTE: Many creeks flow into the Pacific Ocean in this region, most of them unnamed to this day).

Erickson and Ferguson built a small cabin near the creek, then proceeded to filter the flow through a 50-foot-long sluice box, 12" wide, 12" deep and made of 1" X 12" planed boards. The steep banks of the creek were yellow, so the men dubbed their mine "Yellow Banks Gold Mine" and organized a "bona fide" firm known as the Ozette Gold Mining Company.

Each of the two would-be miners staked out a 20-acre area and things looked good for awhile. So good, in fact, that Erickson and Ferguson even elected officers: Ferguson, president and manager; Erickson, secretary. A third man, a hired hand named Lester, was appointed treasurer.

With such a grand organization, the young promoters were certain that things would reach the profit level quite soon. Well, records demonstrate that the grandiose scheme did not quite reach the heights anticipated. The first week's operation yielded $3.00 in gold, the second $4.00. In all the operation struggled its way through seven weeks before the first cold blasts of winter mercifully put an end to it. Perhaps it's just as well it ended as it did. The seemingly well-organized entrepreneurs had never filed for a gold claim at the site anyway! 118, 120

BIBLIOGRAPHY

1. Alcorn, Rowena L. and Gordon D. "Evergreen on the Olympics." *Oregon Historical Quarterly*, 74:1 (March, 1973).

2. Alcorn, Rowena L. and Gordon D. "Memory of Mat Mathias to be Honored - Peak in Olympics to Bear His Name." *The Tacoma News Tribune* (July 23, 1961).

3. Alcorn, Rowena L. and Gordon D. "The Nylund Family, Pioneers of Old Ozette." *Pacific Northwest Quarterly* 53:4 (October, 1962).

4. Alcorn, Rowena L. "Pioneers Settled at Lake Ozette in 1895." *Tacoma News Tribune and Sunday Ledger* (March 15, 1964).

5. Anderson, Helen McReavy. *How, When and Where on Hood Canal.* Everett, WA: Puget Press, Inc., 1960

6. Aldwell, Thomas T. and Company. "Origin of Western Washington Names." *The Seattle Times* (February 2, 1948).

6.5. Archibald, Lonnie. *There Was A Day* 1999. Olympic Graphic Arts, Forks, WA.

7. "Chief Seattle's Challenge." *Off Belay* (February, 1978)

8. *Everett Morning Tribune*, 4:116 (November 22, 1983).

9. "Legendary Mountain Man Helped Open Up Wilderness." *Port Angeles Evening News* (November 28, 1953).

10. *The Mountaineer*, 6: p. 52.

11. "Names in the Olympic Region." *Steel Points*, 1:4:153-158.

12. "Origin of Some Place Names in and near Olympic National Park." Olympic National Park files.

13. Personal communication with Quinault area resident (December 5, 1981).

14. *Port Angeles Evening News* (October 13, 1950).

15. *Port Angeles Evening News* (August 31, 1951).

16. "Rudo Fromme, 91, Dies." *The Daily News* (August 22, 1973).

17. *Seattle Post Intelligencer* (February 13, 1949).

18. *The Seattle Press* (July 16, 1890).

19. "Variations in Place Names for Olympic National Park as Found on Geological Survey Quadrangle Sheets." (Alphabetical list, Olympic National Park files.)

20. Various Olympic Peninsula residents who wish to remain anonymous (1979-1983). 20.5 "Anthropological Report on the Identity, Treaty Status and Fisheries of the Quileute and Hoh Indians." Author unknown. From the files of Attorney Anthony Vivenzio.

20.75. Alexander, Alice B. A Pioneer Family – Homesteading the Upper Elwha River Valley. 1993.

21. Arbeiter, Ildri. Taped Interview by Gunnar and Francis Fagerlund (August 11, 1971).

22. Bailey. "Third Olympic Outing." *The Mountaineer*, 13:1:9-33 (November, 1920).

23. Banks, Mary. "Mountaineers in the Olympics." *The Mountaineer*, 1:1-4 (1907-1908).

24. Barnard, Curt. Personal communication; grandson of Dr. T.J. Appleton (November 24, 1980).

25. Barry, Wendy. Personal communication; Clallam County Ranger (February 1, 1981).

26. Beam, Lyle. Personal communication; hunted Elwha and Dungeness in 1920s and 1930s (December 17, 1982).

26.5 Beckmann, Darryl. *The Life and Times of Alexander, the man who knows: A Personal scrapbook.* Rolling Bay, WA. Rolling Bay Press, 1994.

27. Bowen, George. Personal communication; southeast unit manager of Olympic National Park (November 20, 1980 and March 11, 1981).

28. Brandeberry, Harold. Personal communication; settled on the Hoh in 1906 at the age of 6. (February 2, 1981).

29. Brandeberry, Virgil. Personal communication; settled in western Olympics when two years old (1906). (February 2, 1981).

30. Bretherton, B.J. "Ascent of Mount Olympus." *Steel Points*, 1:4:148-153 (July, 1907).

31. Broadbent, Jack. Memorandum written to the Superintendent of Olympic National Park; Field District Ranger in northeast section Olympic National Park, 1940. (August 10, 1940).

32. Cameron, Amos B. Letter to Victor B. Scheffer, an employee of the Branch of Wildlife Research in Seattle, Washington. (September 5, 1949).

33. Cameron, Eunice, and Howard. Personal communication; Howard's father hunted extensively in the Cameron (February 18, 1981).

34. Cameron, Paul and Margaret. Personal communication; Paul was born (1908) and raised in the Blue Mountain area. (March 16, 1981). 34.5 Campbell Patricia. *A History of the North Olympic Peninsula.* Port Angeles, WA: *The Daily News*, 1977.

35. Campbell, Robert P. *Olympic Peninsula Travel Recreation Map.* Automobile Club of Washington (1976).

36. Carroll, Lewis. *The Annotated Alice - Alice's Adventures in Wonderland* and *Through the Looking Glass.* Bramhall House, a div. of Clarkson N. Potter, Inc. 1960.

37. Carroll, Lewis. *The Hunting of the Snark.* Franklin Watts, Inc. 1970.

38. Clallam County Historical Society. Various news clippings and letters from the Genealogy Library of Clallam County Museum (January 15, 1981).

39. Clark, Ella E. *Indian Legends of the Pacific Northwest.* Berkeley and Los Angeles, CA: University of California Press, 1953.

40. Clelend, Lucile H. *Trails and Trials of the Pioneers of the Olympic Peninsula, State of Washington.* Seattle:facsimile reproduction of original Humptulips Pioneer Association, 1973.

41. Cook, Gordon. Personal communication; Olympic National Park packer from 1951 to 1972. (February 18, 1981).

42. Cornell, Jim. Personal communication; former Olympic National Park ranger. (November 12, 1981).

43. Crawford, Paul. Personal communication; ranger in Olympic National Park for more than eight years. (December 17, 1982).

44. Crisler, Lois. "A Tribute to Billy Everett, Grand Old Man of the Olympic Wilderness." *Olympic Tribune* (October, 1950).

45. Crisler, Lois. "Man for Whom Mt. Christie Named Lives Alone in Canadian Forests." Periodical unknown.

46. Cunningham, Al. Personal communication; ranger in Olympic National Park. (November 2, 1981).

47. Curry, Robert. Personal communication; 27-year employee of Washington State Department of Transportation. (January 22, 1981).

48. Curtis, Asahel. "Storm Bound on Mount Olympus." *The Mountaineer*, 1:1-4 (1907-1908).

49. Dahl, Ron. Personal communication; Lake Crescent area historian. (Fall, 1982).

50. *Visitor's Guide for the North Olympic Peninsula.* Port Angeles, WA: *The Daily News*, 1981.

51. Dalton, Russ. Personal communication; local area historian. (December 16, 1980 and December 7, 1982).

52. Deegan, Harry W. *History of Mason County, Washington.* 1971.

53. Dickenson, Floyd L. Personal communication; packer with Olympic National Forest and Park in the 1920s, 30s, and 40s. (February 2, 1981).

53.5 Doherty, Mike. Personal communication; Quinault ranger in 1970s.

54. Drum, Bill and Wayne Gormley. Written account based on conversation between Carol Kalahar and Bill Drum. Olympic National Park files.

55. Easton, T.S. Letter to Fred J. Overly, Superintendent of Olympic National Park, from his home in Myrtle Point, Oregon. (May 15, 1954).

56. Edwards, W.T. Taped interview; an early Queets settler. Olympic National Park files.

57. Ehlers, Carol J. "A History of Exploring and Mountaineering in the Olympics," Chapter 1. Olympic National Park files.

57.5 Elfendahl, Jerry. Personal communication. (June 24, 1983).

58. Erickson, K.O. Personal communication; longtime Olympic Peninsula resident and son of Ozette pioneer. (January 20, 1981).

58.5 Evans, Gail. "Historic Resources Study." Olympic National Park, 1983.

58.75. Felt, Margaret Elley. *Rivers to Reckon With*. 1985. Graphics Arts, Inc., Forks, WA.

59. Fields, Maynard and Mrs. Personal communication; retired trail foreman and park ranger. (October, 1980).

60. Fish, Harriet U. Personal communication; author and historian. (October, 1980.)

61. Fish, Harriet U. *What's Down That Road?* Port Angeles, WA: Peninsula Publishing, Inc., 1979.

62. Flaherty, Kathryn. Personal communication; daughter of Chris Morgenroth, early U.S.F.S. ranger. (December 10, 1981.)

62.5 Flaherty, Katherine. *Footprints in the Olympics*. Fairfield, WA: YeGalleon Press, 1991.

63. Fletcher, John and Elizabeth. Personal communication; longtime residents of Hoh area. (February 2, 1981).

63.5 Fletcher, Elizabeth. *The Iron Man of the Hoh*. Forks, WA: Olympic Graphic Arts, 2005

64. Fletcher, John and Elizabeth Huelsdonk Fletcher, Myrtle Fletcher Horton, Fred Fletcher, and Lena Huelsdonk Fletcher. Written accounts from interview. Olympic National Park files. (August 29, 1960).

64.5 Fouts, Stan. Personal communication; western Olympics historian. (January 28, 2007).

64.75 Fox, Pat, Personal communication, grandchild of Marvin H. McCartney, who guided the USGS through the Olympic Mountains. (January 14, 2009).

65. Frazier, Ralph and Roland Steinmetz. Personal communication; both are veteran seasonal naturalists of the area. (June 23, 1981.)

66. Fredson, Michael. *Oakland to Shelton, the Sawdust Trail*. Belfair, WA: Mason County Historical Society, 1976.

67. Fromme, Rudo L. *Fromme Memoirs*. Olympic National Park files. 1962.

68. Fromme, Rudo L. Letter to Mr. David Karraker, Chief Park Naturalist for Olympic National Park (November 29, 1966).

69. Funk & Wagnalls. *Standard Desk Dictionary*. New York: Funk & Wagnalls Publishing Company, 1974.

70. Gallison, Glenn D. Letter to Mr. George W. Martin, Registrar of Olympic Community College, Bremerton, Washington, in response to written inquiry; former chief park naturalist of Olympic National Park (April 22, 1960).

71. Gauld, Charles Anderson. "Letter to the Editor – Visitor Recalls Mt. Anderson was Named by Army Expedition for His Grandfather." Early Port Angeles newspaper, publisher unknown.

72. Geerdes, Raymond. "Enchanted Valley and its Chalet." Olympic National Park files (1954).

73. Gilman, S.C. "The Olympic Country." *National Geographic Magazine*, pp. 132-140 (April, 1896).

74. Goodpaster, Bill. Personal communication; longtime Peninsula resident and Olympic National Forest employee from 1923-34. (February 25, 1982.)

75. Gormley, J. Personal communication; lived in Port Angeles area as early as 1912. (January 20, 1981.)

76. Gwinn, Erma. Taped interview by Robert Kaune; Gwinn is an early resident of the southwestern Olympic Peninsula (April 9, 1968).

76.1 Haigh, Jane G. King Con: The Story of Soapy Smith. Whitehorse, Yukon, 2006.

77. Haller, Albert. Personal communication; hunted in Dungeness area for 57 years. (February 17, 1981.)

78. Halsey, William D., editorial director. *Collier's Encyclopedia*. 17, 18, 23, 1980.

79. Hanify, C. Bud. Personal communication; longtime Hoh area ranger. (November 14, 1980.)

80. Hanson, Oscar W. Personal communication; lifelong resident of Indian Valley area (since 1904). (December 9, 1980.)

81. Hart, Frank S. Notarized statement. Olympic National Park files.

82. Hartzell, District Ranger Jim. Office memorandum following conversation with Mr. Smith of Smith Brothers Bottling Works, Port Angeles, Washington (June 9, 1957).

83. Haubrich, Mrs. Al (Geraldine). Personal communication; cabin owners on Ozette Lake. (January 20, 1981.)

83.5 Hay, Clayton. Letter to Helen Payne, employee of *The Daily News* and later *Seattle Times* (Editing and book reviews).

84. Henson, Jack. "Ashes of Chris Morgenroth Rest in Scenes He Loved." *Port Angeles Evening News* (September 25, 1941).

85. Henson, Jack. "About Whiskey Bend." Olympic Outdoors column of Port Angeles Evening News (May 10, 1957).

86. Henson, Jack. Taped interview. Olympic National Park files (February, 1963).

87. Herrick, Burt. Written account of interview. Olympic National Park files.

88. Heuer, Bill. Personal communication; employee of Board of Geographic Names, Menlo Park, California (December 9, 1981).

89. Higley, Orlo. Personal communication; son of Orte Higley and grandson of Alfred Higley, Quinault Valley pioneers. (March 6, 1981.)

90. Hitchman, Robert. "Name Callling – Notes on the Discovery and Exploration of the Olympic Peninsula." *The Mountaineer*, 52:4 (March 1, 1959).

91. Hitchman, Robert. "Washington State Place Name Information." Washington State Historical Society Library, Tacoma, WA.

92. Hoofnagle, Keith. Personal communication; West District Naturalist, Olympic National Park. (June 23, 1981.)

93. Howell, Patricia. *Indian Geographic Names*. Port Angeles, WA, 1947.

94. Hughes, Jack. Personal communication; ranger in Olympic National Park since 1953. (September 6, 1980.)

94.5 "Pioneer Objects to 'Soleduck' River Spelling as Violating Original Name." *Port Angeles Evening News* (January 21, 1953).

95. Hult, Ruby El. *Herb Crisler in the Olympic Mountain Wilds*. Ventura, CA; Crisler, Hult, McAndrew, 1976.

96. Hult, Ruby El. *The Untamed Olympics, The Story of a Peninsula*. Portland, OR: Binfords & Mort, 1954.

96.1 Hult, Ruby E. Unpublished transcript. 1-17-1998.

97. Humes, Grant W. "A 'Lake in Martin's Park.' " - Olympic National Park black and white photo collection. cat. 1207 acc. 142 (1907).

98. Humes, Grant. *Humes Letters*. Olympic National Park files.

99. Humes, Grant W. "Journey to Mount Olympus." *The Mountaineer*, 1:1-4 (1907-1908).

100. Humes, M.D., Will, et al. Very early letters. Olympic National Park files (1897-1934)..

100.5. Hunter, Gay. Personal communication; cultural resources employee Olympic National Park. 2008.,

101. Jones, Nard. *Puget Sound Profiles VI*. Bellevue, WA: Puget Sound Power and Light, 1961-1962.

102. Kaiakaka, Elinore. Personal communication; teacher at Quileute School. (October 26, 1981.)

103. Kassowitz, Roberta Olson. Personal communication; homesteaded just south of Sand(y) Point. (December 14, 1980.)

104. Kauffman, John M. Reminiscences of Harry K. Kittridge, Homesteader on the Queets River as told to John M. Kauffman, Seasonal Park Ranger. Olympic National Park files (November, 1956.

105. Kaune, Robert W., Jr. *Indian Village Nature Trail*. Port Angeles, WA: Olympic Natural History Association and Olympic National Park, 1968.

106. Kaune, Robert W., Jr. Personal communication; Olympic National Park employee for 22 years. (December 16, 1982.)

107. Keller, Ida. Personal communication; daughter of Anders and Johanna Nylund, Ozette pioneers. (January 25, 1981.)

108. Kellogg, Bert and Laura. Personal communication; Bert Kellogg is a noted Clallam County (Washington) collector of historical photographs. (March 4, 1983.)

109. Kelly, Elmer. Personal communication; early maintenance worker on Olympic National Park roads. (December 8, 1980.)

110. Kirk, Ruth. *The Olympic Seashore*. Port Angeles, WA: Olympic National History Association, 1962.

111. Kirkpatrick, Theodora Rixon. Personal communication; daughter of Theodore and Carrie Rixon. (May 24 and October 12, 1981.)

112. Kish, Gary. Personal communication; fire guard in the 1940s for Olympic National Park. (November 14, 1980.)

113. Konopaski, Leo. Personal communication; his father pioneered in the Beaver area. (February 17, 1981.)

113.5 LaChapelle, Dr. Edward. Personal communications, March, 1985.

1.75 Lambert, Mary Ann. The House of the Seven Brothers. 1960

114. Lee, Harold M. Taped interview by Gunnar Fagerlund and Jim Hartzel. Lee is a longtime resident of Clallam County.

115. Lee, Harold M. Taped interview by John Douglas (August, 1978).

116. Leissler, Frederick. *Roads and Trails of Olympic National Park*. Seattle: University of Washington Press, 1957.

117. Lewis, Mrs. Charley (Marie). Personal communication; wife of Charley Lewis, early forest ranger and hunter in the Hoh Valley. (March 5, 1981.)

117.5 Lewis, Marilyn. Personal communication by editors; granddaughter of Iron Man of The Hoh, daughter of Charlie Lewis. (11/25/08)

118. Lofgren, Svante E. *Barth Ar-Kell*, Seattle: Publications Press, 1949.

119. Lotzgesell, Henry. Personal communication; longtime Dungeness area resident. (December 14, 1980.)

119.5 Lujan, Michael. *George Shaube – Pioneer of Olympic National Peninsula*. Michael Lujan is a grandson of George Shaube.

120. Majors, Harry M. *Exploring Washington*. Holland, MI: Van Winkle Publishing Company, 1975.

120.5 Majors, Harry M. "The Hezeta and Bodega Voyage of 1775." *Northwest Discovery - The Journal of Northwest History and Natural History*, 1:4 (October, 1980).

121. Makah Language Program. Maria Parker, Research Assistant; Edith McCarty, Research Assistant; Arlington Flynn, Program Manager; Roger and Lyda Colfax, informants and Makah speakers; Helma Ward, informant and Makah speaker; Hildred Ides, researcher, informant, consultant, and Makah speaker. Makah area map (January 26, 1981.)

122. Marriott, Robert. Personal communication; ranger at Lake Crescent, Olympic National Park. (December 12, 1980.)

123. Marston, Elizabeth. *Rain Forest – From Palms to Evergreen*. Boston: Brandon Press, 1969.

124. Marston, Elizabeth. Personal communication; lived as pioneer in Quinault Valley. (March 12, 1981.)

125. Massick, Sharon. Personal communication; local resident (July 28, 1981).

126. Mattila, Marlys. "Marymere Falls Is a Beautiful Bit of History." *The Daily News* (July 27, 1973).

127. May, Allan. "They Call It the Beach of the Dead." *Everett Herald* (October 10, 1974).

128. McCabe, Julian. Personal communication; trail crew workman, CCC foreman, camp watchman between 1927 and 1938. (December 16, 1981.)

1.5 McCabe, Julian. Interview by Russ Dalton; CCC foreman 1930s. (1981).

129. Meany, Edmond S. "1926 Summer Outing in the Olympics." *The Mountaineer*, 14:1:7-18 (December 15, 1926).

130. Meany, Edmond S. "The Story of Three Olympic Peaks." *Washington Historical Quarterly*, 4:3:182-186 (July, 1913).

131. Meany, Edmond S. *Origin of Washington Geographic Names*. Seattle: University of Washington Press, 1923.

132. Metsker, Charles F. *Metsker's Atlas of Clallam Country*. Seattle: 1955.

133. Metsker, Charles F. *Metsker's Atlas of Jefferson County*. Seattle: August, 1952.

134. Middleton, Lynn. *Place Names of the Pacific Northwest Coast*. Victoria, B.C.: Elldee Publishing Company, 1969.

135. Miles, Emily Lewis. *The Evolution of Emily*. Forks, WA: Creative Communications, 1981.

136. Miles, Rosco and Emily. Personal communication; longtime residents of Olympic Peninsula. (February 18, 1981.)

137. Mowbray, Joe, and Russ Dalton. Written account. Olympic National Park files.

138. Morgenroth, John. Personal communication; son of Chris Morgenroth, early U.S.F.S. ranger. (December 10, 1981.)

138.5 *Morning Olympian*. Olympia WA. August 28, 1929, September 4, 1924.

139. Morse, Samuel Howard. Taped interview by Dona Cloud; Morse lived his entire life in Port Angeles, where his grandparents homesteaded in 1862-3. (November 2, 1973.)

140. Mountaineers, The. *Climber's Guide to the Olympic Mountains*. Seattle: The Mountaineers, 1972.

141. Nattinger, Jack and Florence. Personal communication; Jack Nattinger was an early Olympic National Park ranger. (March 16, 1981.)

142. Nelson, L.A. "The Ascent of Mt. Olympus." *The Mountaineer*, 1:1-4 (1907-1908).

143. Nelson, L.A. "Mount Meany." *The Mountaineer*, 13:1:31-33 (November, 1920).

144. Newell, Gordon R. "The Beach of the Dead - S.O.S. North Pacific." Unidentified local newspaper. Olympic National Park files.

145. Oium, Ben. Written account of interview. Olympic National Park files.

146. Olson, John, Jr. Personal communication; descendant of pioneers of the Quinault Valley. (March 5, 1981.)

1.5 Olympic Mountain Rescue, *Olympic Mountains, A Climbing Guide*. Seattle: The Mountaineers, 2006.

147. Osaki, John. Personal communication; Olympic National Park employee at Ozette Lake. (November 23, 1980.)

148. Overland, Larry. *Early Settlement of Lake Cushman*. Belfari, WA: Mason County Historical Society, 1974.

1.5 Owens, Kenneth. *The Wreck of the Sv. Nikolai*. Lincoln, NE: University of Nebraska Press, 2001.

149. Palmquist, Sam. Personal communication; resident of Olympic Peninsula for 85 years. (February 6, 1981.)

150. Pangratz, Carl. Personal communication; trail crewman and avid Elwha area hiker. (December 18, 1982.)

151. Pargeter, Richard. Personal communication; map publisher and early seasonal ranger for Olympic National Park. (November 19, 1981.)

151.5 Parish, Susan. Joe Jeffers: Tragedy and Legacy. *Strait History* Vol. 5, No.1. Autumn 1989.

152. Parratt, Smitty. Gleaned from topographic maps, hiking the area, and various statements heard and read. (1979-1983).

153. Penn, William E. (Little Bull). Taped interview. (August 5, 1963.)

153.25 Peterson, Oscar Jr. Personal communication by editors; Forks area longtime resident and son of outfitter Minnie Peterson. (11/25/08)

153.50 Peterson/Schaad. *Women to Reckon With*. Forks, WA: Poseidon Peak Publishing, 2007.

153.75 Peterson/Schaad. *High Divide*. Forks WA: Poseidon Peak Publishing, 2005.

154. Peterson, Minnie. Personal communication, early packer in west end (of Clallam County, Washington) valleys. (November 21, 1980.)

154.5 Peterson, Oscar Sr. (Oscar was an Olympic Mt. outfitter and USFS employee from the 1910s to the 1950s) Day Book, August 28, 1929.

155. Phillips, James. *Washington State Place Names*. Seattle: University of Washington Press, 1971.

156. Place Name File. Olympic National Park files. (February 11, 1982.)

157. Polhamus, Bob and family. Personal communication; longtime area residents, descendants of Theodore Rixon. (March 6, 1983.)

158. Port Angeles Centennial. *Port Angeles, Washington: Port Angeles Centennial*, June 14-23, 1962.

159. Putnam, William, Jr. Personal communication; early traveler in southeast Olympics. (Spring, 1983.)

160. Ramsey, Guy Reed. *Postmarked Washington - Jefferson, Clallam and Mason Counties*. Clarksburg, MD: The Depot, 1978.

160.5 Ray, Jimmy. Personal Communication by editors; long time Clallam county resident and son of outfitter, Del Ray, (11/25/08).

161. Reagan, A.B. *Notes on the Olympic Peninsula*. Washington Trans. Kansas Academy, 1909.

162. Righter, Elizabeth. *Cultural Resource Overview of the Olympic National Forest, Washington, Volume 1*. Portland, OR: U.S. Department of Agriculture, contract 006709 (March, 1978).

163. Rivolas. Personal communication; former Low Divide Ranger. (February, 14, 1981.)

164. Rockwell, Jack A. and Karen Logelin. *Index of Geographic Place Names in Olympic National Park*. Port Angeles, WA: Olympic National Park (March 15, 1974).

165. Roose, Gertrude. Interview by Steve Kirsher; niece of Pete Roose, Ozette pioneer. (August 23, 1980.)

166. Russell, Jervis, editor. *Jimmy Come Lately - History of Clallam County*. Port Angeles, WA: Clallam County Historical Society, 1971.

167. Russell, Jervis. Personal communication; publisher and historian. (November 14, 1980.)

168. Sagan, Carl. *Cosmos*. New York: Random House, 1980.

169. Sainsbury, George. "Olympic Names." *Off Belay*, pp. 36-41 (August, 1972).

170. Samuelson, Verne. Taped interview by David Karraker and Benjamin Levy. (September 13, 1967.)

171. Scharf, Janet. Personal communication; East District naturalist, Olympic National Park, former Hoh Naturalist. (November 20, 1980.)

172. Schmid, Merle D. Personal communication; traveled extensively in the Olympics in the 1930s. (September 1, 1981.)

173. Schoeffel, Jean. Personal communication; daughter of Billy Everett and granddaughter of John Everett, pioneer explorers of the Olympics. (August 10, 1981.)

174. Schoeffel, Jean. "Olympic Hot Springs." Olympic National Park files.

175. Schott, Art. Personal communication; settled in Lake Crescent area in 1938. (February 17, 1981.)

176. Schroer, Greg. Personal communication; backcountry seasonal ranger for Olympic National Park. (December 16, 1982.)

177. Scott, John D. "Up Mt. Olympus from the East." *Mazama*, 10:12:17-29 (December, 1928).

178. Shaube, George A. Letter to Bennett T. Gale, Superintendent, Olympic National Park; homesteader on the Queets, Shaube was involved with the initial construction on major Queets River trails. (December 4, 1966).

178.25 Shearer, Ron. Personal communication by editors; longtime resident of Clallam County and son of mountain man and bridge builder, Dan Shearer, (11/26/08).

178.5 Shore, Clyde. "Times Remembered." unpublished memoirs.

179. Sisson, Harold. Personal communication; longtime resident of the Elwha River area. (December 2, 1980 and November 1, 1981.)

180. Smith, Alfred. *Translation of Geographic Names of Indian Origin, State of Washington*. Tacoma, WA: 1938.

181. Smith, Ivor. Taped interview on politics and the development of Port Angeles. (May, 1973.)

182. Smith, Kathe. Personal communication; avid explorer of the Olympics. (October 31, 1982.)

183. Smith, LeRoy. *Pioneers of the Olympic Peninsula*. Forks, WA: Olympic Graphic Arts, Inc., 1976.

184. Smith, Neil. Personal communication; Kalaloch - Queets Sub-district Ranger for Olympic National Park. (May 27, 1981.)

184.5. Spencer, Keith. Personal communication. (January 27, 2008.)

185. Spicer, Rich. Personal communication; naturalist and geologist. (September 26 and 27, 1982.)

186. Spring, Ira and Harvey Manning. *102 Hikes in the Alpine Lakes, South Cascades and Olympics*. Seattle: The Mountaineers, 1978.

187. Streator, Gertrude. "The Olympic Outing." *The Mountaineer*, 6:19-32 (1913).

187.5 Students of Creative Writing of Weatherwax High School, Aberdeen, Washington. "Where Away?" *The Aberdeen Daily World*, circa 1963.

188. Superintendent of Olympic National Park (Macy). Letter to Director, File 731-01, Olympic National Park files (February 15, 1938).

189. Sward, Ric. Personal communication; seasonal naturalist. (December 27, 1980 and June 22, 1981.)

190. Taylor, Marian and Fred. Personal communication; Marian has lived on the Peninsula more than 70 years; Fred has hunted extensively in the Dungeness area. (January 26, 1981.)

191. Thomas, Dick. Personal communication; Lake Crescent Subdistrict Ranger in Olympic National Park. (June 27, 1982.)

192. Thomas, Edward. *Chinook, A History and Dictionary*. Portland, OR: Metropolitan Press Publishers, 1935.

193. Thomas, Martin. History of Lake Ozette. Term paper in Olympic National Park files.

194. Thomas, Russ. Personal communication. (March 12, 1981.)

195. Thompson, Keith. Personal communication; moved to the Olympic Peninsula from Seattle 1911. (January 23, 1981.)

196. Vanderhoof, Myra. Personal communication; Ozette Lake pioneer. (December 14, 1980.)

197. Warder, John. Personal communication; trails foreman for Olympic National Park. (December 15, 1982.)

198. Warren, Henry C. Summary Report on the Queets Corridor and Coastal Strip Additions and Related Controversies. Olympic National Park files, February, 1983.

199. Washington State Associations of County Commissioners and County Engineers in Cooperation with the State College of Washington. *The Book of Counties*. Seattle First National Bank, Standard Oil Company of California and Weyerhaeuser Timber Company, 1953.

200. Webster, E.B. *The Friendly Mountain*. Port Angeles, WA: *The Evening News*, 1921.

201. Wickersham, Don. Personal communication; his father homesteaded in the area of the Hoko River and Don spent many years in Sekiu. (February 17, 1981.)

202. Williams, Richard L. *The Northwest Coast*. New York: The American Wilderness, Time- Life Books, 1973.

203. Williams, Sally. "A Survey of Abandoned Homestead Clearings in the Queets River Valley, Olympic National Park, Washington." Olympic National Park files, 1975.

204. Willis, G. Frank and Michael G. Schene. Historic Resource Study. Olympic National Park files (September 1978).

205. Winters, Larry. Personal communication; spent 20 years as a tour guide in the Olympics. (August 10, 1981.)

206. Wolcott, Ernest W. *Lakes of Washington, Volume 1 - Western Washington*. Olympic, WA: Department of Conservation, Div. of Water Resources, Supply Bulletin 14, 1961.

207. Wood, Robert L. *Across the Olympic Mountains, The Press Expedition, 1889-90*. Seattle, WA: The Mountaineers, 1967.

207.5 Wood, Robert L. Memorandum on Certain Place Names in the Olympics. Unpublished, December, 1984 - January, 1985.

208. Wood, Robert L. *Men, Mules and Mountains - Lieutenant O'Neil's Olympic Expeditions*. Seattle, WA: The Mountaineers, 1976.

208.5 Wood, Robert L. *Olympic Mountains Trail Guide*, Seattle, WA: The Mountaineers, 1984.

209. Wood, Robert L. *Trail Country, Olympic National Park*. Seattle, WA: The Mountaineers, 1968.

210. Worthington, Robert. Personal communication; spent his entire life in the Quilcene area after his father settled here in the 1800s. (December 19, 1980 and January 14, 1981).

210.5 Wray, Jacilee. *Native Peoples of the Olympic Peninsula*. Norman, OK: University of Oklahoma Press, 2002.

1.75 Wray, Jacilee. *Postmistress: Journal Entries and Photographs of Fannie Taylor*. Seattle: Northwest Interpretive Association, 2006.

211. Yanish, Howard. Personal communication; Hoh Sub-district Ranger, Olympic National Park. (June 26, 1982.)

211.1 Yanish, Howard. Personal communication; retired Park Ranger, Olympic National Park, (11/25/08).

The 1984 edition of Gods and Goblins was a landmark study of Olympic National Park place names. Smitty Parratt not only compiled known research, but conducted countless, timely interviews with primary sources. In addition, through hundreds of days in the field exploring the landscape, Smitty and his wife, Shawn, were able to capture the spirit of each locale. The result of their labors became the definitive history of the Park told through its place names.

This 2009 revised and expanded publication honors Smitty's efforts and commitment to the preservation of the Olympic National Park's rich history.

The Bandersnatch

Due to constraints of economics and space, Park Naturalist Keith Hoofnagle's twenty imaginative line drawings are sadly absent from this new edition. It is hoped that the inclusion of new material mitigates this loss.

SECTIONAL MAPS

The following pages contain reprints of the original maps in the first edition of Gods & Goblins (1984.)

These maps are designed for one purpose only: to help the reader locate and identify coordinates referred to in the text. While certainly topographical in nature and accurate, they are not, nor do they purport to be, specific enough to be used as the sole guide for the hikers in the Olympic National Park backcountry.

INDEX TO SECTIONAL MAPS

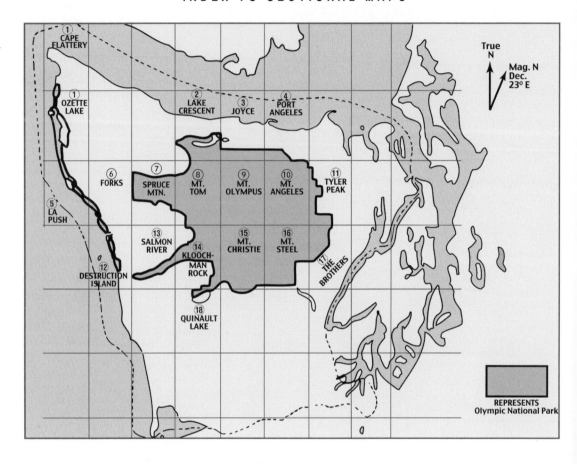

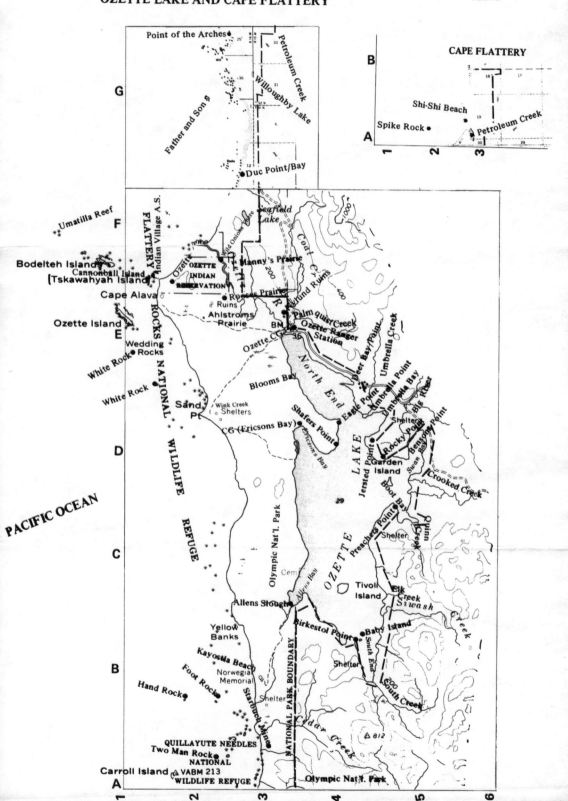

OZETTE LAKE AND CAPE FLATTERY

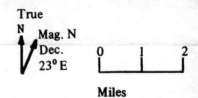

True N
Mag. N
Dec.
23° E

0   1   2
Miles

CAPE FLATTERY

Shi-Shi Beach
Spike Rock
Petroleum Creek

Point of the Arches
Petroleum Creek
Willoughby Lake
Father and Son
Duc Point/Bay

Umatilla Reef
Seafield Lake
Wild Onions Lake
Coal Cr.
Bodelteh Islands
Cannonball Island
[Tskawahyah Island]
OZETTE INDIAN RESERVATION
Manny's Prairie
Cape Alava
Roose's Prairie
Ahlstroms Prairie
Brund Ruins
Ozette Island
Palm quist Creek
Umbrella Creek
BM
Ozette Ranger Station
Wedding Rocks
Ozette Cr.
White Rock
North End
Deer Bay/Point
Umbrella Point
White Rock
Blooms Bay
Eagle Point
Umbrella Bay
Big River
Shelters
Sand Pt
Wink Creek
Shelters
Shafers Point
Shelters
Rocky Point
Benson's Point
CG (Ericsons Bay)
Ericsons Bay
Garden Island
Crooked Creek
Jersted Point
Swan Bay
PACIFIC OCEAN
Boot Bay
Preachers Point
Quinn Creek
Shelter
Olympic Nat'l. Park
Cemy Bay
Allens Bay
Tivoli Island
Elk Creek Siwash
Allens Slough
Birkestol Point
Baby Island
Yellow Banks
Shelter
South End
Kayosla Beach
Norwegia Memorial
South Creek
Foot Rock
Shelter
Hand Rock
Starbuck Mine
Cedar Creek
QUILLAYUTE NEEDLES
Two Man Rock
NATIONAL
Carroll Island
VABM 213
WILDLIFE REFUGE
Olympic Nat'l. Park

CAPE FLATTERY ROCKS NATIONAL WILDLIFE REFUGE
Indian Village V.S.
FLATTERY
Ozette R.
R.
Ozette
LAKE
OZETTE
NATIONAL PARK BOUNDARY

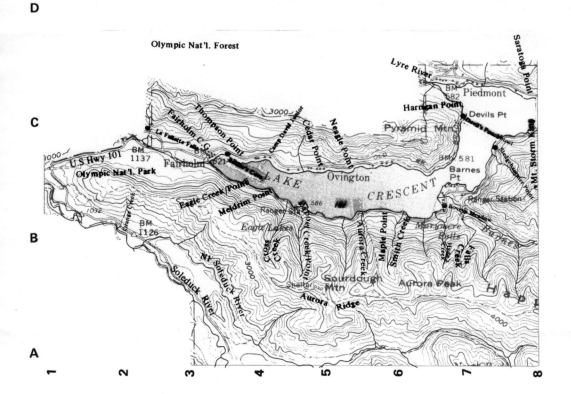

2

True
N
Mag. N
Dec.
23° E

0   1   2

Miles

LAKE CRESCENT

D

Olympic Nat'l. Forest

Lyre River

Saratoga Point

BM 582 Piedmont

Harman Point

Devils Pt

Pyramid Mtn

C

Thompson Point

Fairholm C. Gr.

La Poncie Falls

Camp Davis Junior

Cedar Point

Nettle Point

U.S Hwy 101

BM 1137

Fairholm 621

Olympic Nat'l. Park

OLD

BM 581

Barnes Pt

Shadow Mt. Storm King

LAKE

Ovington

CRESCENT

Ranger Station

Eagle Creek/Point

Meldrim Point

Raogen Falls

Raquel Creek/Point

Aurora Creek

Maple Point

Smith Creek

Marmere Falls

Barnes Creek

Bovees Meadow

B

BM 1126

Orange Creek

N. Soleduck River

Cross Creek

Eagle Lakes

Sheller Bate

Sourdough Mtn

Aurora Peak

H A D

Soleduck River

Aurora Ridge

4000

A

1   2   3   4   5   6   7   8

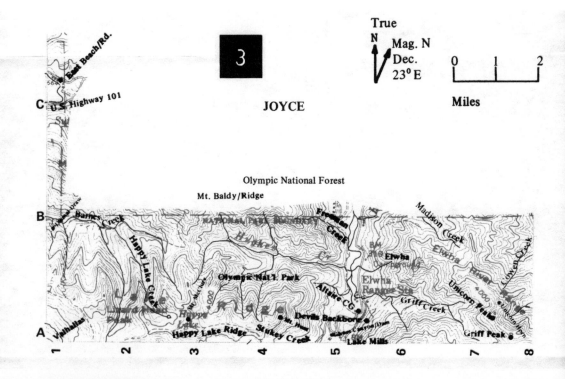

3

True
N
Mag. N
Dec.
23° E

0   1   2

Miles

JOYCE

East Beach/Rd.

C U.S Highway 101

Olympic National Forest

Mt. Baldy/Ridge

B Barnes Creek

Madison Creek

NATIONAL PARK BOUNDARY

Freeman Creek

Hughes

Happy Lake Creek

Elwha

BM Elwha

Elwha River

Elwha Ranger Sta.

Coyote Creek

Unicorn Peaks

Olympic Nat'l. Park

Altaire CG

Griff Creek

Happy Lake

Devils Backbone

Griff Peak

A Valhallas

Happy Lake Ridge

Stakey Creek

Lake Mills

1   2   3   4   5   6   7   8

4

True
N
Mag. N
Dec.
23°E

0   1   2

PORT ANGELES

Miles

D

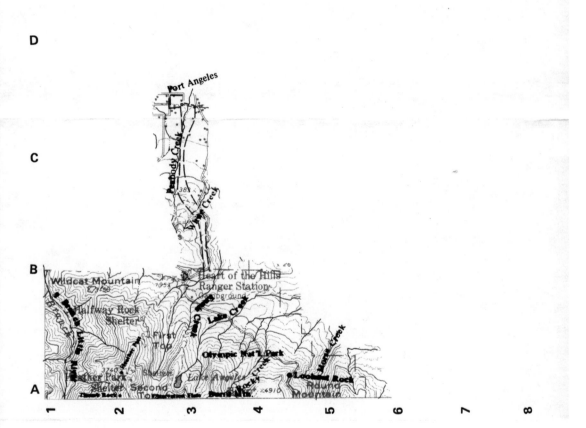

C

B

A

1   2   3   4   5   6   7   8

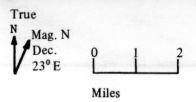

True
N
Mag. N
Dec.
23° E

0   1   2

Miles

5

LA PUSH

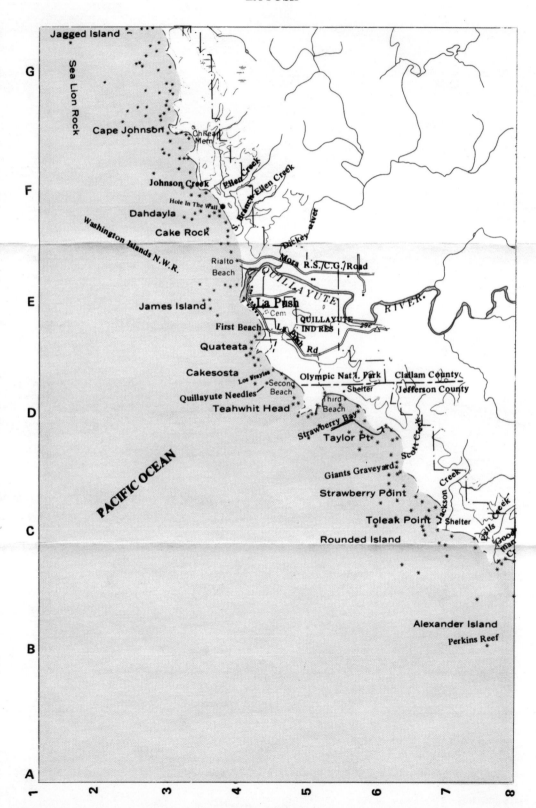

G

Jagged Island

Sea Lion Rock

Cape Johnson

Chiken
Mem

Johnson Creek

Ellen Creek

S. Branch Ellen Creek

F

Hole In The Wall

Dahdayla

Cake Rock

Washington Islands N.W.R.

Dickey river

Rialto
Beach

Mora

R.S./C.G. Road

QUILLAYUTE

E

James Island

La Push

Cem

RIVER

QUILLAYUTE
IND RES

First Beach

La Push Rd

Quateata

Cakesosta

Los Vrayles

Olympic Nat'l. Park

Clallam County

Jefferson County

Quillayute Needles

Second
Beach

Shelter

D

Teahwhit Head

Third
Beach

Strawberry Bay

Taylor Pt

Scott Creek

PACIFIC OCEAN

Giants Graveyard

Strawberry Point

Jackson Creek

Toleak Point

Shelter

Falls Creek

C

Rounded Island

Goodman Cr

Alexander Island

Perkins Reef

B

A

1   2   3   4   5   6   7   8

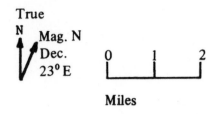

True
N
Mag. N
Dec.
23° E

0   1   2

Miles

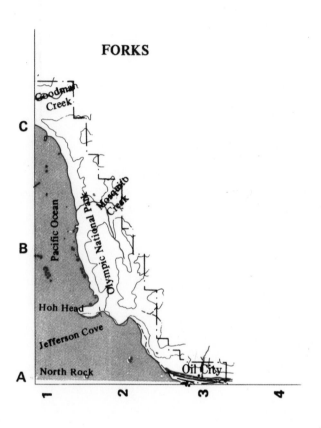

FORKS

C

Goodman
Creek

Pacific Ocean

Olympic National Park

Menasha
Creek

B

Hoh Head

Jefferson Cove

North Rock

Oil City

A

1   2   3   4

True
N Mag. N
Dec.
23° E

0 1 2

SPRUCE MOUNTAIN

Miles

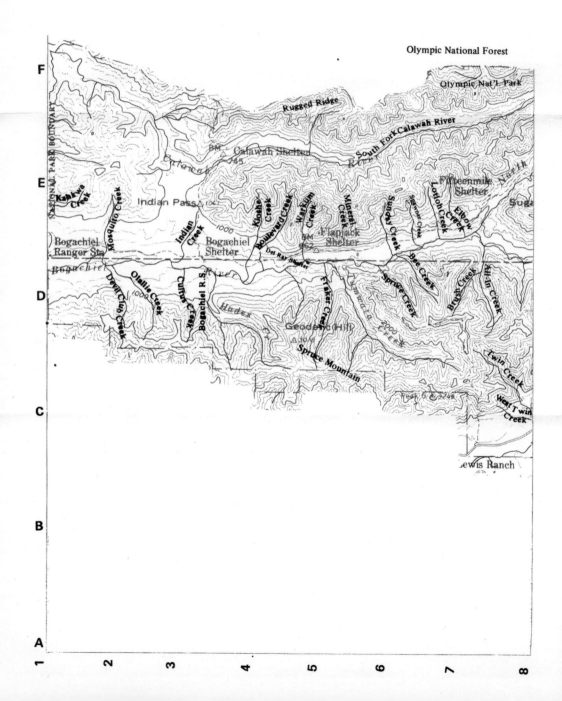

Olympic National Forest

F

Olympic Nat'l. Park

Rugged Ridge

South Fork Calawah River

BM Calawah Shelter
745

Calowah River

North

E

Kahkwa Creek

Indian Pass 1047

Fifteenmile Shelter

Suga

Kloshe Creek

Boulevard Creek

WatKum Creek

Mineral Creek

Sunday Creek

Seawitch Creek

Lottoh Creek

Elbow Creek

Mosquito Creek

Columbio Creek

Indian Creek

Bogachiel Shelter

BM 962
Flapjack Shelter

Bogachiel Ranger Sta

Del Ray Shelter

Bogachiel River

Devil Club Creek

Olallie Creek

Cuttos Creek

Bogachiel R.S.

Hades

Fraker Creek

Leland Creek

Spruce Creek

Bee Creek

Brysk Creek

Ni-in Creek

D

1000

Geodetic Hill
1008

2000

Twin Creek

Spruce Mountain

Peak 6 6 3248

West Twin Creek

C

Lewis Ranch

B

A

1 2 3 4 5 6 7 8

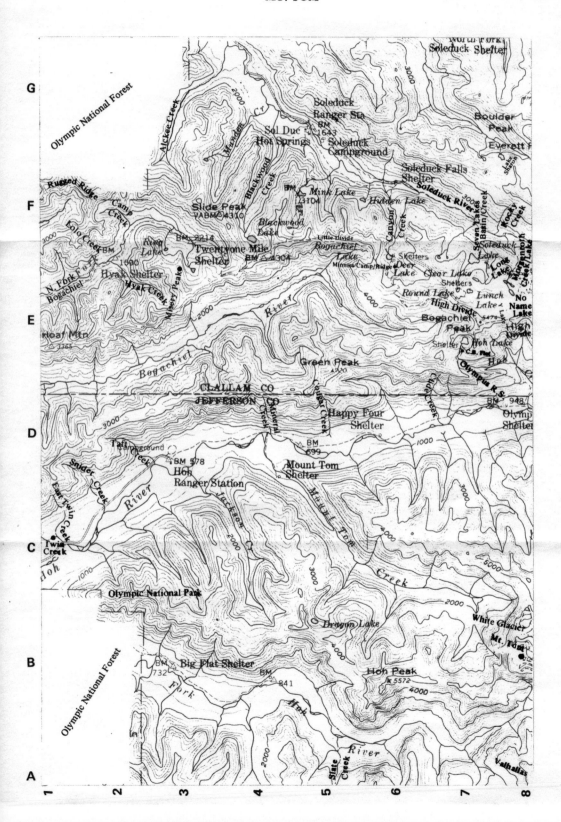

8

True
N Mag. N
Dec.
23° E

0 1 2

Miles

MT. TOM

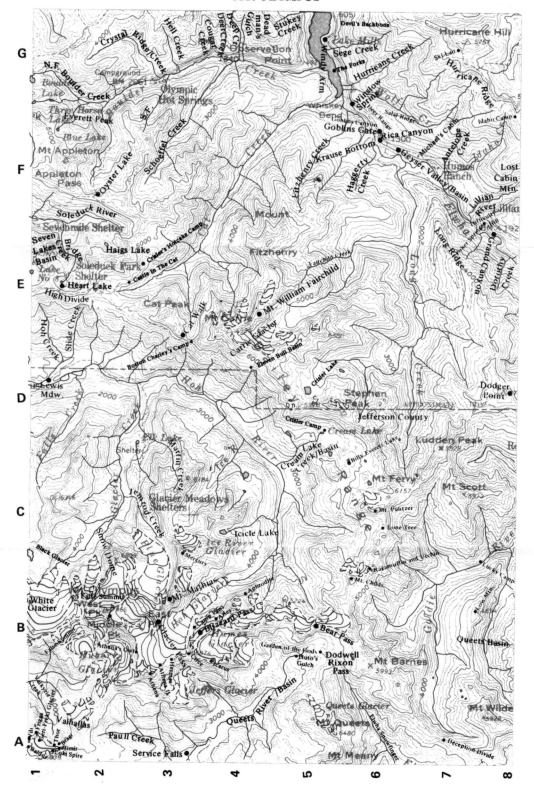

MT. OLYMPUS

True
N
Mag. N
Dec.
23° E

0   1   2

Miles

MT. ANGELES

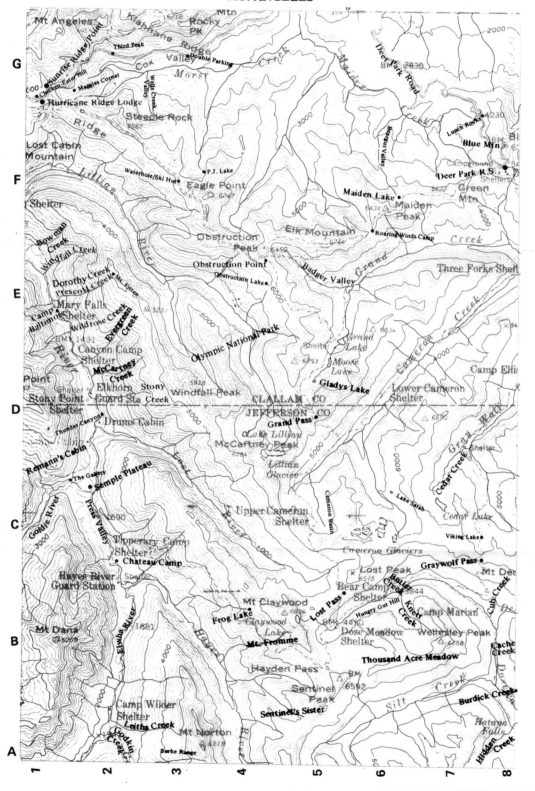

True
N Mag. N
Dec.
23° E

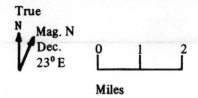

0 1 2

Miles

TYLER PEAK

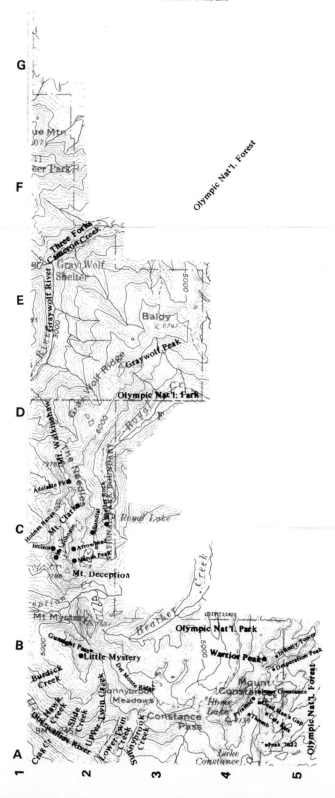

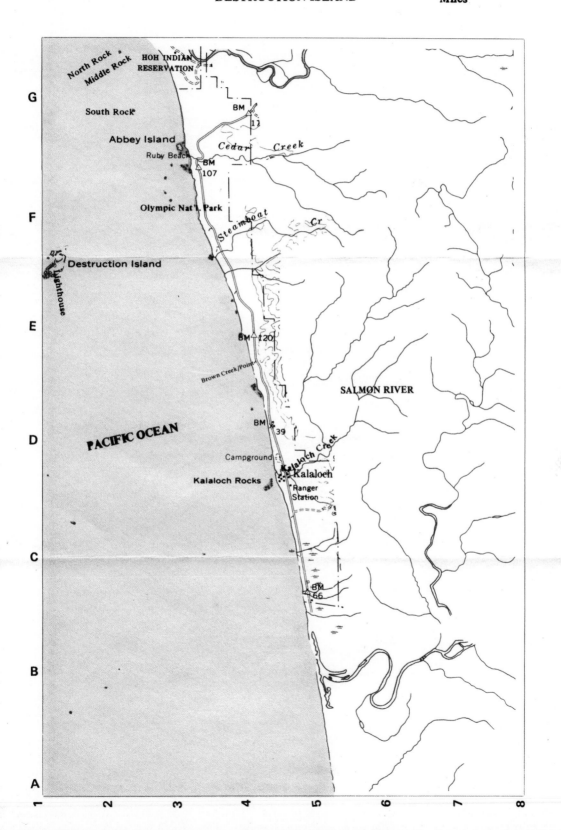

DESTRUCTION ISLAND

True
N
Mag. N
Dec.
23° E

0   1   2

Miles

North Rock
Middle Rock
HOH INDIAN
RESERVATION

G

South Rock

BM
11

Abbey Island

Cedar   Creek

Ruby Beach
BM
107

Olympic Nat'l. Park

F

Steamboat   Cr

Destruction Island

Lighthouse

E

BM 120

Brown Creek/Point

SALMON RIVER

BM
39

D

PACIFIC OCEAN

Kalaloch   Creek

Campground

Kalaloch

Kalaloch Rocks
Ranger
Station

C

BM
66

B

A

1   2   3   4   5   6   7   8

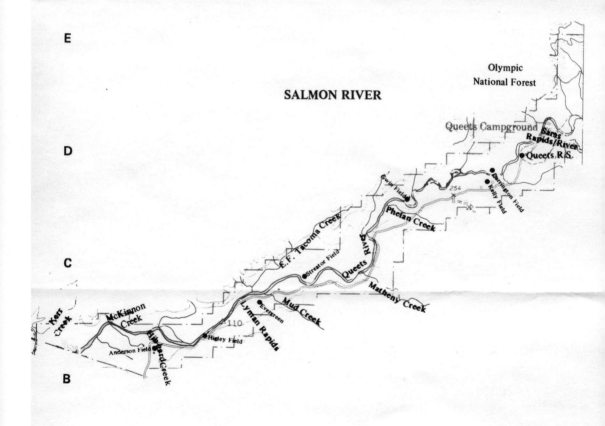

13

True
N
Mag. N
Dec.
23° E

0 1 2

Miles

SALMON RIVER

Olympic
National Forest

Queets Campground
Sams
Rapids/River
Queets R.S.

E

D

C

B

A

1 2 3 4 5 6 7 8

KLOOCHMAN ROCK

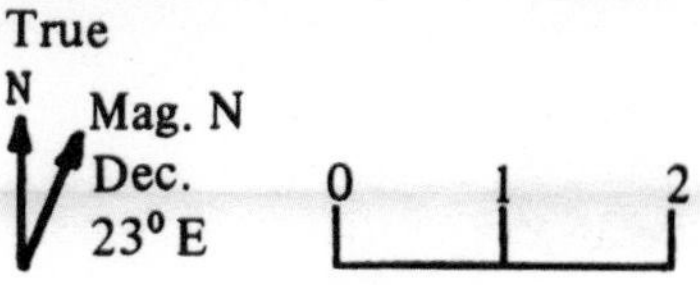

True N
Mag. N
Dec. 23° E

0   1   2
Miles

14

G

F

E

D

C

B

A

Valhallas
Vidar South
Stephen
Vidar North

Pelton

Bob Creek

Paradise Creek

Pelton Creek Shelter

Bob Creek Shelter

Harbor Cr

Pelton Creek

Alta Creek

Tshletshy

Kloochman Rock

River

Tshletshy Ridge

Smith Place

Tshletshy

Creek

Spruce Bottom Shelter

Andrews Field

Queets

Lake Dilly

Round Lake

Olympic Nat'l. Park

NATIONAL PARK BOUNDARY

Sams

Finley Peak

Olympic Nat'l. Forest

Finley Creek

2000

Olympic Nat'l. Forest

Canoe Creek

Kestner Creek

928

BM 257

Higley Peak
Lookout 3025

Quinault Ranger Station

Olympic Nat'l. Park

QUINAULT

RIV

2   3   4   5   6   7   8

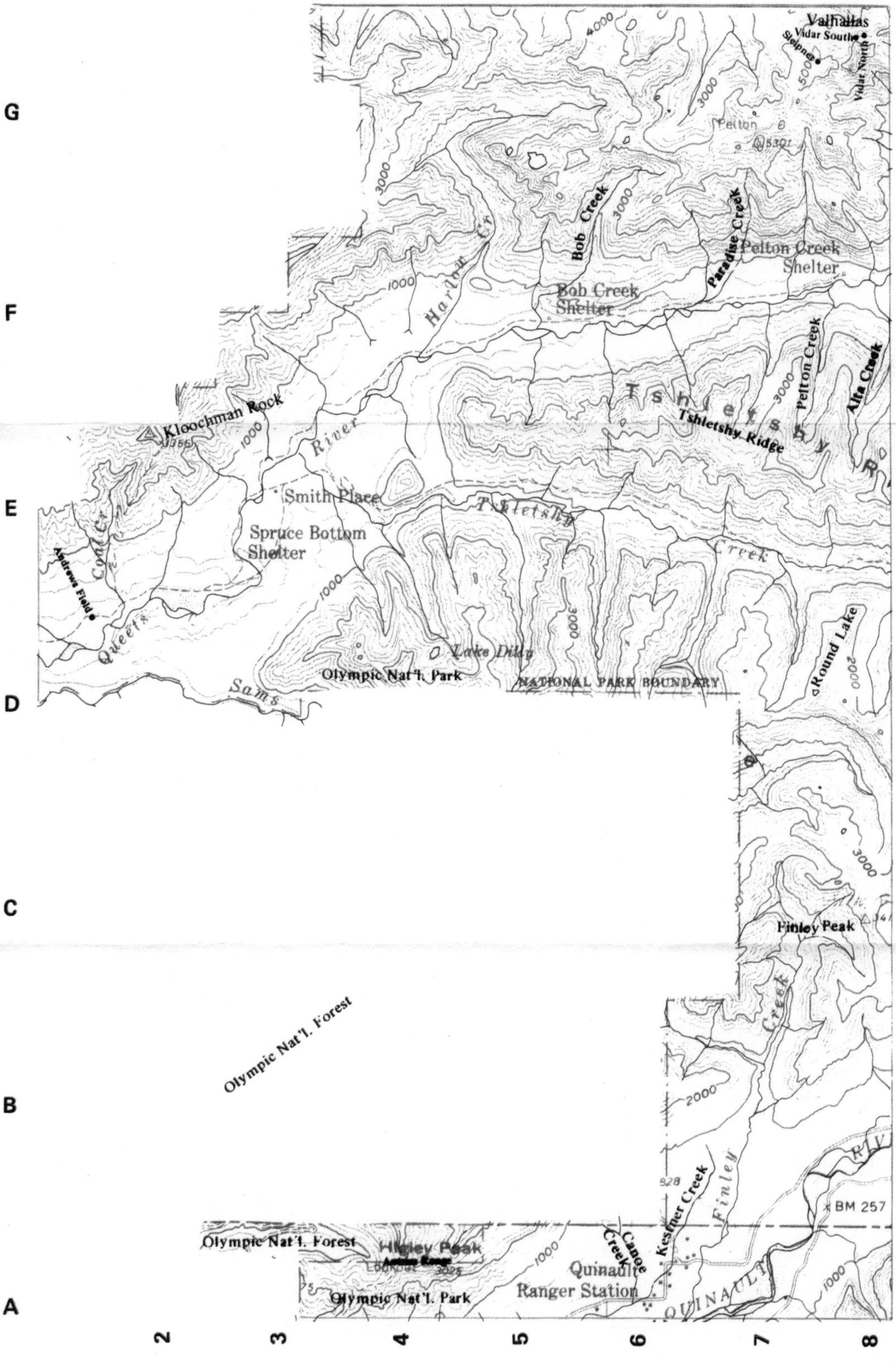

True
N
Mag. N
Dec.
23° E

0   1   2

MT. CHRISTIE

Miles

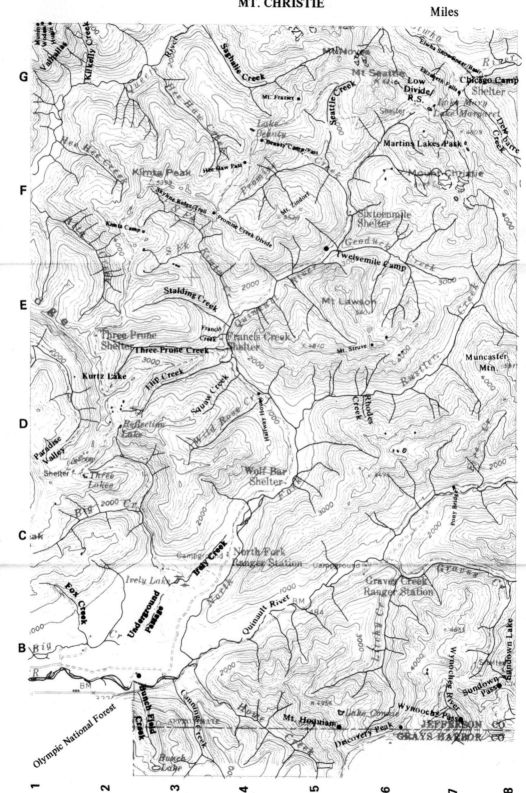

True
N
Mag. N
Dec.
23° E

0   1   2

MT. STEEL   Miles

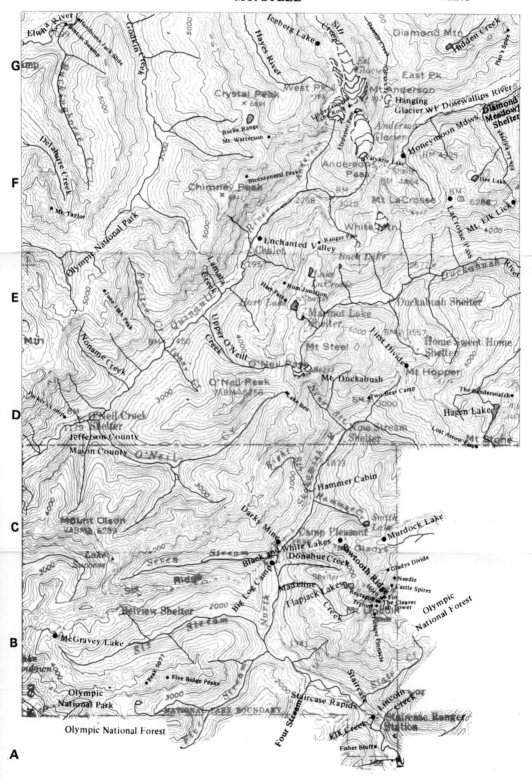

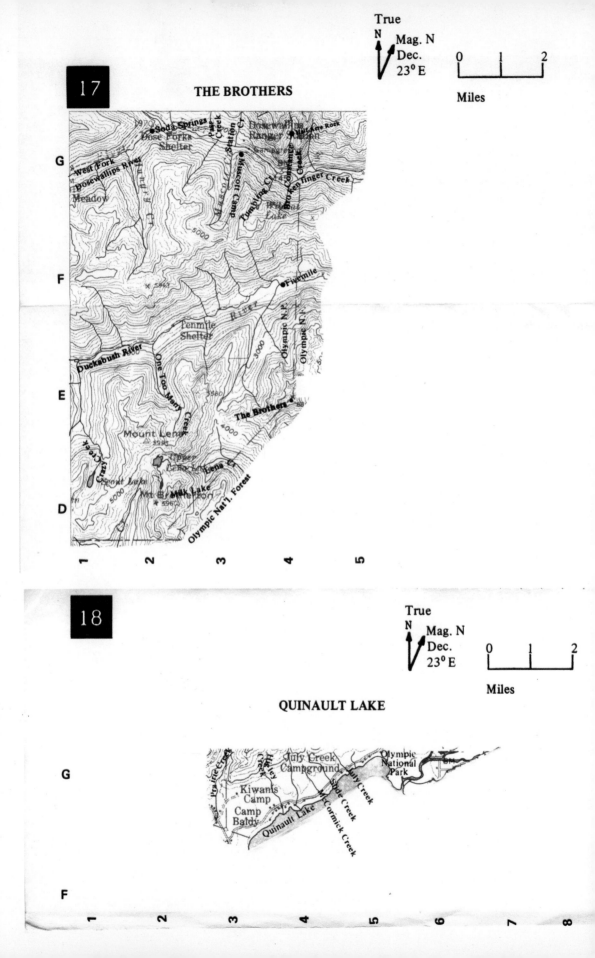